H. L. MENCKEN, LITERARY CRITIC

H. L. MENCKEN

Literary Critic

By WILLIAM H. NOLTE

UNIVERSITY OF WASHINGTON PRESS
Seattle and London

The author is grateful to Alfred A. Knopf, Inc., for permission to quote from the following copyright works by H. L. Mencken: *The American Language,* © 1919, 1921, 1923, 1936; *The Bathtub Hoax and Other Blasts and Bravoes,* © 1958; *A Book of Prefaces,* © 1917; *Happy Days,* © 1939, 1940; *Letters of H. L. Mencken,* © 1961; *A Mencken Crestomathy,* © 1949; *Minority Report,* © 1956; *Prejudices: First Series,* © 1919; *Prejudices: Second Series,* © 1920; *Prejudices: Third Series,* © 1922; *Prejudices: Fourth Series,* © 1924; *Prejudices: Fifth Series,* © 1926; *Prejudices: Sixth Series,* © 1927.

Robinson Jeffers' poem "Thebaid," quoted in part herein, copyright © 1937 by Random House, Inc. and renewed 1964 by Donnan Jeffers and Garth Jeffers. Reprinted from *Selected Poetry of Robinson Jeffers* by permission of Random House, Inc.

The author wishes to thank the editors of *Southwest Review,* the University of Texas *Studies in Literature and Language, The Texas Quarterly, The Midwest Quarterly,* and *New Individualist Review* for assignments of copyright in, or for permission to reprint from, articles by him originally published in those journals that appear in revised form in this book. Specifically, part of Chapter Three appeared in *Southwest Review* (Spring 1964); part of Chapter Four in the University of Texas *Studies in Literature and Language* (Spring 1961; © 1961 by University of Texas Press); part of Chapter Five in *Texas Quarterly* (Autumn 1964); part of Chapter Six in *The Midwest Quarterly* (Summer 1965); and part of Chapter Eight in *New Individualist Review* (Vol. 3, No. 5).

He also thanks the University of Pennsylvania Press for permission to quote brief extracts from *Letters of Theodore Dreiser;* William Manchester for permission to use a letter from Mencken that appeared in his *Disturber of the Peace;* and Simon and Schuster, Inc., for permission to quote a passage from *The Man Mencken* by Isaac Goldberg and another from *Living Philosophies* edited by Will Durant.

Finally, he is incalculably indebted to Alfred A. Knopf and to August Mencken, co-executor of his brother's estate, without whose permission to quote freely from the books, articles, and letters of H. L. Mencken this book could never have been written.

In memory of
my father and my mother

Contents

Preface

MORE than any other twentieth-century American, H. L. Mencken typified the Renaissance ideal of broadness or catholicity. He was never during his long career exclusively any *one* thing—poet, short-story writer, reporter, literary critic, editor, philologist, social philosopher, political analyst, essayist, satirist, humorist, etc. Indeed, his correspondence alone would constitute an active life's work. While his brief career as poet and fiction writer could never distinguish him from the mass of workaday scribblers, the work done in many other areas rises far above the mediocre and oftentimes reaches the stellar regions inhabited by highly select company. Attempts to assign him a place on the shelf have invariably ended, and always will end, in frustration for the one doing the shelving. I like to pigeonhole him as simply "Man Thinking"—not a part of a man, a hand, or foot, or neck (I am borrowing from Emerson, of course), nor "a mere thinker, or still worse, the parrot of other men's thinking." But even this rather broad category cannot contain the man, since he was not just man thinking but man creating as well—that is, he was an artist, a man intent on leaving tangible evidence of his singularity, an image maker, a carver on the wall. Though he believed that the only way in which a man could fully express himself was in the realm of music, he was forced by that accumulation of weights, stresses, strengths, and weaknesses that mold us all to compose his symphonies with word chords. But even this does not quite enclose him. After all, it was the play of ideas that fascinated him; and music is not ideological in the same sense that language is.

Mencken agreed with the eighteenth-century belief that the proper study of mankind is man; we have ample evidence of his interest in psychology, science (particularly the biological sciences), and, rather broadly, epistemology. For all that, he was an avid student of religion or, as he called it, "the ghostly science," though he had none himself. His interest in religion, though, was more anthropological and psychological than metaphysical. He believed that what men attached themselves to, whether religiously, politically, or philosophically, was worthy of critical examination. It was this criticism of general ideas, as he called it, that won him international fame, or notoriety, after World War I. That Mencken should be remembered today as primarily a critic of American foibles is only natural. His greatest acclaim came in the nineteen-twenties when he was editor of the *American Mercury*, a magazine that did much to change the nature of American journalism. The skepticism, the iconoclasm, the Rabelaisian humor, the brilliant Mencken style— these qualities were catnip to the Roaring Twenties, when all wars had been fought, and in vain; when there were no more tomorrows, only the gay, and infinitely sad, today; when America took its dizzy ride slam-bang into the desolate thirties. During the Depression years, people tended to associate Mencken with their great binge. The hangover was severe, and a scapegoat was needed. What could be more natural than to fall on the leader of former days? He neither advocated turning back to a "rich past," as did the New Humanists or the New Critics (in their Agrarian incarnation), nor could he visualize a utopian future under socialism, as did the proletarians. In effect, he was caught in a cross fire and was quickly demolished so far as that period was concerned. In the nineteen-forties his stock rose again, tentatively, with the publication of the *Days* books; they received almost unanimous praise, often of a very high order, and have since been accorded the estate of classics. By the fifties, his name was once more being widely heard in journalistic and critical circles (though his writing career was ended by a stroke in 1948), and today he is as frequently represented in essay collections as any other American. Moreover, much of his work is widely available, both in hard-bound and paperback editions, and is once more being generously attacked and praised.

In this study I have focused attention on the literary criticism, which has not received the attention of his other work. Generally speaking, I have endeavored to do two things in the following pages. First, I try to present, in highly condensed form, just what Mencken thought and wrote about literature and about literary criticism. To do this I employ paraphrase and quotation, of course, but I also endeavor to assess that criticism which lies before me on the operating table. Secondly, and at the same time, I attempt to place Mencken in the history of criticism, to locate him in a critical milieu, to compare and contrast him with his fellows. This involves the use of literary history, of course—or rather my interpretation of that history. Actually, I am more concerned with the major problem of clarification of just what Mencken did in the field than with anything else. If a reader knows what he wrote, he should be able to assess the value of the writing himself; at least he will have some basis for assessment. Hence, I act more as co-ordinator and synthesizer than as critic or historian.

This does not, however, preclude my passing judgments. Indeed, I should make it clear from the beginning that I have certain beliefs on the subject of criticism of belles-lettres which I state with emphasis and some heat—perhaps, alas, to the point of impudence. One of those beliefs, now rather generally shared by literary historians, is that the so-called New Humanism of Irving Babbitt, Paul Elmer More, and various college dons was sterile and totally unfit to live in the world of men. Another is that academic critics have generally been poor critics (almost of necessity, as I try to show), particularly those of thirty or forty years ago—the ones, in fact, whom Mencken battled. I might add that there are several exceptions to the rule and by so saying lay the charge that I am just antiacademy and of a jaundiced disposition. I say all this as a teacher (or pedagogue, if you will) myself and hope that the reader will not find it totally incredible for a teacher to criticize his fellow grape-pickers. I found it amusing and somewhat disturbing to be asked by a professor on my examining board for the Ph.D. degree (this study, now greatly revised and enlarged, was originally a doctoral dissertation) why, since I had so many harsh things to say about the "Prof. Drs.," I had decided to become one myself. Startled by the question, I was unable to make my interlocutor understand that I considered adverse criticism, when the facts called for it, far more healthy or at least invigorating than any amount of approval.

My indebtedness to other Mencken scholars, past and present, has been enormous; and I have used much of the biographical information contained in various books and essays with a liberality that I can only hope never passes beyond the realm of "scholarship" into that of outright pla ᵧ ᵢ.rism—that dark domain lying just east of the scholarly Eden. Frankly, I could not say with any exactness just where I found much of my factual information, since I have almost always synthesized material found elsewhere. I must pay individual respects, however, to various of the biographies, at least. By far the best and most complete of the books is that of William Manchester, *Disturber of the Peace: The Life and Riotous Times of H. L. Mencken* (1951), which is now available in paperback and is, I understand, required reading in certain courses at Yale. The late Edgar Kemler's biography was of little value except for biographical material since Kemler, a political scientist, had little knowledge of books in general and was not at all critically perceptive in his remarks on Mencken's criticism. Actually, he was more interested in Mencken as satirist than he was in the various other sides. One also suspects that he found the subject of his *The Irreverent Mr. Mencken* (1950) more than a little shocking. Moreover, his uncritical veneration of Franklin Roosevelt is largely responsible, I think, for his extraordinarily silly last chapter, in which he interprets Mencken's lack of respect for FDR as being equivalent to fascistic leanings. Reviewers of the book at the time of its publication were quick to dispute the logic of this thesis. (Perhaps I should say that I should probably have voted for Roosevelt had I been old enough to do so, but that does not *ipso facto* prevent me from severely objecting to much he did.) I am indebted to Isaac Goldberg's *The Man Mencken: A Biographical and Critical Survey* (1925) for material on Mencken's family line; and the little book by Ernest Boyd, *H. L. Mencken* (1925), is still a first-rate analysis of the general philosophy. Charles Angoff's amusing, but unconvincing, *H. L. Mencken: A Portrait from Memory* (1956) unwittingly reveals more of its author than of its subject and perhaps should be catalogued under the heading of psychopathology rather than sober judgment. M. K. Singleton's *H. L. Mencken and the American Mercury Adventure* (1962) was of little help since I am primarily concerned with the work Mencken did during the first two decades of the century. Of great aid to me was *H. L. M.; The Mencken Bibliography* (1961), done by Betty Adler with the assistance of Jane Wilhelm; it is a veritable library of references to the thousands of articles and books done by and on Mencken. Under the editorship of Betty Adler, the quarterly *Menckeniana* keeps the bibliography current.

A word on the footnotes: I have avoided the practice of footnoting every word that appears in quotation marks. Hence, instead of two or three thousand footnotes, there are less than two hundred. The source of quotations is usually buried in the text; when quotations are more than a sentence or two, I have made the debt official by using the footnote. I frankly admit that I am not particularly impressed by an author's ability to load his lines with arabic numbers slightly raised. For one thing, I cannot forget Frank Sullivan's famous "A Garland of Ibids for Van Wyck Brooks." For another, I once ran across a footnote number following Plato's name, and on looking at the bottom of the page I was informed that Plato was a Greek philosopher. That just about cured me. On the other hand, I have been somewhat pedantic, I daresay, in my use of dates, often giving the month and year when a statement I am quoting was made.

I wish to thank the reference librarians of the University of Illinois, and Thomas E. Ratcliffe in particular, and the reference librarians of the University of Oregon for their indispensable assistance in locating the forty-six volumes of the *Smart Set* magazine, which has become something of a collector's item. Also, I thank Professor John T. Flanagan, of the University of Illinois, for having read and criticized parts of this study. For her encouragement and cheer during the writing, Dorothy Ridenhour deserves my greatest thanks. Finally, my task was facilitated by a grant-in-aid from the Graduate School of the University of Oregon. The task itself was always more a joy than a labor.

W. H. N.
Eugene, Oregon

H. L. MENCKEN, LITERARY CRITIC

CHAPTER ONE

In the Beginning

N o untoward disturbances of the natural order accompanied the hiring of Henry Louis Mencken as book critic for the *Smart Set* magazine. The eruptions came later, and when they came they came not single spies, but in battalions.

Fred Splint, the new editor of the magazine and late a managing editor under Theodore Dreiser, then in his second year of editorial control of the Butterick Publications, offered Mencken the chance to write a monthly article on books. To convince him that he was the man for the job, Splint enlisted the aid of his assistant editor, Norman Boyer, a former Baltimore newspaperman and acquaintance of Mencken. To begin with, the editors were aware that nothing could entice Mencken away from Baltimore for more than brief periods of time. He had been tendered offers by leading New York newspapers before, but had refused to budge. But now, in the spring of 1908, he was unable to turn down Splint's offer. After all, the job would take him from Baltimore for only a few days a month. Fifteen years later, in his farewell article in the *Smart Set*, Mencken told of his fortuitous entry into the world of professional book criticism.

> The assistant editor of *The Smart Set*, in 1908, was the late Norman Boyer, with whom, eight years before, I had worked as a police reporter in Baltimore. One day I received a polite note from him, asking me to wait upon him on my next visit to New York. I did so a few weeks later; Boyer introduced me

to his chief, Fred Splint, and Splint forthwith offered me the situation of book reviewer to the magazine, with the rank and pay of a sergeant of artillery. Whose notion it was to hire me —whether Boyer's, or Splint's, or some anonymous outsider's— I was not told, and do not know to this day. I had never printed anything in the magazine; I had not, in fact, been doing any magazine work since 1905, when I abandoned the writing of short-stories, as I had abandoned poetry in 1900. But Splint engaged me with a strange and suspicious absence of parley, Boyer gave me an armful of books, the two of us went to Murray's for lunch (I remember a detail: I there heard the waltz, "Ach, Frühling, wie bist du so schön!" for the first time), and in November of the same year my first article appeared in this place.[1]

There is a slight and almost inconsequential error in this remembrance, if we are to believe Mencken's various biographers. Actually, he was first made the offer by mail and asked to call later at the New York office to discuss details. Nor had he given up the writing of fiction and poetry, since he was to write a great deal of both under various pseudonyms during his years on the *Smart Set*.

More importantly, he has failed to mention that one of the most fortunate of accidents occurred that afternoon in the *Smart Set* office: the coming together of Mencken and George Jean Nathan, and hence the beginning of one of the most fruitful friendships in American letters. According to Nathan's account, Mencken introduced himself by thrusting out his hand and exclaiming, "I'm H. L. Mencken from Baltimore and I'm the biggest damned fool in Christendom and I don't want to hear any boastful reply that you claim the honor." Fifteen minutes later, their business in the *Smart Set* office concluded, the two men were toasting each other in the bar of the old Beaux Arts Café a block and a half away. "What's your attitude toward the world?" Mencken asked, continuing before Nathan could open his mouth: "I view it as a mess in which the clowns are paid more than they are worth, so I respectfully suggest that, when we get going, we get our full share."[2] The speech is doubtless apocryphal, for Nathan recalls it over the memory-dimming span of fifty years, but the essence is unimpeachable. The mock seriousness rings true.

A graduate of Cornell and the University of Bologna, erstwhile reporter on the New York *Herald,* and, at one time or another, drama critic for the *Bohemian, Harper's Monthly,* and the *Bookman,* the twenty-six-year-old Nathan was the perfect complement to Mencken. As Burton Rascoe remarked, Nathan was a "New Yorker and man-of-the-world with interests predominantly esthetic and hedonistic, not at all concerned with sociological or political matters, although [he was] quick to see the fallacies and weak points in the arguments of demagogues, Utopians and intellectuals with single-track minds and maliciously shrewd in pointing these fallacies out."[3] In *The World in Falseface* (1923) Nathan stated his credo thus: "What interests me in life is the surface of life: life's music and color, its charm and ease, its humor and its loveliness. The great problems of the world—social, political, economic, and theological—do not concern me in the slightest." Indeed, Mencken often accused Nathan of not knowing who was fighting on which side during World War I; Nathan remained aloof from such vulgar displays of human idiocy. On the other hand, Mencken took a hearty delight in the more absurd antics of politicians and reformers. All of which is not, of course, to say that each man was necessary to the other. Rather, each man acted as both a goad and an auditor for the other; a sort of exuberant competition can be seen in much that the two men wrote.

Their outward personalities offered numerous contrasts. For example, Nathan was a somewhat cold, haughty man, who, according to the novelist Josephine Herbst, an employee in the *Smart Set* office in the early nineteen-twenties, was not much given to familiarity, especially with the hired help. Mencken, on the other hand, was a constant source of delight to the office workers on his brief sojourns in the city. Mrs. Herbst recalls that the entrance of Mencken, clad always in a dark blue suit with blue tie, into the New York office had an effect similar to that produced by champagne on an empty stomach. His secretary immediately went into a state of ecstasy; the office was thrown at once into a turmoil as Mencken declaimed uproariously on the evils that had happily, or unhappily, befallen him while making the trek from Baltimore to the great Babylonian monstrosity of sin and filth; and poor Nathan resigned himself to a week end of insubordination by the office personnel. Whereas Nathan insisted that the secretaries be at work on time and make some attempt to remain busy, Mencken drew them aside one by one and urged them not to waste their precious hours of youth sitting in a drab office when there was little to be done. Rather, he exhorted them to take in a movie, go for a walk in the park, call up a boy friend and arrange a rendezvous for a drink—that is, if one could be found in that drought-ridden time of Christian Endeavor and the Uplift.

But in almost every essential, Mencken and Nathan were blood brothers. Each was ribald, thoroughly Rabelaisian (how utterly unlike the reigning critics of their early days on the *Smart Set!*), and first and last a total skeptic, unwilling to accept any belief, judgment, or standard on its appeal to the masses of men.

If, on the bright afternoon of May 8, 1908,[4] Nathan had already begun to find a place as a drama critic, the name of Mencken was not unknown. By the time of their meeting, he had seen two books of prose through the press: a critical interpretation, and the first ever written, of Shaw's plays (as a young man Mencken was avidly interested in the theater and was for a time the drama critic for the Baltimore *Herald* and, later, the Baltimore *Sun*); and an explication, the first in English, of Friedrich Nietzsche's philosophy. His first published work was a volume of verse, *Ventures into Verse* (1903). He had sold numerous short stories to various magazines— *Short Stories, Munsey's, Ainslee's, Youth's Companion, Everybody's, Hearst's,* the *Redbook,* and *Frank Leslie's Popular Monthly*—and had even impressed Ellery Sedgwick, then editor of *Leslie's* and later editor of the *Atlantic Monthly,* enough so that Sedgwick had offered him, in 1901, the post of associate editor of *Leslie's* at a salary of forty dollars a week and a free pass to Baltimore every month. The young reporter must have been sorely tempted, for at that time he was earning less than half that on the Baltimore *Herald.* But he was head of the house in Baltimore, his father having died in 1899, and had to consider his mother and the responsibility of two younger brothers and a younger sister. This is not to say, however, that he was financially responsible for his family, since his father, August Mencken, had done well as a manufacturer of cigars and had left his widow well provided for.

Aside from his books (*The Philosophy of Nietzsche,* published in 1908, was a popular and critical success) and his short stories, Mencken was also acquiring national renown as the country's foremost journalistic prodigy, having become at the age of twenty-three

America's youngest managing editor and at twenty-four the youngest editor in chief on a big city daily, the Baltimore *Evening Herald.*
In 1906 he moved to the *Sun* and was to be associated with the
Sunpapers, except for a three-year absence (1917–1920), down to
1941, when he retired to write his memoirs. In 1948 he reluctantly
agreed to cover the political conventions for the Sunpapers; in the
fall of that year he suffered an almost fatal, and permanently dis-
abling, stroke.

The "anonymous outsider" who recommended Mencken as a
possible choice to review books for the *Smart Set* was Theodore
Dreiser. That Dreiser would derive incalculable benefit from
Mencken's accepting the job was not then known, of course, but it
does indicate a sort of cosmic justice. When the two men first met,
Dreiser was the editor of the fashionable *Delineator* and of the
Butterick Publications. Among other things, Mencken was acting
as a ghost writer for a Baltimore physician and Johns Hopkins
graduate named Leonard K. Hirshberg. Dr. Hirshberg informed
Dreiser that he wished to do a series of articles which would interpret for the lay public, if possible, some of the more recent advances in medical science. He admitted that as a medical man he
was not a competent writer, but informed the editor that he had
joined with "a young, refreshing and delightful fellow of a very
vigorous and untechnical literary skill," who, as the Doctor's col-
laborator, would most certainly furnish Dreiser with articles of
exceptional luminosity and vigor. In an explanatory note for the
bound volumes in the Enoch Pratt Free Library, Mencken stated
that Ellery Sedgwick had asked him to find a man at Johns Hopkins
who would be willing to write some medical articles for *Leslie's
Weekly*. He found such a man in Dr. Hirshberg, who provided the
facts for the articles which Mencken wrote. "The combination
turned out to be very successful and pretty soon we were deluged
with orders. Among the magazines we worked for was the *Delineator,* then edited by Dreiser. Dreiser ordered a whole series of
articles on the feeding and care of children." That series was published afterward as a book, which was widely popular for years.

As Dreiser tells the story, when he received the first article, it
"seemed to me as refreshing and colorful a bit of semiscientific
exposition as I had read in years." Some weeks later Mencken called
on Dreiser about the articles he had been ghosting. Dreiser was

at once amused by the "taut, ruddy, blue-eyed, snub-nosed youth," whose appearance was that of "a small town roisterer or a college sophomore of the crudest and yet most disturbing charm and impishness, who, for some reason, had strayed into the field of letters." Looking like "a spoiled and petted and possibly over-financed brewer's or wholesale grocer's son who was out for a lark," Mencken promptly ensconced himself in a large and impressive chair placed there to deflate the ego of the overly confident, and from that unintended vantage point beamed on Dreiser "with the confidence of a smirking fox about to devour a chicken." Unable to restrain his laughter at the sight before him, Dreiser asked if his visitor were not "Anheuser's own brightest boy out to see the town." To which Mencken readily replied that he was indeed the son of Baltimore's richest brewer and that his yellow shoes and bright tie were characteristic of his class. Dreiser wrote that they at once dismissed the original purpose of the conference and proceeded to expatiate on "the more general phases and ridiculosities of life, with the result that an understanding based on a mutual liking was established, and from then on I counted him among those whom I most prized—temperamentally as well as intellectually. And to this day, despite various disagreements, that mood has never varied."[5] From that day until Dreiser became popular after World War I, Mencken was to stimulate him as no one else did. After their meeting, a steady flow of letters from Baltimore provided Dreiser with laughter, at least. It is hard to say, as F. O. Matthiessen wrote, which of the two men was farther from his proper work: Mencken as the author of an article on "When Baby Has Diphtheria," or Dreiser as the one who solicited the article.

Not long after he met Mencken, Dreiser was asked by the new editor of the *Smart Set* for advice as to how the magazine could be made better. Dreiser suggested that a book department "with a really brilliant and illuminating reviewer" was just what the magazine needed. And instantly he thought of Mencken as the ideal man for the job. Thus did Mencken begin his fifteen-year association with the *Smart Set*. In the beginning the audience was small, but the stage (I almost wrote *ring*) was bare.

CHAPTER TWO

The Sultry Atmosphere

W<small>HEN</small>, in that quietly innocent, "chemically pure" first decade of the century, Mencken joined the ranks of professional reviewers, there was little being written in the United States that can be read today without perceptible pain. In England and, more and more as time passed, in Ireland, literature still throve, as evidenced by the work of such writers as Kipling, Yeats, "A. E.," Synge, Pinero, Shaw, Galsworthy, Maugham, Barrie, Lord Dunsany, Arnold Bennett, H. G. Wells, George Moore, Hardy, and Conrad—to name some of the major writers. But at home, American letters were sick abed, stultified by a number of paralyzing ills. Though this is no place to rehearse those ailments, a brief survey of the preceding fifty years or so should help clarify the scene.

The American Renaissance of ante-bellum days, grossly overpraised by later American writer-scholars, usually academicians in search of pearls along the shell-strewn shores of New England, had left little more than a wistful memory of days that had been but were no more. Writers of that bygone day, particularly Emerson and Thoreau, had been primarily concerned with declaring their independence and defining their aims—the aims of man thinking. Hawthorne, who came late to bloom, succeeded fully in only one novel, and that one a harsh criticism of our Puritan past. Melville subsided into silence before his fortieth year, leaving behind a handful of competent books and his one gigantic masterpiece. It is hard to tell whether he was the victim of a creative desiccation or of a hostile reading public. Whitman's *Leaves of Grass* appeared in 1855, to the horror of most of its readers. For the next sixty years the poet and his poems were to be involved in the innumerable debates, or battles, over the nature and aims of literature.

It is no longer a secret, even to the most hidebound of conservatives, that the genteel tradition of American literature, stretching roughly from the Civil War to World War I, provides precious little for the judicious reader. Compare American literature in all its facets with that of England or France over the same period of time. It makes one wince. To be sure, there was the brief "Triumph of Realism," as it has been called, in the eighteen-eighties when Howells wrote *A Modern Instance, The Rise of Silas Lapham,* and *Indian Summer;* Twain composed his two greatest books, *Huckleberry Finn* and *Life on the Mississippi;* and James produced *The Portrait of a Lady,* the best of several novels he wrote during the decade. Moreover, Henry Adams' *Democracy* and *Esther,* Hay's *The Bread-Winners,* Cable's *The Grandissimes,* and E. W. Howe's *The Story of a Country Town* belong to the early eighties. Not all of these are great novels, to be sure, but they rise above the mediocre, to say the least.

Again, in the eighteen-nineties Crane and Norris outraged the guardians of public morals by publishing naturalistic novels that were compared to the works of the immoral French. It would be but a slight exaggeration to say that the best work of the period was precisely that which was dismissed as immoral, vulgar, and obscene by the reigning critics. Much of this obtuseness can be attributed to the critics' view of man's place in the universe. "There was still," George Santayana remarked, "an orthodoxy among American highbrows at the end of the nineteenth century, dissent from which was felt to be scandalous; it consisted in holding that the universe exists and is governed for the sake of man or of the human spirit. This persuasion, arrogant as it might seem, is at bottom an expression of impotence rather than of pride."[1] Little wonder that Crane's constant harping on the indifference of the universe should have been considered blasphemous. The remarkable thing about Crane, as Mencken pointed out years later, was not that he was condemned but that he was given a hearing at all. It

would be difficult to imagine a writer more at odds with the prevailing criticism of his time and his country.

Indeed, when one turns his gaze from belles-lettres to criticism
proper, the scene becomes a great deal darker. James Huneker,
probably the most discerning and without doubt the most open-
minded and hospitable critic of the period, rarely so much as mentioned an American artist in his books and articles. Henry James
wrote some excellent reviews of his contemporaries and even drew
fire from other American reviewers for his realism, strange though
that now seems. Still, his brand of realism was always breaking
against the thick wall of prudishness which surrounded all his
writing. He could admire the artistic devotion of Daudet, Goncourt,
and Zola, but was repelled by their "ferocious pessimism and handling of unclean things." His essay on Baudelaire was Victorian
to the core. He could at the same time admire Howells as a naturalist, even write Howells that he did not carry his naturalism
far enough, and raise an eyebrow over *Criticism and Fiction*
(1891): "I am surprised, sometimes, at the things you notice and
seem to care about. One should move in a diviner air."[2] "In a
diviner air"—and yet American reviewers classified James as a
"scientific" novelist who emphasized "morbid analysis," pessimism,
realism, and photographic fidelity at the expense of "the smiling
aspects of life," to use a favorite phrase of Howells, who was himself attacked for the same crimes attributed to James.

In certain respects, Howells outdistanced his friend James as
a critic. Though timid in religious and sexual matters, Howells was
not quite so fastidious as James; and what is more, he was a good
deal more sympathetic to new talent. But in his patronizing manner,
he was often uncritical. Percival Pollard ridiculed Howells for the
"Let them all in!" invitations that characterized his open-door policy
of criticism. Still, it is hard to be severe with a critic who aided
such writers as Frank Norris, Stephen Crane, the early Hamlin
Garland, Henry B. Fuller, and others. In an essay on Howells, entitled "The Dean," Mencken examined the novels and found little
to praise; he thought *The Rise of Silas Lapham* might survive, but
the others would pass with the period in which they were written
—a completely valid criticism that met with general disapproval at
the time it was made. Howells was certainly the most respected

living writer in the country (the essay was written the year before his death in 1920), and with some reason, but his novels had not, Mencken felt, been justly criticized. "For twenty years past his successive books have not been criticized, nor even reviewed; they have been merely fawned over; the lady critics of the newspapers would no more question them than they would question Lincoln's Gettysburg speech, or Paul Elmer More, or their own virginity."[3] Howells was a writer of grace and charm, but had very little to say. "His psychology is superficial, amateurish, often nonsensical; his irony is scarcely more than a polite facetiousness; his characters simply refuse to live. No figure even remotely comparable to Norris' McTeague or Dreiser's Frank Cowperwood is to be encountered in his novels." Mencken believed that all Howells' merited respect as an industrious and inoffensive man was bound, sooner or later, "to yield to a critical examination of the artist within, and that examination, I fear, will have its bitter moments for those who naïvely accept the Howells legend."

On the other hand, Mencken felt that the man's criticism was of real merit, as evidenced by his understanding praise of such as E. W. Howe, Edith Wharton, Norris, and William Vaughn Moody. He had praised and promoted the Russians, and back in the seventies and eighties he had made war on the sentimental novel. Still, his criticism was full of errors and omissions. "One finds him loosing a fanfare for W. B. Trites, the Philadelphia Zola, and praising Frank A. Munsey—and one finds him leaving the discovery of all the Shaws, George Moores, Dreisers, Synges, Galsworthys, Phillipses and George Ades to the Pollards, Meltzers and Hunekers. Busy in the sideshows, he didn't see the elephants go by. . . ."[4] Howells' major defect lay in his temperament, as was best illustrated by his book on Twain, *My Mark Twain.*

> The Mark that is exhibited in this book is a Mark whose Himalayan outlines are discerned but hazily through a pink fog of Howells. There is a moral note in the tale—an obvious effort to palliate, to touch up, to excuse. The poor fellow, of course, was charming, and there was talent in him, but what a weakness he had for thinking aloud—and such shocking thoughts! What oaths in his speech! What awful cigars he smoked! How barbarous his contempt for the strict sonata form! It seems incredible, indeed, that two men so unlike should have found common denominators for a friendship lasting forty-four years. The one

derived from Rabelais, Chaucer, the Elizabethans and Benvenuto—buccaneers on the literary high seas, loud laughers, law-breakers, giants of a lordlier day; the other came down from Jane Austen, Washington Irving and Hannah More. The one wrote English as Michelangelo hacked marble, broadly, brutally, magnificently; the other was a maker of pretty waxen groups. The one was utterly unconscious of the way he achieved his staggering effects; the other was the most toilsome, fastidious and self-conscious of craftsmen.[5]

Other molders of taste, in no way the equals of Howells or James, in the last decade of the nineteenth century were Thomas Bailey Aldrich, Bayard Taylor, Richard Henry Stoddard, E. C. Stedman, Grant White, Richard Watson Gilder—musty names now buried forever in the literary histories. Of this group Stedman was probably the best critic, but he could still chastise Swinburne for not understanding that Whittier, whom Swinburne had thought a bad poet, had fairly depicted "the deep religious sentiment, the patriotism, the tender aspiration, of the best American homes."[6] On the other hand, Stedman was one of the few writers of the age to give Whitman a fair reading, and he even acknowledged the poet's genius. But this was a minority opinion. When the genteel critics were at last forced to admit the existence of Whitman, it was done condescendingly and with hands over eyes, ears, and mouth: a sort of I-hear-no-evil, I-see-no-evil, I-speak-no-evil attitude. Professor George Woodberry admitted that Whitman "wrote a few fine lyrics," which was the common judgment of the professors; and Barrett Wendell explained Whitman's popularity among unmoral Europeans in a manner typical of the whole school of W.C.T.U. critics: "One can see why the decadent taste of Europe has welcomed him so much more ardently than he has ever been welcomed at home; in temper and in style he was an exotic member of that sterile brotherhood which eagerly greeted him abroad."[7]

The numerous female critics of the period were composing articles on "Frailty," "Sentiment," "Melancholy," "Piety," "Love of Nature," "Humanitarianism," "Fashions," and "Decorum" (titles of some of the chapters in an anthology entitled *The Genteel Female*, edited by Clifton J. Furness in 1931). Between the "Lady Critics" and the "Gentlemen of Letters," most of whom resided in the academies of the nation, the only discernible difference is one of gender.

The very prince of gentlemanly critics was the classical scholar or dilettante who ignored living literature altogether and thus attained the ultimate in detachment from ignoble realities. The universities, in their isolation from the market place, provided shelter for the traditionalists and thus helped foster escapism and snobbishness as well as disinterested scholarship. And because of its isolation, the academy was able to prolong the sterility of academic criticism. James Russell Lowell preferred to discuss the masters of the past, especially Shakespeare, Dante, Chaucer, Cervantes, and Spenser. The bulk of his critical writing was essays of appreciation rather than literary criticism per se. To say that Lowell was more interested in the past than in the present is in no way to disparage him (though the Marxian critics were later to damn Lowell violently for his lack of concern for his contemporaries). But one should remember that Lowell wielded great influence on his time; his critical judgments of modern writers, when he consented to make them, were accepted as oracular truth. Of the evolutionary theories that were the storm center of his day, he was completely ignorant, knowing nothing of Darwin or Marx or, what is more, any branch of sociology or science. Although we must assume that he was, in effect, superior to the immediate scene, he could nonetheless sneer at Zola and the other "French so-called realists." He completely misunderstood many writers about whom he wrote, notably Thoreau; and about Henry Fielding he remarked that "he has the merit, *whatever it may be,* of inventing the realistic novel, *as it is called."* (My italics.) High praise, indeed, for the author of the greatest English novel! Lowell has the dubious distinction of having been the precursor of Irving Babbitt, a critic who carried Lowell's old-maidish distaste for the Romantic Movement to its ultimate. Lowell, who died in 1891, anticipated every line of thought and endeavor that occupied the traditionalist critics of the first two decades of the century. If he can be read today, it is because he concerned himself with the past; when the genteel critic attempted to have his say on contemporary literature, he usually became silly.

The leading critics at the turn of the century were only secondarily concerned with the originality or quality of a work of art; their primary problem was to find out if the work under examination were moral or not, if it in any way strayed from the prevailing beliefs—economic, social, religious, aesthetic. For example, Bliss

Perry could say, somewhat smugly, in *The American Mind* (1912) that American literature might not be great, but at least it had the virtue of being clean. There were, of course, ways and means of exorcising the demons of lasciviousness and immorality from the works of the masters; the salty passages in Boccaccio and *The Arabian Nights* and Shakespeare were simply reflections of relatively backward societies. Maurice Thompson, one of the more fervent of the literary policemen of the period, was in constant uproar over the inroads made by the devil Realism—a term that had many meanings and associations during the latter part of the nineteenth century. Thompson charged that the proponents of Realism taught "that marriage is a failure, that home is a brothel, that courtship is lewd, that society is an aggregation of criminals."[8] On Thomas Hardy he wrote: "If the author of *Tess of the d'Urbervilles* would say the truth, he would flatly confess that he wrote that brilliantly fascinating, filthy novel, not to make young girls cling to virtue, not to prevent rich young men from being villains at heart; but to make a fiction that would appeal to human perversity and delectate human animalism."[9] Thompson was, unwittingly, in part right: Hardy did not write his novel to "make poor young girls cling to virtue" or "to prevent rich young men from being villains at heart"; he was much too good an artist ever to ruin a book by loading it with such asinine purpose; he tended to philosophize, but he was no Uplifter. Thompson felt, as did most of his fellow critics, that if "a novel is unfit for open reading at the family fireside [it] is positive proof that it is not wholesome reading for any person at any place." And he could demand self-righteously: "Shall we credit our own civilization with an appetency for the *Kreutzer Sonata, Leaves of Grass,* and *Madame Bovary?* Have we moved no farther than this during these centuries of Christianity?"[10]

We may laugh today at this "moral" approach to literature and wonder if even to bring it up were not to flog a dead horse, but this sort of drawing-room morality is still with us, though in a much more subtle guise. At present it is the fashion to devote oneself to finding, at the expense of almost everything else, the "moral center" of a novel or play or poem. Moreover, one still hears that amorphous word *taste* used over and over in defense of pruderies of one sort or another. In his *Man in Modern Fiction* (1958), Edmund Fuller chastised James Jones because Fuller was unable to read aloud sections of *From Here to Eternity* to his wife. Which, looked at one way, is to say that Jones is responsible for Mrs. Fuller or any other woman who finds his language too coarse—a rather unfair burden to place on the shoulders of Jones. Yvor Winters is probably the best-known preacher of aesthetic morality or moral aesthetics, even going so far as to say that only a moral man can write great literature. Either Mr. Winters knows nothing about the lives of many great writers (Dostoevsky comes to mind at once), or else he disagrees with the accepted opinions as to what the great works of literature are. In one of the most consistently wrongheaded and silly essays written by a contemporary critic, he declared that the poetry of Robinson Jeffers, the subject of the essay, lacked moral meaning of any kind. Though the moralist still exists in criticism, he is now more a curiosity than a moving force.

After the Great Debunking of the nineteen-twenties, the once solid respectability of the genteel age was left tattered and torn, a sort of laughingstock. The war on Victorianism took on all the aspects of a crusade against the Philistines. In his book on *The Beginnings of Critical Realism in America* (1930), V. L. Parrington wrote: "To most Victorians realism meant Zola, sex, and the exploitation of the animal, and all the pruderies of the Age of Innocence rose up in protest against defiling letters with such themes." Such a statement made at that time was not likely to find many objections. It is true, however, that any age or period that is strongly attacked for some time, no matter how much it may deserve the knocks, will invariably find supporters who begin by insisting that "it couldn't be all that bad" and end by finding much to praise where once there seemed to be so little. A case in point is the Middle Ages, which, according to some, were not so dark after all. Moreover, a reaction against a debunking period—for example, the nineteen-twenties—can lead to doubt that the whipping boys of the period were not angels all the while. Such reactions are the natural result of the debunkers' overstatements, which are then overcorrected by the following generations.

But in the first decade of the century, realism in America, after a few unsuccessful starts, was still a bugbear with which to frighten schoolmasters and -marms and other defenders of ideality. When Henry James was getting his due rewards and Howells was reaping more than his share, Dreiser was still being attacked (I use these writers as symbols)—and would continue under anathema for over a decade to come—as the worst outrage yet to afflict the reading parlors of Christendom. The world of James was, after all, one in which "the ideal of joy" remained uppermost; the world of Dreiser —the literary world we still inhabit—was one of harshness and unbending despair, but nonetheless one of somber truth and beauty. It is a long bridge that spans the chasm between contemporary literature and the Genteel Tradition.

CHAPTER THREE

Moldings

I

THERE is at least an element of truth in the often repeated argument that Mencken began life, like Pallas Athena, fully armed and outfitted with a few strong convictions that did him for his long and active career. In his invaluable "Personal Note" to the recently published *Letters of H. L. Mencken,* Hamilton Owens, who was closely associated with Mencken for most of his life, remarked on Mencken's almost instantaneous coming of age. Unlike most of us, who "arrive at maturity with no notion of life's significance or lack of it, no understanding of its myriad complexities, no philosophic system to guide us save copybook and Biblical maxims," Mencken somehow avoided this painful process of coming to terms with man's surroundings. For most people, after they reach maturity, life is filled with changes, compromises, contradictions. Different times bring different beliefs. "It is," as Owens wrote, "only when our arteries begin to harden and we begin the slide toward the funeral parlor that we find it possible to adopt a satisfying or nearly satisfying view of things in general, a pattern or mode of life." Mencken was essentially the same in the first decade of the century when he wrote his books on Shaw and Nietzsche as he was during the teens, when the Uplift and patriotic fervor were in vogue; during the twenties, when ballyhoo, disillusion, and revolt were in the land; during the thirties, when the proletariat had its day (philosophically, if not economically); and during the forties, when another war and its aftermath of revisions and readjustments occupied the people. Those critics who say Mencken was a product of the times—meaning the twenties—somehow overlook the fact that he did the vast majority of his work during the twenty years before and the twenty years after the decade in which he reigned as a kind of literary monarch. To quote Owens once more:

> He would have been his own unprecedented self had there been no World War I, no Woodrow Wilson, no Harding, no Coolidge, no Volstead, no Bible Belt. His riotous vitality, his learning, his skill with words, his sense of the human comedy (closer to farce, for him), his scorn for frauds and hypocrites, his gift for hyperbole and, above all, his deep sympathy for any intelligent man struggling with the riddle of life—all these things would have brought him to the forefront regardless of the times.

Like every other writer of any importance, Mencken acquired his style from several sources, eventually making it both eclectic and distinctive. It would be difficult to use his reading as a means of determining the influence on his style because he was, from early childhood, omnivorous, averaging a book a day during the years when he was primarily a literary critic. (It is absurd in any case to use a writer's "reading" as a means of *proving* that he was influenced by this or that writer. Leon Edel indulges in wishful thinking when he supposes that Faulkner was influenced by Henry James, a writer whom Faulkner dismissed as "a sweet old lady." It appears evident, though, that Faulkner was affected by Cervantes, not just from our reading Faulkner's novels but from his admission that he read *Don Quixote* every year, in the same way that some people read the Bible.) Still, Mencken readily admitted which authors had the most profound effect on his thinking; and he presumably imitated those writers whose style pleased him. In his *Happy Days*, in the chapter entitled "Larval Stage of a Bookworm," he traced his reading from the age of seven to about fourteen. The first long story he ever read was entitled "The Moose Hunters," published in an English annual, *Chatterbox*, in 1887. When he finally finished the tale of adventure, an interval of rough hunting followed in Hollins Street (his lifelong residence) and the adjacent alleys, with imaginary Indians, robbers, and sheep and very real tomcats as the quarry. Shortly thereafter, once more feeling the powerful suction of beautiful letters, "so strange, so thrill-

ing, and so curiously suggestive of the later suction of amour," he
was sweating through a translation of the Grimm Brothers' Fairy
Tales that had been bestowed upon him by F. Knapp's Institute
"for industry and good deportment." Unlike most of his acquain-
tances, he was unable to stomach the books that most boys read;
he forever ran aground in his attempts to read the endless works
of Oliver Optic, Horatio Alger, Harry Castlemon, and the like. "So
far as I can recall, I never read a single volume of it to the end,
and most of it finished me in a few pages."

At the age of nine Mencken discovered *Huckleberry Finn*—a
discovery which he later referred to as probably the most stupendous event of his whole life. Though Mencken's father was not
what might be termed a literary man, he had somehow managed
to collect a rather impressive array of books on widely varied subjects. Certainly Mencken *père* would not have been favorably impressed by his eldest son's choice of profession: "Had he lived into
the days of my practice as a literary critic, I daresay he would
have been affected almost as unpleasantly as if I had turned out
a clergyman, or a circus clown, or a labor leader." Among the
miscellany were the novels of Dickens and George Eliot, the Irish
novels of William Carleton, books on the Civil War, a two-volume
folio of Shakespeare in embossed morocco, encyclopedias, copies
of *Looking Backward, If Christ Came to Chicago, Life Among the
Mormons, Adventures Among Cannibals* ("with horrible pictures
of missionaries being roasted, boiled and fried"), *Uncle Remus,
Ben Hur, Peck's Bad Boy,* and dozens of other such odds and ends.
Most of these tomes "repelled and alarmed" the boy, but among
them he found a set of books by a man named Mark Twain. Noting
that the pictures in the books "were not of the usual funereal character, but light, loose and lively" he proceeded to take down
Huckleberry Finn and sneak it to his room for a closer perusal.

> If I undertook to tell you the effect it had upon me my talk
> would sound frantic, and even delirious. Its impact was genu-
> inely terrific. I had not gone further than the first incomparable
> chapter before I realized, child though I was, that I had entered
> a domain of new and gorgeous wonders, and thereafter I pressed
> on steadily to the last word. My gait, of course, was still slow,
> but it became steadily faster as I proceeded. As the blurbs on
> the slip-covers of murder mysteries say, I simply couldn't put
> the book down. After dinner that evening, braving a possible

uproar, I took it into the family sitting-room, and resumed it while my father searched the *Evening News* hopefully for reports of the arrest, clubbing and hanging of labor leaders. Anon, he noticed what I was at, and demanded to know the name of the book I was reading. When I held up the green volume his comment was "Well, I'll be durned."[1]

Thus began the long *affaire de cœur* between Mencken and the works of Mark Twain. It is significant that he was to read *Huckleberry Finn* at least once a year until he was in his forties. And naturally enough, Twain was one of the Americans whom Mencken was to promote during the early years on the *Smart Set*. It is amusing that James Thurber, in his book on Harold Ross, should have named *Tom Sawyer* as Mencken's favorite American novel. At least he got the right author.

Another novelist who must have done much to shape the style and thought of Mencken was William Makepeace Thackeray. The boy had gone through most of the volumes in his father's secretary, including even Brother Schultz's somber history of Freemasonry in Maryland, and most of Dickens, whom he finished "only by dint of hard labor," when, at fourteen, he discovered Thackeray, and "the English novel really began to lift me." From *Henry Esmond* he was to move back to the eighteenth century and, with a wild surmise, come upon the fine salt of the golden age of English prose masters: Addison, Steele, Swift, Fielding, Johnson, and Boswell. He admired Pope greatly, delighting in his barbed wit. It was but a step back to the Restoration dramatists, the Cavalier poets (Robert Herrick exerted a great influence on Mencken's verse), Ben Jonson, and, above all, Shakespeare. Years later, Edmund Wilson described Mencken's prose style as a blend of American colloquial speech with a rakish literary English that sounded as if it had come out of old plays of the period of Congreve and Wycherley and a tone that was both humorous and brutal in the alive-and-kicking manner of German polemics. On this article, published in the *New Republic* for June 1, 1921, Mencken wrote Wilson: "You have done me far more lavishly than any one else has ever done me, and with a far greater plausibility and eloquence. A little more, and you would have persuaded even me."[2]

Once launched upon the career of bookworm, the boy Mencken read everything he could get his hands on. As Mencken put it in the *Happy Days* chapter: "I began to inhabit a world that was two-thirds letterpress and only one-third trees, fields, streets and people. I acquired round shoulders, spindly shanks, and a despondent view of humanity. I read everything that I could find in English, taking in some of it but boggling most of it." Not until he reached adolescence, when he began "to distinguish between one necktie and another, and to notice the curiously divergent shapes, dispositions and aromas of girls," did he gradually begin to let up.

It is unthinkable that the young Mencken, just learning his trade, could have read Shaw without being, at first, overwhelmed, just as it was natural that he should have cooled toward the great Irishman as the years disclosed Shaw's extreme didacticism. One can imagine no more fitting subject for Mencken's first book of prose, written in 1904, when he was twenty-four (*Ventures into Verse* had appeared the year before). And doubtless Mencken learned much from the Shavian style: the iconoclastic wit, the hyperbolic exaggeration, the use of contrast, often outlandish, even fantastic. Moreover, Shaw always gave a good show. His customers invariably went away moved, if not convinced. At a time when Shaw's influence was just beginning to be felt, Mencken wrote of him as he had written of Ibsen (whom, incidentally, Mencken considered the greatest modern dramatist, primarily for his structural innovations in the drama of realism):

> In the dramas of George Bernard Shaw, which deal almost wholly with the current conflict between orthodoxy and heterodoxy, it is but natural that the characters should fall broadly into two general classes—the ordinary folks who represent the great majority, and the iconoclasts, or idol-smashers. Darwin made this war between the faithful and the scoffers the chief concern of the time, and the sham-smashing that is now going on, in all the fields of human inquiry, might be compared to the crusades that engrossed the world in the middle ages.[3]

Shaw was, Mencken felt, the most gifted of the present-day iconoclasts. Mencken was eager, of course, to take part in the sham-smashing. After all, the two writers who exerted the most enormous influence on his thought—Nietzsche and Thomas Henry Huxley—had spent their lives waging war on popular superstition and prejudice. He realized that the main concern of the vast hordes of aver-

age people was the fixation of belief. It is only natural that man
should wish to believe even that which is demonstrably untrue, for
in belief lie security and a guiding principle, without which there is
no clearly outlined purpose or meaning in life. Like most great
satirists, Mencken felt that the iconoclast proved enough when he
demonstrated the falsehood of some honored belief; there was no
need to hatch a new belief to fill the place of the exploded one. He
seemed to imply, if not overtly state, that a discarded belief left
as a residue the freedom to explore and interpret anew. Indeed,
Mencken felt that progress (what little there was) depended not
so much on the acceptance of new ideas as on the getting rid of
false ones.

In his little book on Shaw, some of the early slap and dash
of the Mencken style is evident, particularly in his discussion of
Man and Superman, which had appeared but recently.

> Measured with rule, plumb-line or hay-scales, *Man and
> Superman* is easily Shaw's *magnum opus.* In bulk it is brob-
> dingnagian; in scope it is stupendous; in purpose it is one with
> the Odyssey. Like a full-rigged ship before a spanking breeze,
> it cleaves deep into the waves, sending ripples far to port and
> starboard, and its giant canvases rise half way to the clouds,
> with resplendent jibs, skysails, staysails and studdingsails stand-
> ing out like quills upon the fretful porcupine.

Though in the play Shaw preached treason to all the schools,
there was no doubt that he had borrowed from earlier thinkers:
"It is a three-ring circus, with Ibsen doing running high jumps;
Schopenhauer playing the calliope and Nietzsche selling peanuts
in the reserved seats." Calling it "the most entertaining play of its
generation," he wondered if Shaw had not written it "in a vain
effort to rid himself at one fell swoop of all the disquieting doctrines that infested his innards." Finally, Mencken called it "a tract
cast in an encyclopedic and epic mold—a stupendous, magnificent,
colossal effort to make a dent in the cosmos with a slapstick."
Note that Mencken was aware of the fundamental fact that the
play was a "tract."

Mencken later remarked, in 1945, that "there was a good deal
of empty ornament in my first prose book, *George Bernard Shaw:
His Plays.* There was also plenty of bad writing in my early *Smart
Set* book reviews, begun in November, 1908. Soon afterward I be-

gan to tone down, and by the time I was thirty I had developed a style that was clear and alive."[4] It is worth noting that as he "toned down" his style, he became less enthusiastic about Shaw. His disenchantment was partially the result, it seems to me, of his realization that Shaw's handling of ideas was too often facile— perhaps of necessity, since he embodied his ideas on the stage. Shaw's facility in handling widely diverse ideas explains his hold on the young, particularly, but that very facility causes the mature student of ideas to be more interested in the Shavian wit than in the gospel being preached. In effect, it is Shaw's manner rather than his matter that continues to please.

The development of Mencken's attitude toward Shaw is most clearly evidenced in his remarks on the plays that appeared between 1910 and 1920. In a review of three plays, in the criticism for August, 1911, entitled "The New Dramatic Literature," Mencken wrote that the prefaces for *Getting Married* and *The Shewing-up of Blanco Posnet* were "far more important than the plays." At the same time, he thought *The Doctor's Dilemma* "an amusing and well constructed piece, in which fun is poked at the medical fellows on the one hand, and that puzzling thing, the artistic temperament, is studied on the other." He concluded by saying that *Dilemma* was the best thing Shaw had done since *Man and Superman*. Still, the antivivisectionist plea in the preface to *Dilemma* drew Mencken's scorn:

> Shaw, like every other anti-vivisectionist, is merely a senti-mentalist who strains at a guinea pig and swallows a baby. In brief, the wild Irishman sinks to the level of a somewhat ridiculous crusader. The trouble with him is that he has begun to take himself seriously. When he was content to write plays first and discuss them afterward, he was unfailingly diverting. But now that he writes tracts first and then devises plays to rub them in he grows rather tedious.

Reviewing a new edition of *Misalliance* in September, 1914, Mencken summed up the Shaw technique: "The formula of Shaw has become transparent enough—a dozen other men now practise his trick of putting the obvious into terms of the scandalous—but he still works with surpassing humor and address." The play's preface, which ran to something like 45,000 words, traversing "the whole field of the domestic relations, with side trips into education, journalism, party politics, theology, criminology and sex hygiene," was one of "the best things, indeed, that he has ever done." There was, however, condescension in the praise, since, after all, it was the obvious that Shaw put on display: "This is the special function of Shaw, the steady business of his life: to say the things that every body knows and nobody says, to expose the everyday hypocrisies, to rout platitudes with superplatitudes." The play would not, Mencken felt, lift Shaw any nearer Shakespeare, but it was excellent reading: "You will not do much snoring over this latest book. It will tickle you and caress you and make you tingle with delight. It is bully good stuff."

But by that date it was evident that Mencken no longer looked up to Shaw as the leader of the iconoclasts; he was now just one of the boys, one of the select few, to be sure, but by no means a saint gifted with divine powers. Moreover, Mencken had begun to find the prefaces more amusing than the plays—which is not to say that Mencken had changed in his critical views so much as it is to say that the prefaces of those later plays were frankly better reading than the plays they preceded.

Mencken's last critical essay on Shaw was his severest indictment of the platitudinarian aspects of the playwright. "The Ulster Polonious" first appeared in the *Smart Set* in August, 1916, as a review of *Androcles and the Lion* and then in a revised and lengthened form in *Prejudices: First Series.* Here Mencken did little more than polish and elaborate his thesis in the *Misalliance* review. Nowhere in Shaw, Mencken stated, was there an original idea; still, he was constantly abused as a heretic almost of the magnitude of Galileo, Nietzsche, or Simon Magus. Why so? Let Mencken, who was always willing to re-use one of his more succinct and melodious phrases, answer in his inimitable fashion.

> Because he practices with great zest and skill the fine art of exhibiting the obvious in unexpected and terrifying lights—because he is a master of the logical trick of so matching two apparently safe premises that they yield an incongruous and inconvenient conclusion—above all, because he is a fellow of the utmost charm and address, quick-witted, bold, limber-tongued, persuasive, humorous, iconoclastic, ingratiating—in brief, an Irishman, and so the exact antithesis of the solemn Sassenachs who ordinarily instruct and exhort us. Turn to his *Man and Superman,* and you will see the whole Shaw machine at work.

What he starts out with is the self-evident fact, disputed by no
one not idiotic, that a woman has vastly more to gain by marriage, under Christian monogamy, than a man. That fact is as
old as monogamy itself; it was, I daresay, the admitted basis
of the palace revolution which brought monogamy into the
world. But now comes Shaw with an implication that the sentimentality of the world chooses to conceal—with a deduction
plainly resident in the original proposition, but kept in safe silence there by a preposterous and hypocritical taboo—to wit, the
deduction that women are well aware of the profit that marriage
yields for them, and that they are thus much more eager to
marry than men are, and ever alert to take the lead in the business. This second fact, to any man who has passed through the
terrible years between twenty-five and forty, is as plain as the
first, but by a sort of general consent it is not openly stated.
Violate that general consent and you are guilty of *scandalum
magnatum*. Shaw is simply one who is guilty of *scandalum
magnatum* habitually, a professional criminal in that department. It is his life work to announce the obvious in terms of the
scandalous.[5]

What lies behind man's inability to face this particular fact, Mencken
felt (and Shaw would agree), is his intellectual cowardice. Mencken
stated it memorably: "Not even the most courageous and frank of
men likes to admit, in specific terms, that his wife is fat, or that she
seduced him to the altar by a transparent trick, or that their joint
progeny resemble her brother or father, and are thus cads."

Assuming Mencken to be correct in his criticism (and I think he
is), it is little wonder that the Shavian drama has an excellent ca-
thartic effect, nor is it a wonder that his plays were constantly
banned by the defenders of hypocrisy. Shaw offers the playgoer
the opportunity to hear truths about himself that he is either too
sentimental or too stupid to admit openly. More, he coats the truth
pill with a candy that is delectable enough to make the medicine
go down without the slightest struggle. In the play and preface of
Androcles and the Lion, for example, Mencken felt the complete
Shaw formula was exposed: "On the one hand there is a mass of
platitudes; on the other hand there is the air of a peep-show. On
the one hand he rehearses facts so stale that even Methodist clergymen have probably heard of them; on the other hand he states them
so scandalously that the pious get all the thrills out of the business
that would accompany a view of the rector in liquor in the pulpit."

Finally, and most importantly, Mencken objected to the moral note in all Shaw's writings, just as he objected to the moral preachments of all artists (he was particularly harsh with D. H. Lawrence on this score). It was dangerous, and usually crippling, he believed, for the artist to allow ethical concerns to dominate the work of art, which rightfully belonged to the realm of aesthetics. (At the present time, moralism in literature is not necessarily considered a defect. Many critics tend to make of literature a kind of religion, wherein are embodied, symbolically in most cases, the moral precepts that organized religions once furnished. F. R. Leavis and Yvor Winters are probably the leading exponents of the New Moralism.) To be sure, the artist could, if he pleased, present his characters involved in moral problems, but he should do so only to portray character and not some battle to the death between good and evil— the proper subject of melodrama or the Uplift.

By the time "The Ulster Polonius" was written, Shaw had all but forsaken the realm of aesthetics for that of ethics and the propagandizing of his beliefs. For this reason, Mencken refused to call Shaw the wholesale agnostic seen by his victims, nor was he even a true Irishman; rather he was "an orthodox Scotch Presbyterian of the most cock-sure and bilious sort—in fact, almost the archetype of the blue-nose." The Irishman was a romantic, who sensed life as "a mystery, a thing of wonder, an experience of passion and beauty. In politics he is not logical, but emotional. In religion his interest centers, not in the commandments, but in the sacraments."

Mencken had admired the Irish writers for years. He published some of Joyce's Dublin stories in the *Smart Set* (and thereby introduced Joyce to the American public). For years he had lauded the work of such Irishmen as George Moore, Lord Dunsany (whose work he introduced to the American reader when it appeared in the *Smart Set*), James Stephens, Lady Gregory, St. John Ervine, and a host of others. He considered Synge "one of the most original and arresting talents of our day and generation," a remark from his criticism for August, 1911. It is not likely that the man who thought *The Playboy of the Western World* the greatest modern comedy should at the same time praise *without qualification* the didactic comedies of Shaw.

The increasing severity of Mencken's criticism of Shaw has led some writers to believe that Mencken was simply an apostate Shavian or, more damning, an upstart who deflated Shaw in order to inflate himself. This latter charge has the least modicum of validity, since Mencken always believed that people enjoy reading attacks. But anyone who knows the least thing about Mencken the man knows that he was intellectually honest. In a recent article, entitled "Apostate Apostle: H. L. Mencken as Shavophile and Shavophobe," Stanley Weintraub, editor of the *Shaw Bulletin,* not only holds this theory but insists that "it is to Mencken more than any other American critic that we owe the popular notion of Shaw as a self-advertising clown and coiner of cheap paradoxes."[6] To hold such a belief is patently to overlook Mencken's early criticism, which should make it clear that he did no about-face in his attitude. Rather, that aspect of Shaw which Mencken liked least became more and more dominant as Shaw became more popular—or, as Mencken put it, as Shaw began to take himself seriously and write tracts. Moreover, Mencken never considered Shaw a "clown" or "a coiner of cheap paradoxes"; to say he did is to go far beyond the facts. But a self-advertiser he certainly was. Few other writers in world literature have so assiduously cultivated a public image of themselves. Shaw was never offstage.

Mencken wrote Upton Sinclair in 1926 that if Shaw were remembered fifty years hence "it will be for his earlier plays and for his uncommonly excellent criticism." The prediction has already proved accurate. (In the same letter he seriously questioned that H. G. Wells, at the time very popular and doubtless a great favorite of the credulous Sinclair, would be remembered in fifty years—the length of time Mencken usually gave as the testing period for artistic immortality.) Shaw, incidentally, stood Mencken's criticism well. In the early twenties, he admitted that he was "obviously and ridiculously out of date," never having heard of Willa Cather, Edith Wharton, or Sherwood Anderson and being under the impression that James Branch Cabell was a senator. But he had read Mencken and found him "an amusing dog, and a valuable critic, because he thinks it more important to write as he feels than to be liked as a good-hearted gentlemanly creature."[7]

As Mencken grew older and more practiced in the art of rhetorical swordplay, he also saw more clearly the tricks, of logic mainly, that Shaw employed in moving his audience—tricks similar to those he himself used. In a letter written in 1930, when he had mellowed somewhat, he admitted that both he and Shaw "were working the same side of the street." Mencken may also have felt that his criticism of Shaw was unjustly harsh, for in compiling *A Mencken Chrestomathy* (1949), in which he included what he considered the best of his writings then out of print, he failed to use a single piece on Shaw. It is also noteworthy that he is very kind to Shaw in the numerous references to him in *The American Language* and the two *Supplements*. Doubtless, Mencken learned a great deal about the art of writing from Shaw, though I think he learned more from both Huxley and Nietzsche.

Still, in their fundamental natures the two men, often so alike in their *manner*, were as far apart as were Joan of Arc and Voltaire. In his biography of Shaw, St. John Ervine produced a masterpiece of understatement when he remarked that Shaw's "credulity was surprising." He then quoted a letter William Archer wrote Shaw on the subject, dated June 12, 1923: "The trouble with you is that you are incurably credulous. Someone comes along and tells you that wool is the only wear; and instantly you go in for woollen boots, which lead, in due course, to a course of crutches." The difference between the two men is evident in their attitude toward language. Mencken meticulously examined the growth and nature of the American language in three fat volumes that stand as one of our great masterpieces of scholarship. Shaw was impatient with growth, with evolution, with the nature of things. He wished to change the language in one fell swoop—in effect, to regiment our speech. Hence, he asked that his sizable fortune be used in developing a new alphabet. Mencken delighted in the different uses of language, in dialects and slang—in all that gave language its timbre and color.

Perhaps the greatest difference between the two men may be seen in their attitudes toward politics and politicians. While each was contemptuous of democracy (Shaw's contempt grew in bitterness and despair; Mencken's became more resigned and stoical, until he could write in the preface to the *Chrestomathy*: "I do not believe in democracy, but I am perfectly willing to admit that it provides the only really amusing form of government ever endured by mankind"), they were at opposite poles in their regard for dictators. Ervine remarked that Shaw's "admiration for dictators was almost unbounded. Hitler, Mussolini, Kemal Atatürk, Stalin—all these absolute rulers received his admiration. He had nothing but disgust for the effete people who formed Cabinets in Great Britain. He gave three hearty cheers when Mussolini referred to the decaying corpse of democracy, and wished that there were a Mussolini in every country." While Mencken believed strongly in rule by an intellectual aristocracy, he was also our greatest champion of the individual and of civil rights in general. He considered the American Bill of Rights the greatest document ever devised by man. Between the two views lies a wide gulf.

II

Probably the three greatest influences on the thought and the prose style of Mencken were exerted by three vastly different men: Friedrich Nietzsche, Thomas Henry Huxley, and James Huneker. Interestingly enough, the only one of these whom Mencken accepted without numerous qualifications was Huxley. Becoming acquainted with Huxley at a very early age (at about the same time he was reading and admiring Herbert Spencer), Mencken imitated his master in several respects. He cultivated a prose style that was always clear, never given to the obscurantism that bedevils and bedamns such a large number of literary critics in their hopeless and rather sophomoric attempts to say things that lie too deep for words; he endeavored to emulate the honesty and courage shown by Huxley in his lifelong war upon superstitious belief backed by tradition; and he never lost faith in science and the scientific method as the only means by which exact knowledge could be obtained. Like Bertrand Russell, Mencken admitted that reason and science may not solve all man's ills (he considered many problems insoluble) or uncover all unknowns, but he insisted that the use of unreasoning impulse or blind faith (the cornerstones of fascism) could in no way do as well. A child of both eighteenth-century reason and nineteenth-century ideology and skepticism, Mencken was a thoroughgoing materialist. At the same time, he was fully aware of the irrationality of the mind and of the extreme importance of emotion as the primary mover. Mencken's writings, particularly those on religion—for example, *Treatise on the Gods*—are as much existential as they are rationalistic. In his early writing there was an element of scientific optimism, but this quickly gave way to a more cautious and skeptical view of human progress. Still, what man knew of his life and his surroundings he had acquired by the use of the intellect rather than by intuition or spirit or blood-knowledge. Mencken was contemptuous, just as was Russell, of the later D. H. Lawrence, for example, and his messianic delusions about the "white psyche" and the "white consciousness" and all the apocalyptic preaching about how the "blood *hates* being KNOWN by the mind" and about how "Blood-consciousness overwhelms, obliterates, and annuls mind-consciousness." He was also a blistering critic of the various forms of New Thought, so popular in the days preceding World War I. Doubtless, he would have subscribed completely to the pessimistic and yet liberating view expressed by Russell in "A Free Man's Worship":

> That man is the product of causes which had no prevision of the end they were achieving; that his origin, his growth, his hopes and fears, his loves and his beliefs, are but the outcome of accidental collocations of atoms; that no fire, no heroism, no intensity of thought and feeling, can preserve an individual life beyond the grave; that all the labors of the ages, all the devotion, all the inspiration, all the noonday brightness of human genius, are destined to extinction in the vast death of the solar system, and that the whole temple of man's achievement must inevitably be buried beneath the debris of a universe in ruins—all these things, if not quite beyond dispute, are yet so nearly certain that no philosophy which rejects them can hope to stand.

During his lifetime Mencken was called upon a number of times to give his credo. Rather than paraphrase any of those statements of belief, and in the paraphrase lose much of the essence that always lies in the Mencken style—which, according to Jacques Barzun, "reveals its subject and conceals its art"—I shall quote from one that appeared in 1931.

> What I believe is mainly what has been established by plausible and impartial evidence, e.g., that the square on the hypotenuse of a right triangle is equal to the squares on the other two sides, that water is composed of oxygen and hydrogen, and that man is a close cousin to the ape. Further than that I do not care to go. Is there a life after death, as so many allege, wherein the corruptible puts on incorruption and the mortal immortality? I can only answer that I do not know. My private inclination is to hope that it is not so, but that hope is only a hope, and hopes and beliefs, it seems to me, can have nothing in common. If, while the taxidermists are stuffing my integument for some fortunate museum of anatomy, a celestial catchpole summons my

psyche to Heaven, I shall be very gravely disappointed, but (unless my habits of mind change radically at death) I shall accept the command as calmly as possible, and face eternity without repining.

Most of the sorrows of man, I incline to think, are caused by just such repining. Alone among the animals, he is dowered with the capacity to invent imaginary worlds, and he is always making himself unhappy by trying to move into them. Thus he underrates the world in which he actually lives, and so misses most of the fun that is in it. That world, I am convinced, could be materially improved, but even as it stands it is good enough to keep any reasonable man entertained for a lifetime.

As for me, I roll out of my couch every morning with the most agreeable expectations. In the morning paper there is always massive and exhilarating evidence that the human race, despite its ages-long effort to imitate the seraphim, is still doomed to be irrevocably human, and in my morning mail I always get soothing proof that there are men left who are even worse asses than I am.[8]

Whether Mencken's admiration of Huxley was a cause or an effect of his lifelong interest in science, and especially in biology, there is no way of knowing, since he showed this admiration and interest almost from the start. It was Huxley, more than any other, who coordinated in Mencken the vague, disordered unbelief which he had inherited from his amiably irreligious grandfather and his contemptuously atheistic father. Indeed, Mencken derived from a long line of aristocratic freethinkers, several of them well-known teachers and scholars at the University of Leipzig. One of them, Johann Burkhard Mencken, Vice-Chancellor of the University, was the author of a book, *The Charlatanry of the Learned* (1715), which was translated from the Latin into German, Dutch, French, and Italian and was read throughout Europe for almost a century. It is amusing to note that this famous book was once banned, without effect, at the request of a powerful Lutheran minister of Leipzig. Otto Mencke (without the final *n*), Johann's father, began as a professor of theology, but was soon to declare himself "the biggest fool that the sun ever shone upon" for his having been taken in. After renouncing theology he cofounded *Acta Eruditorum*, a magazine for the leading scientists and skeptics of Europe. An uncle of Johann, Luder Mencke, was so learned a man that he was called the "living lawbook"; it was this kinsman who employed Johann Sebastian

Bach as choirmaster in his church. Another Mencken, Anastasius (1755? to 1806?), put an end to the scholarly tradition when he deserted academic life for the more glittering surroundings of Frederick the Great's court. Eventually he became officially Frederick's private secretary and unofficially one of the most influential men in Prussia. His extraordinarily beautiful daughter, Luise Wilhelmine, was to marry a cavalry officer named Karl William Ferdinand von Bismarck in 1808, and in 1815 she gave birth to a son, Otto, later known as the Iron Chancellor.[9]

Had Mencken never read Huxley or anyone else of the scientific, agnostic fraternity, for that matter, he would undoubtedly have been a skeptic for a number of reasons. Besides the influence of his family, there is the fact that he was a journalist in some capacity or other from the age of nineteen onward, even serving for a time as a police reporter; and police reporters on large city dailies are, as Mencken would say, lost to all human decency. Considering his intensely practical, common-sensical intelligence, one can hardly conceive of his having anything to do with supernaturalism except perhaps as a phenomenon to study, as an archaeologist might study an artifact. No doubt the clearness and beauty of Huxley's prose style were in great part responsible for the great impression Huxley made on the youth; with his rationality, the "bulldog of Darwin" only provided Mencken with good reasons for his already half-formed agnosticism. More important than the lesson in philosophy, however, was the lesson in composition. In a long letter sent to Burton Rascoe in 1920, Mencken listed Huxley as the greatest influence on his style: "My style of writing is chiefly grounded upon an early enthusiasm for Huxley, the greatest of all masters of orderly exposition. He taught me the importance of giving to every argument a simple structure." The "fancy work on the surface," as Mencken called it, came from other sources, mainly journalistic. Writing of the great Englishman in the Baltimore *Evening Sun* on the centennial of his birth, May 4, 1925, Mencken displayed all the exuberance and youthful ardor of his earlier years in a panegyric that reveals the durable qualities of Huxley's influence.

> Huxley, I believe, was the greatest Englishman of the Nineteenth Century—perhaps the greatest Englishman of all time. When one thinks of him, one thinks of him inevitably in terms of such men as Goethe and Aristotle. For in him there was that

rich, incomparable blend of intelligence and character, of colossal knowledge and high adventurousness, of instinctive honesty and indomitable courage which appears in mankind only
once in a blue moon. There have been far greater scientists,
even in England, but there has never been a scientist who was
a greater man. A touch of the poet was in him, and another of
the romantic, gallant *Homo sapiens,* the superlatively admirable
all-around man.[10]

Mencken felt that Huxley had placed all men, and especially those
of the English-speaking world, in his debt. He had opposed stupidity and tyranny all his life; his battles were all fought for the plain
truth that sets men free. Mencken considered him not only an intellectual colossus but a great artist who knew how to be charming
—one of the highest compliments Mencken could pay a man.
Twenty years later, in discussing his own prose style, Mencken
again paid tribute to Huxley's prose. "It was as far ahead of that
of Macauley as that of Macauley was ahead of the ornate quasi-
Latin of the later Eighteenth Century. No matter how difficult the
theme he dealt with, Huxley was always crystal clear. He even
made metaphysics intelligible, and, what is more, charming. Nietzsche did the same thing in German, but I can recall no one else in
English."[11]

If Huxley provided a model for Mencken's style—its clarity,
simplicity, gracefulness—then Nietzsche was to give Mencken the
perfect example of a style that was explosively alive. Nietzsche
showed the young newspaperman how to express himself in a vibrant, muscular manner, employing a metaphoric language that
was often outlandish and shocking and that possessed, above all
else, the quality of unexpectedness. The Rabelaisian humor of
Mencken was not learned, of course, from the ascetic, somewhat
prudish Nietzsche.

Although Mencken was long considered America's foremost
Nietzschean, having written the first book in English on the philosopher, which was widely read for twenty years, his praise was always qualified. For example, though he enjoyed reading *Ecce Homo,*
he considered it a "semi-insane rhapsody." In a particularly revealing letter to Harry Leon Wilson in 1933, Mencken remarked that
the narrowness of the early training of Nietzsche had an injurious
effect on all his later writing. "As he grew up he could never quite
throw off the ideas rammed into him, and in his most florid revolts

there was always a touch of prissiness. His glorification of mere strength was in large part a reaction from his own feebleness." Nietzsche was an odd fellow, Mencken remarked, and one should always remember that his books were not those of a normal man. Furthermore, Nietzsche lacked a sense of humor, though he had "a considerable bitter wit." And this absence of humor, to Mencken, was more than a character trait; it was a serious limitation.

More than anything else, it was Nietzsche's attacks on the moral interpretation of existence that interested Mencken. When Nietzsche placed ethics among the phenomena, thereby demoting it from its former absolute position, he helped clear the way for an aesthetics free from moral premises. Nietzsche wrote in 1886 that morality had become "a mere fabrication for purposes of gulling: at best, an artistic fiction; at worst, an outrageous imposture." Both the tone and idea may be found again and again in Mencken's writings, particularly in his insistence that the artist should be free from the moral certainties (which were all false anyhow) of inferior men. Putting it another way, it was only the inferior man who professed belief in moral certainties. If art is not *in its nature* a moral concern, then the artist creates in an atmosphere "beyond good and evil." The artist—that is, the man who creates order out of what previously had no order—is a man who makes his own laws, grabs his own rewards, and sets standards for others. That he should be oppressed, especially in a democracy, by the majority which considers itself "right" is, Mencken felt, only natural—and of little importance. "All it amounts to is this: that the artist in America can never have a large audience and must expect to encounter positive hostility—Comstockery, college-professorism, etc."[12]

In *Beyond Good and Evil* Nietzsche wrote that every great philosopher "has always found himself, and always had to find himself, in opposition to his today." Great thinkers have always been "the bad conscience of their time." They applied "the knife vivisectionally to the very virtues of the time," uncovering "how much hypocrisy" and "how many lies were concealed under the most honored type of their contemporary morality, how much virtue was outlived." In other words, the greatest philosophers were iconoclasts. Moreover, it should be remembered that what is today iconoclastic may tomorrow be orthodox. Without intending to make an invidious comparison between Mencken and Nietzsche, I think it is evident that Mencken was out of step with his own time, that he was the "bad conscience" Nietzsche spoke of, and that his knife uncovered more hypocrisy and lies in American society than that of any other surgeon of his day. The pity was that Mencken's iconoclasm in the field of literary criticism became orthodoxy in the period following the First World War, and this caused later critics to forget the great service he performed in the first two decades of the century.

Examining the new translations and critiques of Nietzsche as they came out during those two decades, Mencken assumed the almost impossible task of correcting misunderstandings about the philosopher's thought. Anyone at all familiar with the history of Nietzsche's reputation will readily admit the herculean nature of such an undertaking. For example, there are still numerous people who credit Nietzsche, the great admirer of Jews and the fervent adversary of statism in general and German nationalism in particular, with having been the father of Nazism and German anti-Semitism. He has probably been more widely condemned for things he never said, for beliefs he never professed, than any writer who ever lived. Neither Hegel nor Emerson has been so outrageously misrepresented. In the introduction to his translation of *The Antichrist* (which is by far the "best written" of the half-dozen translations I have looked at), Mencken summed up the essential philosophy of Nietzsche better than anyone has yet done, at least in English. Unfortunately, that thirty-page essay is no longer readily available. Much of it is concerned with the growth of Nietzsche's influence before, during, and just after the war. It also succeeds in clarifying the position of Nietzsche in Western thought. Here is a brief passage:

> The will to power was [Nietzsche's] answer to Christianity's affectation of humility and self-sacrifice; eternal recurrence was his mocking criticism of Christian optimism and millennialism; the superman was his candidate for the place of the Christian ideal of the "good" man, prudently abased before the throne of God. The things he chiefly argued for were anti-Christian things —the abandonment of the purely moral view of life, the rehabilitation of instinct, the dethronement of weakness and timidity as ideals, the renunciation of the whole hocus-pocus of dogmatic religion, the extermination of false aristocracies (of the priest, of the politician, of the plutocrat), the revival of the healthy,

lordly "innocence" that was Greek. If he was anything in a word, Nietzsche was a Greek born two thousand years too late. His dreams were thoroughly Hellenic; his whole manner of thinking was Hellenic; his peculiar errors were Hellenic no less. But his Hellenism, I need not add, was anything but the pale neo-Platonism that has run like a thread through the thinking of the Western world since the days of the Christian Fathers. From Plato, to be sure, he got what all of us must get, but his real forefather was Heraclitus. It is in Heraclitus that one finds the germ of his primary view of the universe—a view, to wit, that sees it, not as moral phenomenon, but as mere aesthetic representation. The God that Nietzsche imagined, in the end, was not far from the God that such an artist as Joseph Conrad imagines —a supreme craftsman, ever experimenting, ever coming closer to an ideal balancing of lines and forces, and yet always failing to work out the final harmony.[13]

Of all American critics, the one who exerted the greatest influence on Mencken's thought and manner was undoubtedly James Huneker. Mencken wrote Dreiser in 1911 that Huneker and William Archer, "two very different men, have given me more ideas than any other living critics." Ludwig Lewisohn did not exaggerate much when he stated that "the entire modern period of American culture is scarcely thinkable without the long energetic and fruitful activity of James Huneker."[14] It would be impossible to know for sure that Huneker "helped more than anyone else to change the cultural climate of America," but there can be no doubt that his influence on and through such men as Mencken, Nathan, Benjamin De Casseres, Carl Van Vechten, Lawrence Gilman, and Paul Rosenfeld was enormous. He stood above all other journalistic critics of the seven arts of his day.

Though he was never a very popular writer with the mass of readers in America, Huneker was always looked up to by the younger critics. There is every reason to believe that he influenced Mencken more than any other of the younger man's contemporaries. To begin with, he was first of all a music critic (his *Chopin: The Man and His Music* [1900] is often considered his best work), and this alone would endear him to Mencken, whose first love was always the tonal art. Such works as *Iconoclasts, a Book of Dramatists* (1905) and *Egoists: A Book of Supermen* (1909) were concerned with precisely those whom Mencken most admired. One-fourth of Mencken's *A Book of Prefaces* (1917) was devoted to discussing

Huneker's criticism, and in his *Smart Set* articles he was forever praising and popularizing him. Between June, 1909, when he reviewed *Egoists* in the *Smart Set,* and 1929, when he selected and prefaced a volume of *Essays by James Huneker,* Mencken wrote a dozen reviews of, or essays on, Huneker's work. "Huneker: a Memory," written shortly after Huneker died in 1921, is probably the best essay ever done on the man. First printed in the *Century* in June, 1921, it then appeared in *Prejudices: Third Series,* and was later collected in the *Chrestomathy.*

Avoiding all the wild movements of his age, Huneker preferred to follow the dictates of his cultured taste rather than those of some school of criticism. Today he is generally catalogued, accurately enough, as an impressionist. In thus "disposing" of him, we should remember that *all* competent critics are, in varying degrees, impressionistic. The mischief is that the decidedly impressionistic critic too often allows his "impressions" to take the place of analysis, when the two should go together. Moreover, the impressionist, like Henry James, for instance, frequently lacks the judicial temperament so necessary to *judging* the work of art. Rather than outfit Huneker with any such broad, and often misleading, tag, Mencken wrote:

> If he bears a simple label, indeed, it is that of anti-Philistine. And the Philistine he attacks is not so much the vacant and harmless fellow who belongs to the Odd Fellows and recreates himself with *Life* and *Leslie's Weekly* in the barber shop, as that more belligerent and pretentious donkey who presumes to do battle for "honest" thought and a "sound" ethic—the "forward looking" man, the university ignoramus, the conservator of orthodoxy, the rattler of ancient phrases—what Nietzsche called "the Philistine of culture." It is against this fat milch cow of wisdom that Huneker has brandished a spear since there was a Huneker.[15]

Mencken felt that Huneker had accomplished precisely what all good critics accomplish: he had introduced his readers to a number of true artists and had done so in a charming and ingratiating manner. He was, according to Mencken, the first American "to write about Ibsen with any understanding of the artist behind the prophet's mask"; as far back as 1888 he saw the "rising star of Nietzsche"; he saw the importance of Shaw's criticism long before Shaw became known as a dramatist; he wrote of Hauptmann and

Maeterlinck before they were accepted in their own countries; his criticism of Sudermann, written in 1905, "may stand with scarcely the change of a word today"; he aided Strindberg, Hervieu, Stirner, and Gorki, and later helped Conrad; "he was in the van of the MacDowell enthusiasts; he fought for the ideas of such painters as Davies, Lawson, Luks, Sloan and Prendergast (Americans all, by the way: an answer to the hollow charge of exotic obsession) at a time when even Manet, Monet and Degas were laughed at"; among American writers he early fought for were Norris, Dreiser, Crane, and H. B. Fuller.[16] Mencken lauded Huneker's intellectual alertness, his catholic hospitality to ideas, his artistic courage, and, above all, his powers of persuasion. Without the charm of his style, Huneker could never have persuaded others to see and understand the artists about whom he wrote.

In "Huneker: a Memory" Mencken pointed out that Huneker's intensely impressionistic style, with its extravagant name-dropping, was at times a fault insofar as it tended to group the giants with the pigmies indiscriminately. Also, he was too fond of rebels just for the sake of rebellion; hence, he sometimes overpraised the sort of revolutionist who was here today and gone tomorrow. But he also championed artists whose reputations eventually became secure— Ibsen, Nietzsche, Brahms, Richard Strauss, Cézanne, Stirner, Synge, the Russian composers and novelists. "He did for this Western world what Georg Brandes was doing for Continental Europe— sorting out the new comers with sharp eyes, and giving mighty lifts to those who deserved it." And he accomplished his goal with verve and grace; he represented "a glorious deliverance from schoolmastering." In Huneker's conversation, just as in his writing, there were zest and the scent of vine leaves.

In his early days, when he performed the tonal and carnal prodigies that he liked to talk of afterward, I was at nurse, and too young to have any traffic with him. When I encountered him at last he was in the high flush of the middle years, and had already become a tradition in the little world that critics inhabit. We sat down to luncheon at one o'clock; I think it must have been at Luchow's, his favorite refuge and rostrum to the end. At six, when I had to go, the waiter was hauling in his tenth (or was it twentieth?) Seidel of Pilsner, and he was bringing to a close *prestissimo* the most amazing monologue that these ears (up to that time) had ever funnelled into this consciousness. What a stew, indeed! Berlioz and the question of the clang-tint of the viola, the psychopathological causes of the suicide of Tschaikowsky, why Nietzsche had to leave Sils Maria between days in 1887, the echoes of Flaubert in Joseph Conrad (then but newly dawned), the precise topography of the warts of Liszt, George Bernard Shaw's heroic but vain struggles to throw off Presbyterianism, how Frau Cosima saved Wagner from the libidinous Swedish baroness, what to drink when playing Chopin, what Cézanne thought of his disciples, the defects in the structure of *Sister Carrie*, Anton Seidl and the musical union, the complex love affairs of Gounod, the early days of David Belasco, the varying talents and idiosyncrasies of Lillian Russell's earlier husbands, whether a girl educated at Vassar could ever really learn to love, the exact composition of chicken paprika, the correct tempo of the Vienna waltz, the style of William Dean Howells, what George Moore said about German bathrooms, the true inwardness of the affair between D'Annunzio and Duse, the origin of the theory that all oboe players are crazy, why Löwenbräu survived exportation better than Hofbräu, Ibsen's loathing of Norwegians, the best remedy for Rhine wine *Katzenjammer*, how to play Brahms, the degeneration of the Bal Bullier, the sheer physical impossibility of getting Dvořák drunk, the genuine last words of Walt Whitman.[17]

There is doubtless a great deal more art than exact truth to this record, as Mencken would be the first to admit, but it is easy to believe him when he said it took two days to sort out his impressions and formulate some coherent image of the man. If Huneker was allusive in his books, then he was ten times more so in his discourse—

a veritable geyser of unfamiliar names, shocking epigrams in strange tongues, unearthly philosophies out of the backwaters of Scandinavia, Transylvania, Bulgaria, the Basque country, the Ukraine. And did he, in his criticism pass facilely from the author to the man, and from the man to his wife, and to the wives of his friends? Then at the *Biertisch* he began long beyond the point where the last honest wife gives up the ghost, and so, full tilt, ran into such complexities of adultery that a plain sinner could scarcely follow him. I try to give you, ineptly and grotesquely, some notion of the talk of the man, but I must fail inevitably. It was, in brief, chaos, and chaos cannot be described.[18]

No doubt Mencken admired Huneker for what he was *not* as well as for what he was. The fact that Huneker's criticism was

almost the diametrical opposite of academic criticism would by itself have impressed Mencken favorably. Nowhere in all his books
could Mencken find him "doing the things that every right-thinking
Anglo-Saxon critic is supposed to do—the Middleton Murry, Paul
Elmer More, Clutton-Brock sort of puerility—solemn essays on
Coleridge and Addison, abysmal discussions of the relative merits
of Schumann and Mendelssohn, horrible treatises upon the relations
of Goethe to the Romantic Movement, dull scratchings in a hundred
such exhausted and sterile fields." Huneker never indulged in au-
topsies; he never engaged in the professorial game of re-evaluating
the masters. Rather, he brought gusto and life into American criticism, long known for its sober dullness. In short, Huneker brought
back into vogue the alive and kicking manner of Poe. It is remarkable that his "ethical atheism," as Mencken called it, which was
at once strange and abhorrent to Americans, should have exerted
so much influence on the critics who followed him. It is evident
that in comparing literary criticism with scholarship, Mencken was
confusing the issue, at least insofar as he expected one to do the
work of the other. Such confusion of these two related but quite
different fields is, of course, more evident than ever today. Mencken
was well within his rights, however, when he castigated those dull-
ards of the academy who were often wont to forsake scholarship
for the more lively enterprise of criticism—an enterprise for which
they were totally unfit. In commenting on the influence of Huneker,
Mencken contrasted his aesthetic criticism with the moralistic
didacticism of his contemporaries.

> What [Huneker] brought back from Paris was precisely the
> thing that was most suspected in the America of those days:
> the capacity for gusto. Huneker had that capacity in a degree
> unmatched by any other critic. When his soul went adventuring
> among masterpieces it did not go in Sunday broadcloth; it went
> with vine leaves in its hair. The rest of the appraisers and criers-
> up—even Howells, with all his humor—could never quite rid
> themselves of the professorial manner. When they praised it
> was always with some hint of ethical, or, at all events, of cul-
> tural purpose; when they condemned that purpose was even
> plainer. The arts, to them, constituted a sort of school for the
> psyche; their aim was to discipline and mellow the spirit. But
> to Huneker their one aim was always to make the spirit glad—
> to set it, in Nietzsche's phrase, to dancing with arms and legs.
> He had absolutely no feeling for extra-aesthetic valuations. If

a work of art that stood before him was honest, if it was original, if it was beautiful and thoroughly alive, then he was for it to his last corpuscle. What if it violated all the accepted canons? Then let the accepted canons go hang! What if it lacked all purpose to improve and lift up? Then so much the better! What if it shocked all right-feeling men, and made them blush and tremble? Then damn all men of right feeling forevermore.[19]

Mencken here exaggerates Huneker's role in the battle between the aesthetics and the moralists; his own influence was far greater, in this particular conflict, than was Huneker's. Furthermore, Huneker was not nearly so iconoclastic as Mencken implies; at least he was not *consciously* iconoclastic. It was Mencken, not Huneker, who knocked heads about—and delighted in the knocking. Though their relationship could hardly be called a teacher–student one, it is nonetheless clear that Mencken learned a great deal about the art of criticism from the cosmopolitan Huneker. Together they were largely responsible for the great upheaval in critical philosophy; they led American criticism out of the wilderness of academic stultification. As Benjamin De Casseres remarked, "Huneker and Mencken did more than any other two men of the century to thin the ranks of the literary stud-horses from Vassar and the fillies from Harvard."[20]

CHAPTER FOUR

First Premise

IT is a sad commentary on the huge army of the critics of criticism that they very often overlook the fact that criticism, if it is to outlive the day of its birth, must be interesting. It is obvious that the man who writes well has an enormous advantage over the man whose prose is a task rather than a joy to read. The clumsy writer might gain a degree of fame in his own day, but posterity has a merciful habit of letting dust cover his work. To be sure, one constantly hears that it is impossible to separate *what* is being said from *how* it is being said; in other words, to separate content and style. This is, of course, patently false. Every reader distinguishes between an author's matter and his manner. Long before the birth of those of us who insist to undergraduates that those two aspects are insolubly wed, Mencken was saying the same thing —and then contradicting himself in the next breath. The argument is at times useful, so we use it. At other times, we feel the need to distinguish between the two, so we suddenly become critical dualists.

One thing at least is certain: the writer of grace and charm will be read long after the pedestrian maker of sentences is forgotten, even though the two may have expressed essentially the same ideas. Schopenhauer is more widely read than Kant, not because he was a more profound thinker—for he was not—but simply because he was a better "writer." In like manner, we read Nietzsche while

Hegel gathers dust on the shelf because (other things being equal) Nietzsche wrote with gusto and Hegel wrote such atrocious German that no one has yet been able to render it gracefully even in translation. Voltaire will always be widely read because of the clarity, vigor, and euphony of his style, not because of the profundity of his thought. In Voltaire's prose, we see the *whole* man, not just the intellect. He exemplifies perfectly Thoreau's remark: "We cannot write well or truly but what we write with gusto. The body, the senses must conspire with the mind."

Before saying anything of Mencken's critical philosophy, I think it might help to comment on, and illustrate through quotation, the guiding principles for all his criticism. He credited Robert I. Carter, managing editor and drama critic for the Baltimore *Herald, circa* 1900, with having taught him "that the first desideratum in criticism is to be *interesting*."[1] In the same letter (to Burton Rascoe) he wrote that Huxley had taught him the value of apt phrases and the need for an extensive vocabulary. "I believe that a good phrase is better than a Great Truth—which is usually buncombe. I delight in argument, not because I want to convince, but because argument itself is an end." An exaggeration, certainly—another of Mencken's efforts to play the bad boy by eschewing any semblance of *moral* earnestness in his writing. The fact was that he wished very much to convince that small body of readers he referred to as the "civilized minority." As for the large body of readers, we may safely believe Mencken when he tells us that it was a matter of no importance to him whether he was accepted or rejected. He was much too arrogant to care. And in this disdainful arrogance, with its concomitant faith in the "good phrase," lie both great strength and weakness. It helped make him the consummate artist that he was; and it caused, and causes, readers to take much of what he wrote with a grain of salt. On the one ha 1, it helped raise Mencken to a power never possessed, before o. .fter, by an American writer. Not even Shaw in England wielded the power over his fellow countrymen that Mencken had in America for over a decade. But on the other hand, Mencken's skepticism, so foreign to Americans, made him vulnerable to the charge of insincerity. It was easy to label him as little more than a phrase-maker. But what phrases!

Reviewing *Prejudices: Third Series* in 1922, Newton Arvin praised Mencken for his willingness to attack humbug in all its forms and for his style, which, "as a style, is a medium of perfect efficiency; it is vibrant, athletic, vascular. He should take rank among our first-rate prosateurs." In his essay-review, Arvin stated that Mencken had by that time become a recognized national figure and was perhaps America's first literary dictator. He felt that Mencken would be remembered primarily as a humorist, an assessment that is much too common among Mencken's critics. The fact that Mencken was a humorist of high rank has, I think, caused many people to think of him as *primarily* a wit, whereas the humor is really a means to an end, not an end in itself. Laughter, particularly derisive laughter, was a weapon in his arsenal with which to goad the thick hides of self-complacent men. It was a shaft to be turned on "unwarranted pretension," the avowed target of his writing, especially in the nineteen-twenties. His work, whether it took the form of burlesque, serious criticism, or mere casual controversy, always sought "to expose a false pretense, to blow up a wobbly axiom, to uncover a sham virtue."[2] A negative view, one might say, but no less a noble enterprise. Walter Kaufmann has wisely said, "The critic who attacks idolatry does the most serious thing of which a man is capable." Still, it is a natural human tendency, especially in England and America, to accord the humorless clod who spouts his nonsense with funereal seriousness a higher position than we give to the hearty rascal who leavens his common sense with laughter.

Arvin also paid homage to the libertarianism of Mencken, remarking that the Baltimore Sage came like a gust of fresh air into the sultry atmosphere of the period around 1910 and had been giving humbug and cant and bigotry a spirited run for their money ever since. "He has been a gadfly to the State, a voice crying in the wilderness, a mouthpiece of the Lord. All that is vulgar and cheap and craven in American life has had its due from him; and is certainly less secure than it would have been without him." Moreover, unlike Carlyle, Mencken had no "Messianic delusion"; rather, he performed his services as a freer and more robust Mark Twain.[3]

In the first of the 182 criticisms he was to write for the *Smart Set*, covering the span from November, 1908, to December, 1923, Mencken set the pattern to which he adhered more or less throughout the fifteen-year period. He began his initial piece, entitled "The

Good, the Bad and the Best Sellers," by endeavoring in the opening paragraphs to lure or charm his reader into following his arguments and reading his criticism:

> Platitudes have their uses, I have no doubt, but in the fair field of imaginative literature they have a disconcerting habit of denouncing and betraying one another. Separate a single platitude from the herd, and you will find it impeccable, inviolable and inevitable; comfortable, amiable and well-mannered. But then lead out another and try to drive them tandem; or three more and try to drive them four-in-hand; and you will quickly land in the hospital—your collar-bone broken, your head in a whirl and your raiment muddy and torn.

Mencken then indulged in a brief parody of an example of the platitude that can stand alone (viz., It is wrong for the rich to rob the poor) which becomes absurd when placed beside a brother platitude (viz., Only the poor are happy). He then asked, apropos of his preliminary material, what platitudes have to do with the divine art of literature. And, more particularly, what they have to do with Upton Sinclair's "new romance," *The Moneychangers.* Answering his own rhetorical question, he concluded: "Simply this: that hordes of the *bacillus platitudae* have entered Sinclair's system and are preying upon his vitals. They have already consumed his sense of humor and are now fast devouring his elemental horse sense. The first result is that he is taking himself and the world seriously, and the second result is that he is writing tracts." And the tract, with the exception of "explanatory programs from symphony concerts," is, Mencken said, the lowest of all forms of literature. In order to write a play, a novel, a poem, or even a newspaper editorial, "one must first ensnare an idea. To write a tract one needs but leisure, a grouch and a platitude." Lamenting the fact that Sinclair had not fulfilled his early promise, Mencken pointed to the great success of *The Jungle,* which had appeared two years before, as the point in Sinclair's career when "the afflatus of a divine mission began to stir him, and he sallied forth to preach his incomprehensible *jehad.* Today he is going the road of Walt Whitman, of Edwin Markham, of the later Zola, all of whom began as artists and ended as mad mullahs." (I shall discuss Mencken's review again in the following chapter on his critical credo.)

Another example of Mencken's method of approaching the first,

and usually longest, criticism in his articles, which generally ran
to five thousand words each, will help to illustrate his strong belief
that the prime requisite of all writing, and especially criticism, is
that it be charming and readable:

> When George Moore looks at human life he sees it as a
> conflict between the flesh and spirit, the impulse to have a high
> old time and the yearning to get to Heaven; when Thomas
> Hardy looks at it he sees it as a hopeless tragedy; when Joseph
> Conrad looks at it he sees it as a meaningless and insoluble
> riddle. I might go on thus for pages, pointing out the differences
> in point of view which set off author from author, school from
> school, philosophy from philosophy. Rabelais and Thackeray
> were cynics and so they saw life as a great game of make-
> believe, with all of the participants wearing grotesque cloaks
> and masques; Dickens was a maudlin sentimentalist and so he
> saw it as an affecting morality play, with hymns by the choir
> and a collection for the orphans; Sterne and Congreve were
> liquorish revelers and blacklegs and so they saw it as a wild
> carouse. Our American manufacturers of best sellers, having the
> souls of fudge-besotted high school girls, behold the human
> comedy as a mixture of fashionable wedding and three-alarm
> fire, with music by Frédéric François Chopin; the pornographic
> lady novelists of England, having the outlook of elderly and
> immoral virgins, see it as a Paris peep show. Finally, there are
> the happy fellows who see life as a joke—not as a hollow and
> mirthless joke, but as one of innocent merriment all compact,
> with a faint undercurrent, let us say, of honest sentiment. To
> that select and genial congregation belongs W. J. Locke, author
> of *Simon the Jester*.[4]

From this opening gossip, Mencken went on to compare the novel
with an earlier Locke work, *Septimus*, which he had reviewed and
praised a few months earlier.

It would be a rare specimen of humanity who could read
Mencken and be bored. It is not difficult to imagine a literate
reader disagreeing with him; indeed, it would be difficult to imagine anyone agreeing with everything Mencken said; but it is all
but inconceivable that anyone could be indifferent to him. He
always insisted that the critic not bury the work of art by writing
like a tired mortician. While airing his discontents with American
criticism in a series of articles that appeared in the *Atlantic* a few
years back, Alfred A. Knopf remarked that we have had no critic
since Mencken who could make his reader actually want to pur-

chase a book. Indeed, Henry Mencken "could even sell a book by denouncing it, so arresting was his invective."

Perhaps the most salient feature of the Mencken style is its vigor (Edgar Kemler remarked that "no writer, except Rabelais, ever argued a case with such animal spirit or visceral force"). In reviewing a book of James Huneker's criticism (*The Pathos of Distance* [1913]), Mencken wrote, "Huneker stands head and shoulders above the general, for he gets into his prose the quality of gusto, the air of one enjoying the making of it, and that is something which very few other Americans show." Mencken went on to say that the national style possessed a heaviness that was scarcely matched in England and Germany. Even "our newspapers are written in the fashion of a death warrant" and "our prevailing criticism smells of the pulpit, the Chautauqua, the schoolroom. [. . .] But Huneker writes like a Frenchman—like those misplanted Frenchmen, Friedrich Nietzsche and George Henry Lewes." Furthermore, Huneker met George Gissing's demand that the artist should be free from everything like moral prepossession. He never denounced an idea just because it happened to be unusual, nor was he one "to measure first-rate men with the yardstick of the rabble; he is wholly free from that national Puritanism which attempts to reduce all art to terms of a windy and puerile morality; he doesn't apply the theology of the 'Jubilee Songs' to concepts of civilized men."[5]

Like Huneker, Mencken could be wrong at times, as he himself always admitted, but he was never lifeless. In an early article, in 1909, he ended his review of Owen Johnson's *The Eternal Boy* thus:

> Here is a writer who knows the young male of the human species as thoroughly as a Maryland blackamoor knows the roosting customs of the domestic fowl—knows him from his frowsy head to his stubbed toe, from his felonious mind to his insatiable stomach, from his loose incisor to the scab on his shin. Here we have a whole gallery—a principality, a cosmos— of boys, and every one of them is alive, human and irresistible.[6]

In the same article he praised H. G. Wells's *Tono-Bungay*, calling it the best novel of the month: "There are pages that show the insight of George Moore, and other pages that show the comic sense of Kipling. But more important than the story itself is the criticism of British civilization that Mr. Wells formulates in telling it." Also in that article is a good example of Mencken's ability to write a thoroughly excoriating review which is without malice or hate. Benjamin De Casseres condensed this quality perfectly in a brief sentence: "I discover a miracle in Mencken's work: good-natured anger, burbling venom, chortling frenzy." Here is the review in its entirety:

> And now let us jump from Paradise to Gehenna, which is to say, from the three excellent books we have been discussing to the Rev. Thomas Dixon's *Comrades* (Doubleday-Page, $1.50). The first few chapters of this intolerably amateurish and stupid quasi-novel well-nigh staggered me, and it was only by tremendous effort that I got through them at all. After that, I must confess, the task became less onerous, and toward the end the very badness of the book began to exercise a nefarious fascination. I was exploring new worlds of banality, of vapidity, of melodrama, of tortured wit. I felt the thrill of the astronomer with his eye glued upon some new and inconceivable star—of the pathologist face to face with some novel and horrible *coccus*. So I now look back upon the two hours with *Comrades*, not with a shudder, but with a glow. It will lie embalmed in my memory as a composition unearthly and unique—as a novel without a single redeeming merit. It shows every weakness, fault, misdemeanor known to prose fiction, from incredible characterization to careless proofreading, and from preposterous dialogue to trashy illustrations.
>
> No, I am not going to tell you the plot. Buy the book and read it yourself. The way to happiness lies through suffering.

As a note of Americana it might be pointed out that it was this Rev. Thomas Dixon who wrote the scenario for *The Birth of a Nation* (1915), which was based on two of Dixon's white-supremacy novels, *The Leopard's Spots* (1902) and *The Clansman* (1905). In the September, 1925, issue of the *Mercury*, Mencken included a long review, actually a riotously funny "paraphrase," of Dixon's *The Love Complex*, in which the author leaned heavily on Freudian psychology for interpretation of his characters' behavior. After simply annihilating the novel, Mencken marveled that Dixon was a Baptist clergyman: "The Baptists are not commonly regarded as artists. One hears of them chiefly as engaged in non-aesthetic or anti-aesthetic enterprises—ducking one another in horse-ponds, scaring the darkeys at revivals, acting as stool-pigeons for Prohibition agents, denouncing the theatre and the dance, marching with the Klan. But here is one who has felt the sweet kiss of beauty; here is a Baptist who can dream."

In his review of Waldo Frank's *Our America* in 1920, Mencken praised the author's realistic estimate of Americans. In attempting to define the American for foreign readers, Frank differed from the "touring professors of the Henry van Dyke kidney," who were wont to ladle out "dose after dose of heavy balderdash about American idealism, the 'soul' of America, and other such stuff"; Frank stuck to the horrible facts, "to wit, that America has, as yet, no more soul than a cow in a pasture—that the country is still in the preliminary stage of developing a mind—that it must get rid of a lot of bad blood before ever it presents to the world a spiritual and cultured face." When the van Dykes scanned the American scene, they saw the sorry spectacle of "110,000,000 enraptured Presbyterians, all pure in heart, all bursting with nobility, all *Höfrate* of the Lord God Jehovah." Americans to Frank were "a people who are still in the baby stage of playing with their toes." Mencken ended his review in a typically exuberant manner by admitting that perhaps he was "a bit softish" about the book "because the author, in one place, says that I am a meritorious fellow, for whose ease and happiness Yorktown and Gettysburg were not fought in vain." This praise Mencken doubted:

> for in the same paragraph he calls me middle-aged, and puts me alongside such doddering bags of bones as Huneker and Dreiser. The charge will stick in my gizzard a good while longer than the kiss is felt on my brow. To be middle-aged is to be —well, *what* is it? It is to have hope without expectation, courage without strength, desire without the fire. It is to be a nearsighted man at a burlesque show. It is to shimmie with the lumbago. Nay, I don't want to be middle-aged. Let me be young until suddenly, one frosty day, I am old, and then let me die. . . . And let Frank taste hell for that libel.[7]

In everything Mencken wrote there are just such joy and gusto. Even in *The American Language,* in which he outscholared the scholars and which the scholars have praised almost unanimously, Mencken composed a delightfully alive book on a subject (philology) that has never been known for the qualities of excitement or joy. His lifelong interest in language was not, however, always "scholarly" in a serious sense. For example, he enjoyed "coining" words that had satiric intent. From President Harding came the verb: "*Gamalielize.*—To reduce a proposition to terms of such imbecility that it is immediately comprehensible to morons. (From *Gamaliel,* an American prophet and hepatoscopist.)" More than any other American Presidents, Harding and Coolidge delighted Mencken, for their persons constituted prima-facie evidence that democracy was a scrofulous disease afflicting dunderheads, politicians, and idealists. He failed to see that any political system which could raise such men to power and eminence and still survive must have some fine, or at least enduring, qualities.

For the entertainment of his *Smart Set* readers, Mencken constantly contributed definitions (for example, "Puritanism—An attempt to repeal physiology"), aphorisms, buffooneries of all sorts. In the section entitled "Pertinent and Impertinent," which began appearing under the pseudonym of Owen Hatteras in April, 1913, Mencken, Nathan, and Willard Huntington Wright created a shower of sparks with their slashing satire and debunking of the American creed. Mencken contributed most of this section and all of the material that concerned the American's speech. He constantly gave examples of "The Eloquent American Language": for instance, "I never seen nothing I would of rather saw" and "I usen't to like olives, but them times ain't no more." He also contributed such buffooneries as the following:

Sample Program of a woman's club meeting ten years ago:
1. "The Genius of Richard Harding Davis."
2. "How to Understand 'Lohengrin.'"
3. "Milton, Goethe and Henry Van Dyke."
4. "Recent Advances in Infant Feeding."

Sample Program of a woman's club meeting today [in 1913]:
1. "Tricks of White Slave Traders."
2. "Should a Divorced Husband Be Forced to Take the Children?"
3. "Readings from Wedekind's 'The Awakening of Spring.'"
4. "Surgical Interference as a Moral Agent."

Mencken satirized the American's penchant for creating and joining all sorts of fraternal orders:

Suggestions for New Orders:
The Jolly Brotherhood of Honorary Pallbearers.
The Despondent Sorority of Esoteric Virgins.

The Fascinating Order of Gesticulating Gentlemen.
The Perfumed Knights of the Macaroon.
The Caparisoned Worshipers of Mystic Flubdub.
The Valiant Vermin of the Radiant Rat.
The Liquorish Louts of Hideous Hieroglyphics.
The B. U. G. S.
The Mysterious Brotherhood of the Epileptic Handshake.

The Dionysian element is especially evident in Mencken's writings on music, his first and last love. In attempting to describe the beauty of one of Richard Strauss's works, he finally gave up, remarking: "Roget must be rewritten before 'Feuersnot' is described. There is one place where the harps, taking a running start from the scrolls of the violins, leap slambang through (or is it into?) the firmament of Heaven. Once, when I heard this passage played at a concert, a woman sitting beside me rolled over like a log, and had to be hauled out by the ushers." This is not to say that Mencken was just glib in his discourses on music; far from it. He has been called by learned men one of the best music critics this country has produced. But the chuckle and satanic glee were in everything. He ended a piece on Johann Strauss in typical fashion:

> I venture to say that the compositions of Johann Strauss have lured more fair young creatures to complaisance than all the movie actors and white slave scouts since the fall of the Western Empire. There is something about a waltz that is irresistible. Try it on the fattest and sedatest or even upon the thinnest and the most acidulous of women, and she will be ready, in ten minutes, for a stealthy smack behind the door—nay, she will forthwith impart the embarrassing news that her husband misunderstands her, and drinks too much, and is going to Cleveland, O., on business tomorrow.[8]

In the May, 1912, issue of the *Smart Set* this appeared:

> Wagner—The rape of the Sabines . . . a *kommers* in Olympus.
> Beethoven—The glory that was Greece . . . the grandeur that was Rome . . . a laugh.
> Haydn—A seidel on the table . . . a girl on your knee . . . another and different girl in your heart.
> Chopin—Two embalmers at work upon a minor poet . . . the scent of tuberoses . . . Autumn rain.
> Richard Strauss—Old Home Week in Gomorrah.
> Johann Strauss—Forty couples dancing . . . one by one they slip from the hall . . . sounds of kisses . . . the lights go out.

Puccini—Silver macaroni, exquisitely tangled.
Debussy—A pretty girl with one blue eye and one brown one.
Bach—Genesis I, 1.

Mencken often said that his one genuine regret, on the day of his hanging, would be that he was not better instructed in music as a youth. He believed that music was the sole art that could be made absolutely pure and thus totally satisfying. "Letters deal only incidentally with aesthetic ideas; their main concern is always with philosophical and moral ideas." No poem or novel or drama was wholly without philosophical or moral content. And Mencken admitted that most philosophical ideas struck him as being dubious and futile; more often than not, moral ideas simply enraged him. "If I could write a string quartette I'd put things into it that I really feel and believe in. But I lack the necessary technique, and am too old to acquire it. Thus I shall go down to infamy without ever having expressed myself freely and fully. It is sad, but damme if I know what is to be done about it."[9]

In *Notes on Democracy,* in which Mencken voiced his multifarious reasons for regarding democracy—or, as he interpreted it, the political philosophy of the common man—as inimical to everything that is great in man, there are among the arguments occasional flashes of ribaldry and sacrilege. After pointing out that democratic government gave the mob man a feeling of importance that he easily translated into the belief that he was as good as anyone else and could, with a little luck, one day become a U.S. Senator or even President—and, in fact, someone of the mob often does attain high office under American democracy—Mencken stated that the true charm of democracy is not for the democrat but for the spectator. And that charm is a direct result of the common man's grotesque false pretenses:

> The fraud of democracy, I contend, is more amusing than any other—more amusing even, and by miles, than the fraud of religion. Go into your praying-chamber and give sober thought to any of the more characteristic democratic inventions. Or to any of the typical democratic prophets. If you don't come out paled and palsied by mirth then you will not laugh on the Last Day itself, when Presbyterians step out of the grave like chicks from the egg, and wings blossom from their scapulae, and they leap into interstellar space with roars of joy.

Mencken defined democracy as "the worship of jackals by jack-asses," and as "the theory that the common people know what they want, and deserve to get it good and hard," and, again, as "the art and science of running the circus from the monkey-cage." And yet once more—the most unkindest cut of all:

Democracy is that system of government under which the people, having 60,000,000 native-born adult whites to choose from, including thousands who are handsome and many who are wise, pick out a Coolidge to be head of the state. It is as if a hungry man, set before a banquet prepared by master cooks and covering a table an acre in area, should turn his back upon the feast and stay his stomach by catching and eating flies.

The influence of Ambrose Bierce, whose *Devil's Dictionary* Mencken considered his best work, can perhaps be seen in many of the Menckenian aphorisms. The following examples also make it clear why Mencken should have admired the wit of Oscar Wilde.

Theology—An effort to explain the unknowable by putting it into terms of the not worth knowing.

Archbishop—A Christian ecclesiastic of a rank superior to that attained by Christ.

Hymn of Hate, with Coda—If I hate any class of men in this world, it is evangelical Christians, with their bellicose stupidity, their childish belief in devils, their barbarous hoofing of all beauty, dignity and decency. But even evangelical Christians I do not hate when I see their wives.

Pastor—One employed by the wicked to prove to them by his own example that virtue doesn't pay.

Creator—A comedian whose audience is afraid to laugh.

Puritanism—The haunting fear that someone, somewhere, may be happy.

Courtroom—A place where Jesus Christ and Judas Iscariot would be equals, with betting odds in favor of Judas.

The believing mind reaches its perihelion in the so-called Liberals. They believe in each and every quack who sets up his booth on the fair-grounds, including the Communists. The Communists have some talents too, but they always fall short of believing in the Liberals.

Coda

To sum up:

1. The cosmos is a gigantic fly-wheel making 10,000 revolutions a minute.
2. Man is a sick fly taking a dizzy ride on it.

3. Religion is the theory that the wheel was designed and set spinning to give him the ride.

Mencken was, it should be remembered, an ardent student of theology, and he wrote two books on the subject (*Treatise on the Gods* [1930] and *Treatise on Right and Wrong* [1934]), which are well worth reading. *Treatise on the Gods,* the better of the two books, was reprinted nine times before a revised second edition appeared in 1946. It has sold steadily for thirty years and is now available in paperback.

If Mencken is remembered for nothing else, he must be thought of as a demolition expert without rival in American letters. That he led the revolt against sentimentality, against puritanism, against the "Prof. Drs.," against all the fly-by-night hawkers of flaccid idealism, is a fact attested to by almost all the commentators on the national scene, from Edmund Wilson to Van Wyck Brooks to Joseph Wood Krutch to Alfred Kazin to Gerald Johnson—the list could go on indefinitely. There are, of course, many individuals who can see no good in the practice of destructive criticism. They simply give notice that such and such book has been published, mention the book's contents, and pay the author some sort of compliment for having got words on paper. Indeed, a markedly unfavorable review is so rare that the appearance of one is enough to cause excited comment on the hidden "intent" of the critic.

Not only was Mencken a "hard-minded" critic; he was also—most rare of traits!—an honest man. When a book was badly written or childish, he pointed this out, even if it meant insulting a friend. Though he was uncommonly affable and thoughtful as a man, liked by nearly everyone who talked with him for more than five minutes (according to several sources, even the various comstocks, lay and clerical, who met Mencken thought highly of the man and regarded him as a prince of decorum and fair-mindedness), he wrote with a surgical indifference to feelings. Also, he was the first to admit that his criticism of books was colored by his "prejudices" ("opinions" is a much better word, since Mencken, the author of six volumes of *Prejudices,* was, at least during his years as a literary critic, one of the most open-minded critics America has produced; moreover, it should be clear that the deeply prejudiced individual never thinks he is prejudiced; like the husband with an unfaithful wife, he is the last to know). With typical exaggeration, which is a *device,* incidentally, and not a prejudice, he admitted that he was an earthy sort:

> I am by nature a vulgar fellow. I prefer *Tom Jones* to "The Rosary," Rabelais to the Elsie books, the Old Testament to the New, the expurgated parts of *Gulliver's Travels* to those that are left. I delight in beef stews, limericks, burlesque shows, New York City and the music of Haydn, that beery and delightful old rascal! I swear in the presence of ladies and archdeacons. When the mercury is above ninety-five I dine in my shirt sleeves and write poetry naked. I associate habitually with dramatists, bartenders, medical men and musicians. I once, in early youth, kissed a waitress at Dennett's. So don't accuse me of vulgarity; I admit it and flout you. Not, of course, that I have no pruderies, no fastidious metes and bounds. Far from it. Babies, for example, are too vulgar for me; I cannot bring myself to touch them. And actors. And evangelists. And the obstetrical anecdotes of ancient dames. But in general, as I have said, I joy in vulgarity, whether it take the form of divorce proceedings or of *Tristan und Isolde,* of an Odd Fellows' funeral or of Munich beer.

Mencken even admitted that he found it much easier to damn a book than praise one. Certainly he praised a high number of books during his years as a literary critic, and many of his laudatory reviews were in themselves minor works of art, but he was at his most delightful when garbed in the black robes of the hangman. He began his article for February, 1910, as usual, by attempting to gain the reader's attention:

> When a book is a good one and worth the price asked for it by the book selling banditti, the best thing for the reviewer to do is to say so in plain words and have done. Any attempt to enlarge upon that bald verdict is not only gratuitous and useless, but also extremely fatiguing to the reviewer. The customary vocabulary of his art fails him, for it is made up almost entirely of terms derogatory and infuriate, and when he seeks to make use of the ordinary phrases of praise he finds them flat to the taste. In addition, he discovers that his processes of ratiocination, usually so fluent and accurate, are impeded by his novel emotions. He is in the impossible position of a man trying to read Kant in the vestry room while waiting for his bride to arrive at the church, or of a woman trying to recite the Lord's Prayer with a mouse nibbling at her ankle. Take my word for it, the enterprise is one of staggering difficulties.

If an editor came to my laboratory today and asked me to write an intelligible review of *Huckleberry Finn, The Antichrist* or *The Old Bachelor,* I should have to charge him a thousand dollars for it to pay for the wear and tear on my system; but if he asked me to fill a few pages with observations upon a book by Sir Oliver Lodge, Marie Corelli, E. Phillips Oppenheim or Edward Bok, I should be glad to do it for three dollars, with one hundred dollars extra if he demanded that I read the book.

From this "preliminary," Mencken went on to review and praise H. G. Wells's *Ann Veronica* as the most important book of the month.

The majority of novels, collections of essays and poetry, and printed plays are not, of course, worth reading. For every good book there are a hundred bad ones and at least as many more indifferent ones. And masterpieces come few to a decade or even generation. In an effort to review twenty or thirty books a month, Mencken necessarily read a vast amount of trash. De Casseres commented on the high price Mencken paid to be a literary critic: "My God!, the years Mencken has spent—wasted—in mentally rolling in tons and tons of dried dung: American fiction! Can he ever be cleansed? Such is the price an honest workman must pay for thoroughness. (Dante's River of Dung—was that a vision of American fiction to come?)"[10] Although unable to look at all the new books, Mencken invariably read, or tried to read, the productions of all the better-known writers. He always paid some sort of tribute to the best sellers. When one learns who the popular writers, *circa* 1910, were, he can understand the severity of many of the Mencken reviews. The popular writers, English and American, of that period were Marie Corelli, E. Phillips Oppenheim, Edward Bok, Sir Oliver Lodge, Hall Caine, Harold MacGrath, Richard Harding Davis, Gene Stratton Porter, John Fox, Jr., Kate Douglas Wiggin, and the fabulous Harold Bell Wright. From the pens of these masters came such works as *Freckles, The Trail of the Lonesome Pine, Rebecca of Sunnybrook Farm,* and *The Shepherd of the Hills.* Interestingly enough, *The Winning of Barbara Worth* (1911) sold 1,500,000 copies in twenty-five years. Needless to say, the genius of these writers was praised by such pseudo critics as Hamilton Wright Mabie and Clayton Hamilton.

In his fourth article for the *Smart Set,* Mencken admitted that American novels and poetry were sadly inferior to those produced in Europe, especially England. American drama was so bad that it could not even be compared to what the English or Russians or Scandinavians were producing. Mencken and Nathan were to be instrumental in bringing the young rebels of the theater, particularly Eugene O'Neill, to public notice in the years during and after the war. In his first years as a professional critic, Mencken praised the work of various Europeans: Conrad, Galsworthy, Arnold Bennett, George Moore, Shaw, Gorki, Andreev, Max Beerbohm, Sudermann, Hauptmann, H. G. Wells, George Meredith, Chesterton, Havelock Ellis, Synge, and various other writers of the Irish Renaissance. He also praised the work of Henry James, whom he labeled an Englishman, though he never considered him the profound psychologist seen by a few later academicians. In 1920 he wrote that James was "a sort of super-Howells," a superb technician, but beyond that he refused to go.

It should be remembered that during this period around 1910 Robert Frost grew potatoes and wrote poetry on the side, Edgar Lee Masters practiced law, Sherwood Anderson manufactured paint, Edwin Arlington Robinson worked in a customhouse, Robinson Jeffers had yet to come to his "inevitable place" on Carmel Bay, Wallace Stevens practiced law in New York City, T. S. Eliot was in college, Dreiser edited at Butterick's, Willa Cather worked on the staff at *McClure's Magazine,* Sinclair Lewis and Ring Lardner labored on newspapers, and O'Neill lived the life of a hobo, as yet unaware that his inner turmoil might be transformed into art. It must also be remembered that that was the heyday of Anthony Comstock, the great "Smuthound" (Mencken's coinage), who had convicted enough "lewd" writers to fill sixty-one passenger coaches. American literature, in brief, was stale, flat, and unprofitable. A critic was needed who could inject gusto and energy into the national letters—one who could enliven the corpse. A lover of roughhouse was in demand—someone who would knock heads together and "stir up the animals." As chance would have it, Mencken happened along.

Mencken divided books into two major groups: the generally bad ones, from which the best sellers came, and the few works of art, which were almost always the products of foreign hands. Never a snobbish critic, Mencken admitted that a certain knack was required to write a best seller, and in his reviews there is even a dim glow of admiration for the professional who can turn out book after book and consistently please a large public. If the writer had the qualities of a competent artist, as did Jack London, and insisted on writing for the mob, then Mencken chastised him for the prostitution of his gifts. But if he was a hack who was sincerely doing his best, Mencken was always willing to pay him a kind of praise. For example, this review of a Hall Caine novel:

> *The White Prophet* [. . .] rises superior to all estimate and analysis. It is a mammoth tome of over six hundred closely printed pages, in which every conceivable problem of human life is disposed of. The canvas is a thousand miles wide, with its bottom edge in the waters under the earth and its top in the empyrean heights. There is room for a whole race of people— to wit, the race of modern Egyptians. How they rise against the domineering English and how, in the end, they work out their destiny—this is the main story. Engrafted upon it are tales of love, honor and simple faith. It is magnificent, and if you like Hall Caine you won't stop to inquire if it is also art.[11]

In his November, 1913, article, entitled "Marie Corelli's Sparring Partner," Mencken stated that Caine's latest novel was just as bad as all his others but admitted his rare ability to reach the popular audience:

> Here is the tested stuff, the immemorial stuff, the sure stuff. And here it is with new frills, new magnetos, new sauces. A dash of mental telepathy, a pinch of white slavery, a drop or two of frenzied finance, a garnish of polar exploration—and behold, the Duchess and Augusta Evans have become Hall Caine! Is the Montessori method missing? Is there no mention of eugenics? Does one seek in vain for the initiative and referendum? Have patience, beloved! Hall is still in the prime of life. He will write other books. Besides, he has a certain conservatism, a fastidious disinclination for the too new. A novelty must prove its worth before he embalms it in his amber. He will reach the Montessori method along toward 1915, the recall of judicial decisions the year after, sex hygiene in 1917.

Far more interesting than Caine's novels was Caine himself, at least to Mencken. Indeed, after reading and criticizing Caine's autobiography (reviewed simultaneously with the autobiography of another fascinating specimen of *Homo sapiens,* John D. Rockefeller), Mencken maintained that "it would take a whole seminary of Thackerays, working day and night, in eight-hour shifts for a geological epoch, to create a character as interesting as Hall Caine himself." Mencken enjoyed the autobiography because it offered one of the rare opportunities to get so intimate a view of a common mind. After all, to view such a mind was of itself a lesson of great importance:

> Suppose you could actually look into the cerebellum of the man who mows your chin, or of the woman who dusts your office, or of your trousers presser, your ward leader, your father-in-law, or any other human blank of your acquaintance: what a host of interesting discoveries you would make! You would learn in one easy lesson why it is that sentient beings, theoretically sane, join fraternal orders, march in parades, go to political meetings, wear badges, read the poems of Ella Wheeler Wilcox and weep over the plays and novels of Hall Caine. As it is, the thing is an impenetrable mystery, and it will remain so until someone establishes a science of comparative psychology and gives exhaustive study to the embryology of mental processes. Meanwhile, it helps us a bit to examine the anatomy and physiology of a mind that is obviously in tune (to borrow a phrase from wireless telegraphy) with the mass mind of the fraternalists, the paraders, the badge wearers. At all events, the book throws some light upon the elusive psychic states which precede the genesis of a platitude and are necessary to the evolution of bathos.[12]

Mencken at times praised the workmanlike novels of E. Phillips Oppenheim or Robert W. Chambers or Harold MacGrath, but he never slipped in the manner of a Clifton Fadiman and called their work art. For example, after paying brief notice to a MacGrath story in 1914, Mencken ended his review: "This Mr. MacGrath is no blacksmith. He writes deftly, amusingly, bouncingly. He knows how to tell a bad story well. He is even able to poke a bit of sly fun at it in the telling." Just so long as a writer told his story well, Mencken could forgive him the misfortune of not having been born a Conrad or a Thackeray. Certainly, Mencken has been criticized for the extreme emphasis he placed on style, but it should be remembered that he could also praise a writer for his art and castigate him at the same time for his shoddy manhandling of the language, as his remarks on Dreiser readily show.

An excellent example of the popular novelist during the first two decades of the century was the Kansas editor William Allen White. White simply borrowed the most maudlin traits of the Victorians—

that is, those like Felicia Hemans, Samuel Smiles, and Dickens at his most lachrymose—and went a step further. His black-and-white novels always presented two opposing forces—the forces of good and evil. Reviewing White's *In the Heart of a Fool* in 1919, Mencken found it the usual and inevitable thing of its kind.

On the one side are the Hell Hounds of Plutocracy, and their attendant Bosses, Strike Breakers, Seducers, Nietzscheans, Free Lovers and Corrupt Journalists. On the other side are the great masses of the plain people, and their attendant Uplifters, Good Samaritans, Poor Working Girls, Inspired Dreamers and tin-horn Messiahs. These two armies join battle, the Bad against the Good, and for 500 pages or more the Good get all the worst of it. Their jobs are taken away from them, their votes are bartered, their women debauched, their poor orphans are turned out to starve. But in the third from the last chapter someone turns on a rose spot-light, and then, one by one, the rays of Hope begin to shoot across the stage, and as the curtain falls the whole scene is bathed in luminous ether, and the professor breaks into "Onward, Christian Soldiers" on the cabinet-organ, and there is happy sobbing, and an upward rolling of eyes, and a vast blowing of noses. In brief, the finish of a chautauqua lecture on "The Grand Future of America, or, The Glory of Service." Still more briefly, slobber.[13]

In an essay on White in *Prejudices: First Series,* Mencken summarized the novelist's accomplishments over the years. They were unique. They were thoroughly American. Certainly they furnished what a large segment of the population, unpolluted by intelligence, wanted. On the merit side, White used a graceful English and had been known to write excellent editorials in the Emporia *Gazette* (Mencken later solicited and obtained articles from White for the *Mercury*). He was a surviving relic, albeit an immensely popular one, from a past period. As early as 1909, Mencken had referred to him in a *Smart Set* article as the last of the Victorians, and he used that epithet for the title of his later essay. The opening three sentences should suffice: "If William Allen White lives as long as Tennyson, and does not reform, our grandchildren will see the Victorian era gasping out its last breath in 1951. And eighty-three is no great age in Kansas, where sin is unknown. It may be, in fact, 1960, or even 1970, before the world hears the last of Honest Poverty, Chaste Affection and Manly Tears."

Although Mencken at times singled out an especially popular

book to satirize, he spent the vast majority of his time seeking out the few worthy books to praise. When he was criticized for being too severe, he answered:

> Criticism itself, at bottom, is no more than prejudice made plausible. The judicial temperament, like moral beauty, is merely a phrase that men use to fool themselves. When I put on my hangman's gown of criticism and buckle on my celluloid sword, I make a mental oath that I will be as fair, as honest and as charitable as any judge on the bench. I succeed, like the judge, in being as fair, as honest and as charitable as any lawyer at the Bar.[14]

If it is possible for a critic to be unfair to silly books by condemning them, then Mencken must be ranked as America's most iniquitous man of letters.

There are numerous ways to do execution on flapdoodle. Some feel that the best plan is simply to ignore it. But this is tacitly to give it permission to exist and thrive. Mencken preferred to assume the role of judge and jury, to waylay the popular gods, and even to indict the whole of American literature. Before the publication of *A Book of Prefaces* (1917), Mencken performed his demolition work in the *Smart Set* by periodically satirizing the "message" books, the myriad of New Thought volumes, the White Slavery novels, the tomes devoted to the various forms of Uplift. First there is what might be called the "brief dismissal" technique:

> *Apologies for Love*—by F. A. Myers. (Badger, $1.50)
> " 'Do you remain long in Paris, Miss Wadsworth?' Earl Nero Pensive [!!!] inquired, as he seated himself beside her. His eyes, like beaming lights out of a shadowless abysm, were transfixed upon her as by magic force. . . ." Thus the story begins. God knows how it ends![15]
> *Views and Reviews*—by Henry James. (Ball Pub. Co., $1.50 net) Early essays by Henry James—some in the English language.[16]
> *Entering the Kingdom*—by James Allen. (Fenno & Co., 50 cents) A dissertation on virtue, with a roadmap of Heaven. Good reading for the chemically pure.[17]
>
> Finally, there is My *"Little Bit,"* by Marie Corelli (Doran), not a novel but a collection of essays in the author's best marshmallow manner. It is a tall and stately book. I advise you to buy it for your pastor.[18]

Mencken had this to say of *The Autobiography of Calvin Coolidge,* which was written after Coolidge's famous decision not to seek re-election in 1928:

> The Coolidge volume, on all imaginable critical grounds, is abominable beyond compare. It is vilely written, it is full of transparent fraudulences and evasions, and there is a pious and puerile unction in it that recalls a Y.M.C.A. secretary lecturing on sex hygiene. But these deficiencies cannot conceal the man; on the contrary, they only serve to make him the more vivid. The volume deserves to be read prayerfully by every American patriot. It is a shameless and amazing demonstration of what the public service has come to among us. Here is a man who sat in the chair of Washington and Jefferson, Lincoln and Cleveland, for nearly seven years, hymned and greased by the Washington correspondents, revered by millions, and with more power in his hands than forty Czars of Russia—and yet the net content of his cranium, revealed innocently by himself, turns out to be hardly distinguishable from what fills the brain-pan of an average garage attendant. Having got through his appalling self-revelation, horrified and yet spellbound, I hasten to apologize to the readers of this great family magazine for my writings about him in the past. He was, as President, a great deal worse than I ever made him out—nay, a great deal worse than I ever, in my most despairing moments, suspected. I can only promise to be more careful about Hoover.[19]

Mencken sometimes dismissed a novel or collection of poetry by simply paraphrasing it or quoting lines from it. In his *Mercury* review (March, 1925) of Henry van Dyke's *Six Days of the Week: A Book of Thoughts About Life and Religion,* Mencken simply offered twelve brief quotations, setting them off ostentatiously on the page. The "review" begins thus:

> I offer a specimen:
> As living beings we are part of a universe of life.
> A second:
> Unless we men resolve to be good, the world will never be better.
> A third:
> Behind Christianity there is Christ.

And so on down to the twelfth, after which Mencken danced glee-fully on the mound of platitudes: "Tupper *est mort! Hoch* Tupper! *Hoch, hoch! Dreimal hoch!*" In such reviews there was always humor: Mencken invariably laughed at, rather than cried over, the idiocies of man; no modern writer has better demonstrated that laughter is the most powerful of all weapons. At times in the early years he wrote lengthy "paraphrases," but usually he allowed the mushy works only a short paragraph.

> In *The Winning Game,* by Madge Macbeth (Broadway Pub. Co., $1.50), we come upon the sad story of a charming young American girl married to a drunken and dissolute Englishman. How to save him from his highballs and hussies—here is a tough problem indeed! But his fair young wife solves it. Against his intolerable polygamy she proceeds by disguising herself as one of his harem beauties. When in pursuance of his routine he drags her to his den of iniquity, she strips off her disguise and sears his soul with the hot flash of her indignant eye. His lesson learned, he promises to break the seventh commandment no more. But he is still a drinking man—a lusher, in fact, with one foot constantly upon the rail. How to cure him? Again that resourceful wife of his is equal to the task. What would be easier than feigning drunkenness? She is familiar with the outward symptoms of that condition, and she gives an astonishingly realistic performance. He is horrified, disgusted—cured! Such a story![20]

In the years just preceding World War I an amazing number of popular books on New Thought poured from the presses. It would have been impossible for any critic who endeavored to acknowledge the important works of his time to avoid the mania completely. And Mencken, who was always fascinated with the average American, was one of the most violent opponents of all forms of mystical flubdub. Although he admitted that the whole of New Thought was just windy and harmless nonsense, he was amazed by its extreme popularity. After reviewing *The Miracle of Right Thought* by Orison Swett Marden, Mencken marveled that 21,000 copies of one of Marden's books had been sold. In an essay-review of Havelock Ellis' *The World of Dreams* (1911), Mencken contrasted the intelligence of Ellis, "a diligent and sapient inquirer, a brave enemy of pseudo-scientific flapdoodle, a writer of sense and charm," with the mountebankery of the frauds of science. He summed up the lunacy thus:

> The New Thought, taking it by and large, is probably the most prosperous lunacy ever invented by mortal man. Every one of its multitudinous sub-lunacies, from psychical research to anti-vaccination, from vegetarianism to the Emmanuel Movement,

and Zoophilism to Neo-Buddhism, is gaining converts daily and making excellent profits for a horde of male, female and neuter missionaries. Why work at gravel roofing or dishwashing in the heat of the day when you can open a table tapping studio in any convenient furnished room house and rake in the willing dollars of the feeble-minded, the while you make their eyes bulge and the xanthous freckles on their necks go lemon pale? As a communicative New Thinker of my acquaintance once said, Mind is a darn powerful thing. What causes chilblains to afflict the slaves of error, banjoes to tinkle in dark cabinets, veiled (and fat) she-wizards to read the number of your watch, dogs to die of non-existent rabies, dreams to come true? Mind! Matter is a mere symbol of Mind—a sort of effigy, shadow or greenback. And of the two halves of Mind (for, like all other things, it has two halves) the most potent and protean is the Subconscious that awakens you in the middle of the night to deliver a telepagram from the coroner at Zanesville, O., saying that your mother-in-law, dear old girl, has died of lockjaw. It is the Subconscious, again, that cures you when pink pills, camomile and five doctors have failed. It is the Subconscious, yet again, that plucks the banjo in the cabinet and lifts the table from the floor and strokes you with damp, uncanny hands— while the medium's *de facto* husband, out in the ante-room, is searching your overcoat for cigars.[21]

At one with the New Thought books were the "message" tomes. These books were often preachments on the evils of alcohol or tobacco or on the invidious wiles of white slavers (who evidently were performing their hellish deeds with great success around the turn of the century). In his criticism for May, 1913, entitled "Weep for the White Slave!" Mencken attacked the Uplifters, particularly those most concerned with spreading the gospel about the white-slave trade. He reviewed in particular two books—*The Necessary Evil* and *My Little Sister*—that were destined to be best sellers because of their lachrymose rendering of the "facts." Mencken felt that they were in many ways comparable to the greatest of Uplift novels, *Uncle Tom's Cabin*. A public which found such stuff to its taste could hardly be expected to approve the labors of a Dreiser or any other competent artist, for that matter.

To this "public" Mencken addressed the venom of his pen. If it is impossible to reason with a man, you can at least shock him into taking a closer look at himself; you can at least put him on the defensive. In a series of articles ("The American," June, 1913; "The

American: His Morals," July, 1913; "The American: His Language,"
August, 1913; "The American: His Ideas of Beauty," September,
1913; "The American: His Freedom," October, 1913) in the *Smart
Set*, Mencken attempted to define the undefinable—the typical
American:

> that sub-brachycephalous and sentimental fellow, with his sud-
> den sobs and rages, his brummagem Puritanism, his childish
> braggadocio, his chronic waste of motion, his elemental humor,
> his great dislike of arts and artists, his fondness for the grotesque
> and melodramatic, his pious faith in quacks and panaceas, his
> curious ignorance of foreigners, his bad sportsmanship, his prim-
> itive feeding, his eternal self-medication, his weakness for tin
> pot display and strutting, his jealous distrust of all genuine dis-
> tinction, his abounding optimism, his agile pursuit of the dollar.

Incidentally, Mencken did not think that the American's concern
for the dollar was in any way a native trait of distinction; actually,
the average American was no more greedy than the average German or Englishman or Frenchman. But in all the essays, it was the
shortcomings of the American that Mencken concentrated on.

In his essay on the American's ideas of beauty, Mencken pointed
to the deep-seated distrust of all professional artists as a leading
reason for the artist's inability to find favor in his own country.
Mencken believed that America had produced more than one great
artist and many lesser ones of respectable capacity and that some
of these artists were intensely national in feeling, but he found no
spontaneous recognition of any of them. He pointed to Poe, who
had to be "discovered" for Americans by the French. He pointed to
Whitman:

> who made no more impression upon his countrymen, taken in
> the mass, than a third-rate pugilist. If they thought of him at
> all, during his seventy-three years of life among them, it was
> chiefly, if not wholly, as a wholesaler of the obscene. He never
> appealed to them as a great poet, as an eloquent and impas-
> sioned prophet of their democracy, but merely as a man who
> took long chances with the postal laws. When, in reward for
> *Leaves of Grass*, he was deprived of his modest place in the In-
> terior Department and denounced donkeyishly by some forgot-
> ten Tartuffe, public sentiment approved both the dismissal and
> the denunciation. Even today, by one of fate's little ironies, all
> appreciation of Whitman is confined to a narrow circle of ad-
> mirers, most of whom are professed immoralists. That average

American in whom he believed so resolutely, and whose thirsts and struggles he celebrated so feelingly, is no more moved by him than by Johann Sebastian Bach.

There was perhaps an exception in the case of Mark Twain, a writer known to most Americans—an exception until we learn that he was remembered as a sort of Artemus Ward, Bill Nye, and Chauncey M. Depew. Twain was remembered not as an artist of high caliber, but as an entertainer, an after-dinner speaker, a man who wore white suits, a "sort of super-clever clown." As a writer, Twain was known as the author of "The Jumping Frog," a "mere anecdote, borrowed in its substance and but little dignified in the telling." The average American thought of our greatest writer up to that time as the author of children's stories. Incidentally, Mencken once remarked that he had been more violently attacked for his belief that *Huckleberry Finn* was a masterpiece than he ever was for his denunciation of the popular writers of his day.

In the last chapter of *Prejudices: First Series,* Mencken reminded his readers in memorable fashion of the American's respect for his artistic countrymen. I quote the final part of the brief chapter (the first two parts are concerned with Emerson and Poe), which is entitled "Three American Immortals," as an excellent example of the sort of thing that helped induce the rebellion of the nineteen-twenties and make Mencken the major force of the decade—a decade in which American literature came to the fore and began setting standards for the other nations of the Western world.

Memorial Service

Let us summon from the shades the immortal soul of James Harlan, born in 1820, entered into rest in 1899. In the year 1865 this Harlan resigned from the United States Senate to enter the cabinet of Abraham Lincoln as Secretary of the Interior. One of the clerks in that department, at $600 a year, was Walt Whitman, lately emerged from three years of hard service as an army nurse during the Civil War. One day, discovering that Whitman was the author of a book called *Leaves of Grass,* Harlan ordered him incontinently kicked out, and it was done forthwith. Let us remember this event and this man; he is too precious to die. Let us repair, once a year, to our accustomed houses of worship and there give thanks to God that one day in 1865 brought together the greatest poet that America has ever produced and the damndest ass.

Contained in miniscule in this brief passage are some of the major characteristics—both weaknesses and strengths—of Mencken's criticism. To begin with, this is ideological criticism, or "criticism of ideas," and only secondarily literary criticism. Mencken is more concerned with Harlan—that is, with what Harlan represents —than he is with Whitman. By immortalizing Harlan, Mencken was in effect burying the man and the moralism which he symbolized in the deepest circle of hell. More important to Mencken, at this late day, than the slain was the slayer. Which is to say, Mencken was more interested in the American's *concept* and *reception of* the artist than he was in the artist himself. Admittedly, this is an isolated example, and indeed a very minor little vignette, not intended as literary criticism in the first place; but I think it is indicative of Mencken's growing interest in man en masse, and more particularly in American man, and his loss of interest in the *art* of literature. The younger men of the nineteen-twenties who accused Mencken of not being a literary critic in the pure sense of the word were perfectly correct. Mencken was not a *pure* critic in that he confined himself to discussing just the work of art before him, but then no *purist* has ever lived beyond his own day. Ironically, Mencken agreed with his prosecutors; indeed, he went far beyond the indictment. "All my criticism is, at bottom, a criticism of ideas, not of mere books."[22] After the war in Europe he became more and more interested in "the follies and imbecilities of men." The important thing is that though Mencken was to write excellent criticism for years to come, it was to be done with the left hand and only incidentally. After 1920 he played his stream on the forces moving about in the national caldron and left the individual effects to the younger men to dissect. Moreover, Mencken was henceforth more the artist or creator than the critic of other men's creations, as "Memorial Service" amply illustrates. But all this sounds like the cock at midnight heralding a dawn that had not yet gathered light beneath the eastern horizon. After all, in *Prejudices: First Series* there are a dozen first-rate essays of literary criticism, including the extraordinary "Criticism of Criticism of Criticism." And in all of them there is a freshness and immediacy that only the artist could give to critical writing.

CHAPTER FIVE

Critical Credo

A<small>T</small> a time when criticism threatens to replace fiction (not to mention poetry, which has not been widely read for over thirty years) as the favorite topic of discussion among the more serious students of literature, it is perhaps presumptuous to speak of the aims and functions of criticism—presumptuous because of the plethora of widely divergent views as to the proper concern of criticism. If not paradoxical, it is certainly ironic, at least, that amid all these critics of criticism and critics of criticism of criticism there are so precious few men now writing who can compose an intelligent review of a new book and make that review both discerning and delightful to read. One would think that with all the critical apparatus now at the disposal of the critic, our magazines and quarterlies would be brimming over with incisive analyses of the new books— many of them, as I have said, on criticism. Obviously—too obviously —this is not the case. Aside from occasional reviews of high merit that appear in the *New Yorker* and a few of the quarterlies, there is little being written on contemporary books that would warrant a second look. Moreover, the best criticism, now as always, is being done by writers properly describable as journalists. All of which leads one to the belief that it is the man and not the theory that makes for the best criticism.

This critical bankruptcy results, I am convinced, from at least two ills which act as cause and effect of each other. On the one hand, the extreme interest in criticism (fostered by the teachers of literature in our colleges and universities primarily) has nourished the belief that aesthetic judgments are somehow akin to mathematical equations; that is, that the *right* critical answer may be given only if the proper procedure of analysis is followed. The problem then becomes one of method or procedure. Having chosen from among the multitude of "methods" the *one* correct way, the critic is then faced with a further problem: the acquisition of a vocabulary elevated enough to give his exegesis the aspect of lofty wisdom. More often than is pleasant to contemplate, the critic will borrow terms from metaphysics with which to ennoble his utterance, giving it a kind of bastard profundity; which is to say, he cloaks his ideas in obscure terminology or in unwieldy syntax; which is to say, he writes abominably. I do not propose that all ideas are readily comprehensible; rather I object to those who make more difficult an already difficult idea, who, whether consciously or through incompetence, move in the opposite direction from one of any critic's primary functions—the clarification of the obscure. Walter Kaufmann has commented on the process by and through which obscurantism helps make respectable that which is incomprehensible, "until eventually whatever is comprehensible is *eo ipso* considered relatively shallow." In criticizing the obscure and/or the incomprehensible, the critic is furnished with material with which he may build topless towers of the palpably absurd. As Kaufmann perfectly put it: "Terminology supplants thought; exegesis, vision." For those critics who can think only *reactively*—that is, who must read before they can think—the proliferation of terminology is much to be desired: nothing provides more work, and hence the chance to shine, than the obscure work of art and an occult terminology.

It is to Mencken's everlasting praise that he never laid down a set of ironclad rules concerning the novel or drama or poetry. He never tired of scornfully dismissing all the dogmatic theorists with their tight, narrow little definitions as to what a book had to be before it could be called a novel, or what a poem must be before it can be called a lyric or an epic or what-have-you. (Imagine what Mencken would have done with that Pope of modern pigeonholers, F. R. Leavis!) In this he might be called a romantic, though the terms "romantic" and "classicist" are so vague as to be almost meaningless. Though never a pigeonholer, Mencken did have a theory

of literature and a theory of criticism, both of which were rather
severely revised between the early years on the *Smart Set* and the
period of the *Mercury*. When, in his first criticism for the *Smart
Set*, Mencken severely chastised Upton Sinclair for mouthing platitudes in his novel *The Moneychangers* and at the same time predicted that the artist in Sinclair would be destroyed by his messianic delusion, he accompanied his censure with the reminder that
"an economic struggle, to make material for fiction, must be pic-
tured, not objectively and as a mere bout between good and evil,
but subjectively and as some chosen protagonist sees and experiences it." He insisted that the interest the reader or viewer has in
a novel or drama lies, "always and inevitably, in some one man's
effort to master his fate." Even in this first criticism Mencken was
distinguishing between surface realism that slid easily into melodrama, and what might be called "subjective" realism, which in its
interpretation and its concern with the enigmatic in life went far
deeper than the photographic could ever go. In criticizing Sinclair,
Mencken might well have been thinking of his favorite English
novelist, Joseph Conrad. He believed then, as he did later, that
Lord Jim was the greatest novel in the language.

To say nothing more about Mencken's attitude toward Sinclair
would be to give a partially false impression. To be sure, he never
admired Sinclair's fiction, for the same reasons that he never admired any didactic fiction, but he did find some of the nonfiction
worthy of praise. For example, in 1923 he lauded *The Goose-step*,
a muckraking examination of the administrative side of our universities. In his review, which he included in *Prejudices: Fifth Series*,
Mencken went far beyond the book at hand and addressed himself
to the subject. Rather than do an analysis of the book, he wrote an
excellent essay, using the book as a take-off—an essay which still
has immediacy even though Sinclair's book is nearly forgotten. After
commenting at some length on the professors' loss of prestige since
the end of the World War ("In universities large and small, East,
West, North and South, the very sophomores rise in rebellion against
the incompetence and imbecility of their preceptors, and in the
newspapers the professor slides down gradually to the level of a
chiropractor, a press-agent or a Congressman"), Mencken briefly
rehearsed the shortcomings of two of Sinclair's critiques: *The Brass
Check*, on yellow journalism, and *The Profits of Religion*. But in

The Goose-step the expected weaknesses were absent. Sinclair had left off "his customary martyr's chemise" and allowed the narrative to tell itself.

> There is no complaining, no pathos, no mouthing of platitude; it is a plain record of plain facts, with names and dates—a plain record of truly appalling cowardice, disingenuousness, abjectness, and degradation. Out of it two brilliant figures emerge: first the typical American university president, a jenkins to wealth, an ignominious waiter in antechambers and puller of wires, a politician, a fraud and a cad; and secondly, the typical American professor, a puerile and pitiable slave.

From this general statement, Mencken goes on to provide specifics in support of his dark view. Such reviews belong, of course, not to the narrow realm of *literary* criticism, but rather to the broader area of the critical essay.

Mencken began his third *Smart Set* article, in January, 1909, by giving his definition of the novel—a definition designed to both instruct and please:

> *Q.*—What is a novel?
>
> *A.*—A novel is an imaginative, artistic and undialectic composition in prose, not less than 20,000 nor more than 500,000 words in length, and divided into chapters, sections, books or other symmetrical parts, in which certain interesting, significant and probable (though fictitious) human transactions are described both in cause and effect, with particular reference to the influence exerted upon the ideals, opinions, morals, temperament and overt acts of some specified person or persons as may come into contact, either momentarily or for longer periods, with him, her or them, either by actual, social or business intercourse, or through the medium of books, newspapers, the Church, the theater or some other person or persons.
>
> This definition represents the toil of several days and makes severe demands upon both eye and attention, but it is well worth the time spent upon it and the effort necessary to assimilate it, for it is entirely without loophole, blowhole or other blemish.

It should be noted that in this intentionally high-flown definition, Mencken placed a great deal of emphasis upon the necessity of the novelist's providing credible causes for the effects he describes. If a novel does not accurately "represent" some aspect of the human comedy or dilemma, it can never be considered really excellent. It should also be noted that this definition insists that the novel is an "undialectical" form. More than one competent novelist, from Sinclair and Jack London to D. H. Lawrence in the twenties and John Steinbeck in the thirties, would be censured for violating this canon.

But the most important comment on the novel in this article showed Mencken's naturalistic bent. The great novel, Mencken wrote, must tell, with insight, imagination, and conviction, the story of some one man's struggle with his fate, at the same time displaying, "like a vast fever chart, the ebb and flow of his ideas and ideals, and the multitude of forces shaping them." Such a novel would provide an accurate picture of a protagonist being driven, tortured, and fashioned by the blood within him and the world without. As an admirer of the fiction of Zola, Frank Norris, Dreiser, Hardy, Bennett, and Conrad, Mencken felt that it was the "background" that chiefly marks the good novel; and after the background, the normality of the people under observation. Abnormality was more the subject matter for the psychologist than the novelist; Mencken would never call many of the highly praised books of today great because they are less concerned, many of them, with the average man and his immemorial struggle with life than they are with the freaks and perverts and "case studies" of the warped minority. Moreover, this typical man must fit in some kind of recognizable environment.

> The aim in a genuine novel is not merely to describe a particular man, but to describe a typical man, and to show him in active conflict with a more or less permanent and recognizable environment—fighting it, taking color from it, succumbing to it. If that environment sinks into indistinctiveness or unimportance, if it might be changed, let us say, from the England of 1870 to the England of 1914 without materially modifying the whole character and experience of the man—or, as the ancient Greeks used to call him, the protagonist—then the story of his adventures is scarcely a novel at all, but merely a tale *in vacuo,* a disembodied legend, the dry bones of a novel. The better the novel, indeed, the more the man approaches Everyman, and the more the background overshadows him.[1]

Such a theory is the natural result of Mencken's conviction that life is a struggle, that each man battles for his place in the sun. And, be it added, man's struggle with his environment, although he battles heroically, valiantly, ends inevitably in his "succumbing to it."

In other words, fiction must not endeavor to contradict the most important facts of life. The influence of Darwin, Spencer, and Huxley on Mencken's thought is here clearly present. At this stage in his career his aesthetic theory is inextricably bound to biological science. I am referring to his attitude toward "serious" literature, not to comic writing, which he criticized much in the manner of a contemporary existentialist commenting on the absurd.

Although Mencken later felt that the hero of major fiction was a superior man, "a salient individual" in conflict with "harsh and meaningless fiats of destiny" (such phrases appear again and again), he always insisted that recognizable traits of Everyman must be seen in the hero. For one thing, the really exceptional man is the most difficult to portray convincingly. Of Somerset Maugham's *The Moon and Sixpence* (1919), Mencken wrote that "it is a book which tackles head-on one of the hardest problems that the practical novelist ever has to deal with, and which solves it in a way that is both sure-handed and brilliant. This is the problem of putting a man of genius into a story in such a fashion that he will seem real—in such fashion that the miracle of him will not blow up the plausibility of him." Mencken admitted that he was surprised by Maugham's success, even considering the fact that *Of Human Bondage* (1915) was a "curiously sagacious and fascinating composition —very un-English in its general structure, almost Russian in some of its details," since the novelist began as a writer of bad comedies filled with "labored epigrams strung upon a thread of drawing-room adultery." Still, there it was. Charles Strickland was a major accomplishment, and the thing had been done very simply.

Maugham's success, in fact, lies a good deal less in what he positively does than in what he discreetly leaves undone. He gets the colors of life into his Charles Strickland, not by playing a powerful beam of light upon him, but by leaving him a bit out of focus—by constantly insisting, in the midst of every discussion of him, upon his pervasive mystery—in brief, by craftily making him appear, not as a commonplace, simple and completely understandable man, but as the half comprehended enigma that every genuine man of genius seems to all of us when we meet him in real life. The average novelist, grappling with such a hero, always makes the fatal error of trying to account for him wholly—of reducing him to a composite of fictional rubber-stamps. Thus he inevitably takes on commonness,

and in proportion as he is clearly drawn he loses plausibility as
a man of genius. Maugham falls into no such blunder. Of Strickland, the unit of human society—the Strickland who eats, sleeps,
travels about, reads the newspapers, changes his shirt, has his
shoes polished, dodges automobiles and goes to business every
morning like the rest of us—we get a portrait that is careful,
logical and meticulous—in brief, that is brilliantly life-like. But
of the vaster, darker Strickland who is a man of genius—the
Strickland who deserts his family to go to Paris to paint, and
there plods his way to extraordinary achievement, and then
throws away his life in the South Seas—of this Strickland we
see only an image made up of sudden and brief points of light,
like flashes of Summer lightning below the horizon. He is, in one
aspect, made convincingly vivid; he is, in the other, left in the
shadow of mystery. That is precisely how we all see a man of
genius in real life; he is half plain John Smith and half inscrutable monster.[2]

Mencken concluded his review by comparing Maugham's device of
presenting his story through the medium of an onlooker, "himself
fascinated and daunted by the enigma of it," with that of Conrad,
who, though not the first to use the device, handled it better than
anyone else, past or present.

If the great novel depicted man heroically struggling with his
fate, it was but a short, logical step to Mencken's belief that the
second-rate novel, or "the average best seller," has for its hero a
creature who is superb, irresistible, and wholly autonomous. "He is
the easy master of every situation that his environment confronts
him with; he is equally successful at killing cannibals, snaring bur-
glars, operating airships, terrorizing the stock market or making
love. He is not the product and plaything of fate, but its boss. The
world is his oyster."[3] The hundreds of novels which displayed the
protagonist as the master of his fate, the captain of his soul, occa-
sioned high mirth in the skeptical newspaperman and critic. Having
viewed society on all its layers, Mencken concluded that all men
are in large part products of a conditioning process that began at
the instant man first crawled out of the primeval mud. Again, cor-
roboration was readily found in science.

If, then, good fiction is less concerned with what the characters
do than with what is done to them, we must insist that the novelist
have some view of the world. The writer with no philosophy of life
can hardly be expected to account for what befalls his victim-

protagonist. Did not all the great artists in history have some "comprehensible and credible philosophy of life, born of a mighty personality"? Also, the philosophy of an artist will invariably set him off in an unmistakable way from all other interpreters of motive and acts. It would be impossible to think of Dickens, for example, "without recalling his sentimental view of the world, with its cardinal doctrine that all human ills are to be cured by love. And in the same way, we cannot detach Thackeray from his tolerant cynicism, nor Shakespeare from his proud resignationism, nor Milton from his lofty idealism, nor Fielding from his buoyant optimism, his belief in mankind, his firm conviction that the mere being alive is sufficient for happiness."[4] Moreover, it is the philosophy of an artist which, underlying everything he writes, enables the reader to gain from reading him and to face life with more understanding and comfort.

Mencken felt that the absence of a philosophical viewpoint in the works of Hermann Sudermann, who shared with Gerhart Hauptmann the distinction of being Germany's leading man of letters in the period just preceding World War I, denied him the rank of a great writer. Although Sudermann (whose *The Song of Songs* [1910] Mencken reviewed in this particular article) was an observer of extraordinary shrewdness, he was unable to interpret his observations satisfactorily. "It is not that he is struck by the notion that life is meaningless—for that notion, as the case of Joseph Conrad proves, is not inconsistent with clear thinking—but that he seeks to read hazy, antagonistic and often puerile meanings into it."[5] One missed in Sudermann's works "the passionate earnestness and certainty, the clear, clean cut logic" to be found in such novels as *Germinal, Barry Lyndon,* and *Anna Karenina.* Rather than present one consistent view, Sudermann sought to be alternately an idealist and a realist, a revolutionary and a reactionary, a pessimist and an optimist; hence, his writings lost vitality because there was no dominant master note in them expressive of the one man only. In an essay on Sudermann, in *Prejudices: First Series,* Mencken commented again on this absence of any prevailing point of view. He remarked that when Sudermann, like Hauptmann, was finally oppressed by "the emptiness of naturalism," he was unable to change satisfactorily. Rather, he began to dilute his naturalism with a sentimentality that, in *Magda,* his best-known play, recalled Augier's *Le Mariage d'Olympe.*

Like Coleridge before him, Mencken amalgamated theory and practice, which is to say that before, or while, pointing out the weakness or strength in a given work, he would comment on certain broad principles which govern, for example, the creation of character. In criticizing Gertrude Atherton's *Julia France and Her Times* (1912), Mencken revealed his critical credo when he stated that the fallacy of Mrs. Atherton's method lay in the fact that it left her characters unaccounted for, "that it describes them too much and explains them too little. She shows them doing all sorts of amazing things, and in the showing she is infallibly brisk and entertaining, but she seldom gets into their acts that appearance of inevitability which makes for reality." Mencken did not feel that the novelist had got beneath the surface of her people; to him she had neglected "the first business of a serious novelist, which is to interpret and account for her characters, to criticize life as well as describe it." In this "sense of inevitability" which Mencken constantly insisted upon, there may be seen a leading classical concept: to wit, the concept of a *natural* order and harmony deriving from the "relatedness" of all phenomena.

At this point, the reader of Mencken should be aware of what appears to be an essential contradiction in his entire critical credo. In the first place, Mencken believed that life, in general or philosophical terms, was flatly meaningless; there was no particular purpose in man's existence—his existence being but one of the many results of natural selection—any more than there would have been had he never existed; which is to say, no intelligent, foresighted being created man to fulfill a specific need in the cosmic process. Belief in such an intelligent being is nothing more than anthropomorphism, no matter how you cut it, and Mencken felt that all anthropomorphic gods were creatures of man's imagination. Bearing this apparently nihilistic theory in mind, the reader might assume that Mencken was one of those who then concluded that "everything is permissible," in the manner of a Dostoevskian character. Mencken believed no such thing, of course; he was much too *irre*-ligious ever to be a nihilist, who, so far as I can make out, is either a religious man deprived of his dogmatic belief, or else a callous half-wit. (The two men whom Mencken admired most, T. H. Huxley and Nietzsche, were violent opponents, in their different ways, of all that nihilism stood for. It may help to remember that Nietzsche's war on Christianity was in effect a war on the nihilism to which it inevitably led, with its *de*naturizing of both the world and man, its abnegation of *this* life, its elevation of pity as the highest virtue, and its promise of celestial kingship to the weak and the unfit for no other reason than that they were weak and unfit.) The assumption that man resided in a world created for his benefit, for the purpose of his playing at the little game of saints and sinners, was a result of his ability to *imagine* it possible to rescind the laws of physics and biology and move beyond his humanity. Such imaginings were nothing more than evidence of man's almost incredible egotism and his no less amazing refusal to accept existence as the product of something like chemical necessity. As the contemporary existentialists say, man is free of ultimates; in effect, he is free of anything like divine guidance and its concomitant duty. But unlike the existentialist, Mencken would not extend that freedom to the entire realm of existence, as Sartre, for example, has so illogically done. Sartre seems to say that since man is freed from the shackles of anthropomorphism (Mencken insisted that the anthropomorphic theory, though idiotic, would continue to be popular with the mass mind for ages to come, and probably forever), he is also free in his existential state; that is, he is free to choose what course of action he will take; which is to say, he is free to *determine* his own fate. Not so at all, Mencken would insist, since man's freedom from the gods is really meaningless when we realize that his struggle has always been with nature and its fiats, though at times man translates the terms of natural existence (man as the result of biological and psychological forces) into terms of supernatural dependence (man as the result of laws or intelligent design outside the natural order). Sartre says man is pretty much free to do as he wishes, both morally and physically; Mencken said that man was "free" to do whatever he was most strongly motivated to do. Hence his demand that the serious, not the comic, writer provide ample causes to show that his effects are in large degree necessary and thus believable. The comic writer was not so bound, for his success often depended upon his describing actions and events that seemed to contradict the normal cause–effect relationships found in most human activity. Hence, the laughter.

My point is that there is really no contradiction between Mencken's numerous (perhaps too numerous) remarks about the meaninglessness of life on the one hand and, on the other hand, his demand that a writer give meaning to his portraiture by having some consistent philosophy of existence. He was not much different in this, of course, from Joseph Conrad, who was skeptical in almost the same manner as Mencken. But he was at opposite poles from the vast majority of American critics. Mencken's "rage for order" was similar to that of Stephen Crane, whose short stories, particularly, Mencken admired. Also, one thinks of the ironic Wallace Stevens, who perhaps better than any modern poet has sung of the order man gives to the meaningless universe in which he resides.

To see Mencken's critical credo in action (and a credo is as useless as sorrow until it becomes active), we should examine his criticism of various writers, particularly those whose work he reviewed over a period of years. Conrad offers the best example, perhaps, insofar as his work received the approval of Mencken. But for the present purpose it would be well to examine his remarks on writers who elicited a mixed blessing. In the objections a critic has to a given work, we may readily observe his criteria for the perfect work —which exists as a standard only, never in fact.

Among the writers whom Mencken praised most highly during his first three years as a book critic was H. G. Wells. In April, 1909, he called *Tono-Bungay* one of the best novels to appear in months. In February, 1910, he lauded *Ann Veronica*. In July, 1910, in a review of *The History of Mr. Polly*, he stated that Wells was the successor of Dickens in that he concerned himself with the much-neglected English middle class (the two novelists were, of course, poles apart in their treatment of character: "Dickens regarded his characters as a young mother regards her baby; Wells looks at his as a porkpacker looks at a hog"). "I know very well that the author of *David Copperfield* was a greater artist than the author of *Mr. Polly*, just as I know that the Archbishop of Canterbury is a more virtuous man than my good friend, Fred the Bartender; but all the same, I prefer Wells and Fred to Dickens and the Archbishop. In such matters one must allow a lot to individual taste and prejudice."

Less than a year later, Mencken reviewed *The New Machiavelli* and found in it evidence that Wells had the inside track in the race to claim the laurels of the recently deceased George Meredith. Only Conrad, Hardy, and Moore had as much to say that was worth saying, and they were all entering the twilight of their careers. "If [Wells] keeps on as he has started, the world in ten years may choose to forget that he once wrote thrillers in the manner of Jules Verne, just as it has chosen to forget that Richard Wagner once wrote romanzas for cornet-a-piston." Mencken was more reserved in his praise of *Marriage,* which he reviewed in January, 1913. Wells still promised a great deal, but he was not delivering on schedule. Two more years passed, and Mencken began to despair of his white hope. *Marriage* and *The Passionate Friends* were both disappointing after the success of *Tono-Bungay,* and now, in January, 1915, Mencken openly panned *The Wife of Sir Isaac Harman:* "We are now familiar with his suffragettes, his tea-swilling London uplifters, his smattering of quasi-science, his Thackerayan asides, his chapter sections, his journalistic raciness. And, being familiar with these things, we begin to grow a bit weary of them." Mencken went on in his review to comment on the numerous English novelists of ability who wrote two or three good books and then moved backward (as examples he listed Leonard Merrick, W. J. Locke, Galsworthy, Hugh Walpole, and Wells). The only two English novelists who continued turning out good work year after year, mellowing and improving their method, were, according to Mencken, Joseph Conrad and Henry James, "the one a Pole and the other an American!"

As the months turned into years and as book after book by Wells came off the presses, Mencken became more and more acerb, at last pitiless in his reviews. Had not Wells proved that he could turn out competent work? Then why this continuous flow of fustian, this obsession with every fad of the day? Mencken called *Bealby,* reviewed in June, 1915, unspeakably bad and remarked that Wells was a superficial thinker whose only virtues were a deceptive cleverness and a journalistic facility for plausible writing. Five months later, he castigated *The Research Magnificent:* "He is not only clumsy; he is downright stupid. In the past year he has published no less than four books, and all of them have been intolerably bad."

Finally, in December, 1918, Mencken gave up on Wells and

composed an essay-review of *Joan and Peter,* which he entitled
"The Late Mr. Wells." The same title was given to a rather lengthy
obituary in *Prejudices: First Series,* in which Mencken endeavored
to account for the alarming disintegration of Wells the artist. The
essay may stand today as an accurate assessment of the novelist.
According to Cameron Rogers, writing in the *Outlook and Independent* (November 21, 1928), it outraged people at the time it
appeared but was accepted as gospel within a few years—a fate
shared by numerous of Mencken's essays. It was not the war,
Mencken asserted, that swallowed Wells; he was patriotic, but
never went totally insane as so many others had done:

> What has slowly crippled him and perhaps disposed of him is
> his gradual acceptance of the theory, corrupting to the artist
> and scarcely less so to the man, that he is one of the Great
> Thinkers of his era, charged with a pregnant Message to the
> Younger Generation—that his ideas, rammed into enough skulls,
> will Save the Empire, not only from the satanic Nietzscheism
> of the Hindenburgs and post-Hindenburgs, but also from all
> those inner Weaknesses that taint and flabbergast its vitals,
> as the tapeworm with nineteen heads devoured Atharippus of
> Macedon. In brief, he suffers from a messianic delusion—and
> once a man begins to suffer from a messianic delusion his days
> as a serious artist are ended.[6]

More important than the causes of Wells's artistic decline, at
least for the present purpose, are Mencken's remarks concerning
the nature of serious art (notice again that his condemnation is
accompanied by an aesthetic theory). In this essay, he repeated
his belief that a novelist must not only have a point of view but
have one that is in no way dependent on any craze of the moment.
Merely to describe existence was not enough—an answer to those
who endeavor to pigeonhole Mencken as nothing more than a
"naturalistic" critic and who define "naturalism" in a most shallow
way in the first place. The novelist's point of view, Mencken contended, must regard the internal workings and meanings of existence and not just its superficial appearances. And the writer must
be consistent in his over-all view of existence: another of Mencken's
unwavering demands. Even though the artist may be unable to
find any meaning in life, still that meaninglessness can be displayed
with clarity and consistency, as such skeptics as Conrad, Hardy,
Dreiser, and Anatole France have shown. In brief, Mencken in-

sisted that the sound work of art must do at least two major things: it must represent accurately, and it must interpret convincingly. Moreover, "a current of feeling" must co-ordinate and inform the representation and the interpretation. And here are Horace's *dulce et utile* in modern clothing. The work of art must be both sweet and useful; that is, it must both please in its structure and instruct or interpret in its content. The "current of feeling" Mencken referred to is nothing more than the consistent philosophy or manner of viewing life which he insisted must be found in the best art. The two aspects or functions—the *dulce et utile*—are not, of course, mutually exclusive; they are not divorced as structure on the one hand, content on the other. Rather, they are interlocking, dependent on each other.

Today Mencken is credited, quite rightly, with having been the leader of the forces for realism that triumphed so completely in the nineteen-twenties. But here again it is necessary to examine what he meant by the terms "realism" and its didactic cousin, "naturalism." After reading an essay on Joyce's *Ulysses,* which praised it "in high, astounding terms as a complete and exact record of a day in the life of its people," Mencken objected:

> It is, of course, nothing of the sort. At least nine-tenths of its materials came, not out of the Bloom family, but out of James Joyce. Even the celebrated unspoken monologue of Marion at the end is his, not hers. There are long sections of it that even the professional psychologists, who are singularly naïve, must detect as false—that is, false for Marion, false for a woman of her position, perhaps even false for any woman. But they are not false for Joyce.[7]

Still, Joyce was a realist, according to Mencken's definition. "Realism," he wrote, "is simply intellectual honesty in the artist. The realist yields nothing to what is manifestly not true, however alluring. He makes no compromise with popular sentimentality and illusion. He avoids the false inference as well as the bogus fact. He respects his materials as he respects himself."[8] And Joyce did this. Mencken refused to believe that such a thing as realism, grounded on objective fact, existed. The artist does not copy the real world (Mencken had almost no respect for what was called "photographic realism"); rather he interprets and criticizes, and his interpretation and criticism are of necessity subjective. It was, in other words, not the subject matter which determined whether a writer was a realist; it was rather his honesty with his material and, above all, with himself. Thus Mencken believed that Jane Austen was one of the great realists, as were Anatole France and Conrad, who were often near the border line of the fantastic. It is also clear that in this definition Mencken is taking a swipe at the opponents of realism (mostly academicians, who still constituted a small phalanx in the nineteen-twenties when this was written). Clearly, the implication he makes is that only the nonrealists are dishonest. How Irving Babbitt, Paul Elmer More, and Henry van Dyke must have cried out at such foul casuistry!

Naturalism was something else again. It was a type, rather than a method. Mencken saw clearly that the naturalistic novel, so called, often dabbled in filth for the simple hoggish joy of being repulsive (he spoke of the "meticulous nastiness that is so often the undoing of the naturalistic novelist" and of "flea-hunting naturalism"), but he also saw the enormous asset derived from such writers as Zola. In a long essay-review of three new translations of Zola's minor works, Mencken paid tribute to the great novels of the "Rougon-Macquart" series and especially to his influence on other writers.

> Allow all you please for Zola's ardent pursuit of scientific half-truths, for his air of an anatomist dismembering a corpse, for what Nietzsche, in a bitter moment, called his "delight to stink," and you still have an extraordinarily acute and penetrating observer of the human comedy, a creator of vivid and memorable characters, an accomplished workman in large forms, the high priest of a new cult in art. Zola, I am aware, did not invent naturalism—and naturalism, as he defined it, is not now the fashion. But it must be obvious that his propaganda, as novelist and critic, did more than any other one thing to give naturalism direction and coherence and to break down its antithesis, the sentimental romanticism of the middle Nineteenth Century—*Uncle Tom's Cabin, David Copperfield, La Dame aux Camélias*—and that his influence today, even if he has few avowed disciples, is still wide and undeniable.[9]

That influence, Mencken felt, could be seen in the works of Moore, Hardy, Wells, and Bennett in England, Sudermann and Wedekind in Germany, Norris and Dreiser in America, Gorki and Andreev in Russia, and in a whole school of writers in Scandinavia. His impression on individual writers was not so great, however, as the effect he had had on the novel as an art form. He was one of the first great writers to view man as a mammal, "swayed and fashioned, not by the fiats and conspiracies of a mysterious camorra of arbitrary gods, but by natural laws, by food and drink, by blood and environment. He taught his fellow-craftsmen to sit down in patience before a fact, to trace out its cause, to see it largely, not as something *in vacuo*, but as something fitting into an inevitable and unemotional process." Though perhaps an exaggeration of Zola's influence (I do not know whether it is or not), this statement perfectly illustrates Mencken's concern with character motivation. It was not a character's acts that were of first concern; rather, it was the novelist's depiction of the causes of action that mattered.

There was, however, a danger in following too closely any kind of "objective" naturalism. In his reviews of various writers, Mencken remarked the inability of the naturalist to do the one thing necessary to the highest form of art; that is, involve his reader emotionally with the central figures of his creation. No matter what the art form—drama, music, sculpture, fiction, painting, poetry—the "viewer" must be "taken in" by the artist and become one with the subject. Such a concept is very close, of course, to Aristotelian catharsis. In an exceptionally acute essay on Bennett that appeared in *Prejudices: First Series* (a volume which contained some of Mencken's best literary criticism, particularly in the essays on Wells, Bennett, Howells, Veblen, Sudermann, George Ade, Shaw, Nathan, and finally the essay on criticism, "Criticism of Criticism of Criticism"), Mencken further clarified his position on the necessity of emotional involvement in the plight or fate of the fictional hero. Beginning the piece by likening Bennett's "extraordinarily fluent and tuneful" journalese to that of Wells ("The Late Mr. Wells" is the preceding chapter of the volume), Mencken then contrasted the "matter" of the two men.

> Wells has a believing mind, and cannot resist the lascivious beckonings and eye-winkings of meretricious novelty; Bennett carries skepticism so far that it often takes on the appearance of a mere peasant-like suspicion of ideas, bellicose and unintelligent. Wells is astonishingly intimate and confidential; and more than one of his novels reeks with a shameless sort of autobiography; Bennett, even when he makes use of personal experience, contrives to get impersonality into it. Wells, finally, is a sentimentalist, and cannot conceal his feelings; Bennett, of

all the English novelists of the day, is the most steadily aloof and ironical.

In this aloofness Mencken saw both the great strength and the no less great weakness of Bennett the artist. On the one hand, the irony set him free from the messianic delusions that had "engulfed such romantic men as Wells, Winston Churchill and the late Jack London, and even, at times, such sentimental agnostics as Dreiser." But on the other hand, it had left him "empty of the passion that is, when all is said and done, the chief mark of the true novelist." Unable to involve himself in his characters' struggles against destiny, Bennett was unable "to arouse in the reader that penetrating sense of kinship, that profound and instinctive sympathy, which in its net effect is almost indistinguishable from the understanding born of experiences actually endured and emotions actually shared." Possessing little sympathy for his characters, Bennett was unable to create a figure that haunted the memory as did Lord Jim or Carrie Meeber or Huck Finn or Tom Jones. In explaining why Bennett was unable to create memorable characters, Mencken expressed a theory that is near to being irrefragable. The reason for this inability:

It lies in the plain fact that [Bennett's characters] appear to their creator, not as men and women whose hopes and agonies are of poignant concern, not as tragic comedians in isolated and concentrated dramas, but as mean figures in an infinitely dispersed and unintelligible farce, as helpless nobodies in an epic struggle that transcends both their volition and their comprehension. Thus viewing them, he fails to humanize them completely, and so he fails to make their emotions contagious. They are, in their way, often vividly real; they are thoroughly accounted for; what there is of them is unfailingly life-like; they move and breathe in an environment that pulses and glows. But the attitude of the author toward them remains, in the end, the attitude of a biologist toward his laboratory animals. He does not *feel* with them—and neither does his reader.

Actually, Bennett's chief concern was not so much with individuals as with large groups. In the long series of Five Towns books he had done his best work. "Better than any other man of his time he has got upon paper the social anatomy and physiology of the masses of average, everyday, unimaginative Englishmen." But in depicting this middle-class milieu, Bennett employed an irony that was, in the end, disquieting to the reader. Striving for what Mencken called a French objectivity, Bennett eventually arrived at a cynicism that was crippling to his art. Finding life without meaning, he seemed to conclude that it was futile to read a meaning into it.

> The reasoning, unluckily, has holes in it. It may be sound logically, but it is psychologically unworkable. One goes to novels, not for the bald scientific fact, but for a romantic amelioration of it. When they carry that amelioration to the point of uncritical certainty, when they are full of "ideas" that click and whirl like machines, then the mind revolts against the childish naïveté of the thing. But when there is no organization of the spectacle at all, when it is presented as a mere formless panorama, when to the sense of its unintelligibility is added the suggestion of its inherent chaos, then the mind revolts no less. Art can never be simply representation. It cannot deal solely with precisely what is. It must, at the least, present the real in the light of some recognizable ideal; it must give to the eternal farce, if not some moral, then at all events some direction. For without that formulation there can be no clear-cut separation of the individual will from the general stew and turmoil of things, and without that separation there can be no coherent drama, and without that drama there can be no evocation of emotion, and without that emotion art is unimaginable.

The last two sentences of this critique deserve to be emblazoned in gaudy lights above every artist's work table. Think how many dull evenings at the theater and under the reading lamp would be spared us if all artists could recognize the elemental truth of those succinct statements.

Though Conrad, Mencken wrote, was a far more implacable ironist than Bennett and just as unshakable an agnostic, still his novels were inundated with a sardonic pity that was contagious to the reader. What one got from Bennett's novels was "not the impression of a definite transaction, not the memory of an outstanding and appealing personality, not the after-taste of a profound emotion, but merely the sense of having witnessed a gorgeous but incomprehensible parade, coming out of nowhere and going to God knows where." He had done what Balzac and Zola, from whom he derived, had done before him: "he has painted a full-length portrait of a whole society, accurately, brilliantly and, in certain areas, almost exhaustively. The middle Englishman—not the individual, but the type—is there displayed more vividly than he is displayed anywhere else that I know of." And if he failed to scale the peaks where the greatest fiction may be found, he still produced a body of work that must be respected.

One of the key passages in this criticism of Bennett refers to his ability to create *types*, but not *individuals*. As we have seen, Mencken was most interested in fiction that had as its central figure a person who approached Everyman; but this person must have some salient qualities that enable the reader to admire and sympathize with his struggle against the forces hemming him in. In other words, the reader must be able to take an interest in the conflict of the novel not for the sake of the conflict but for the sake of the victim. It was this ability to make us sympathetically share the fate of Conrad's and Dreiser's protagonists that made those writers, more than any others of their day, so appealing to Mencken, as we shall see later.

CHAPTER SIX

Criticism of Criticism

I

I F Mencken had certain set ideas concerning the novel, it is nonetheless clear that those ideas leave room for the artist to move freely about, to experiment, to blaze new paths. Thus it was necessary that the critic be a man hospitable to change, which is to say, a man who was not bound by a theory that would leave in outer darkness the artist who wished to innovate. Such a man was James Huneker. It has also been shown that Mencken constantly discussed the standards of art against which he evaluated a specific work. But to know what those standards were is not quite the same thing as to know precisely what he considered to be the function of the critic. To learn that, we must go to two essays in particular, two widely divergent and at times somewhat contradictory essays, one of them placing the critic in the role of a catalyst and insisting that "The really competent critic must be an empiricist," and the other depicting the critic as a man who is primarily concerned with expressing himself in his individual reaction to the work of art. I refer to "Criticism of Criticism of Criticism" and "Footnote on Criticism." While the latter essay has been much the more widely anthologized of the two, I feel that a knowledge of both is requisite to an understanding of Mencken's philosophy of criticism. It is also well to bear in mind that Mencken finally came to doubt that criticism—that is, literary criticism per se, as opposed to what he called "criticism of ideas"—was a worth-while pursuit for a man who possessed more than average creativity. But that hard-nosed conviction came after he had spent several years reviewing books— after, in fact, he had become the reigning monarch of criticism in America.

In its original form, "Criticism of Criticism of Criticism" was an essay-review of Joel Spingarn's *Creative Criticism* (1917). Two years after its appearance in the *Smart Set,* Mencken resurrected and revised the review for the first volume of his *Prejudices* series. Since he changed the phraseology in various places and rather widely extended the essay, I shall use the later version. The title refers, incidentally, to Mencken's criticism of Spingarn's criticism of criticism. The essay begins in a typically Menckenian manner:

> Every now and then, a sense of the futility of their daily en-deavors falling suddenly upon them, the critics of Christendom turn to a somewhat sour and depressing consideration of the nature and objects of their own craft. That is to say, they turn to criticizing criticism. What is it in plain words? What is its aim, exactly stated in legal terms? How far can it go? What good can it do? What is its normal effect upon the artist and the work of art?

After asking his questions, he then proceeded to give the answers offered by the various critical schools of thought. This es-say, written at the height of what has come to be called "The Battle of the Books," summarizes the various theories as succinctly as any, and more objectively than most, of the numerous expositions on the subject. The very crudeness (and the essay is certainly crude compared to more recent studies of the subject) of Mencken's sum-mary is an asset in that he goes at once to the heart of each critical system. It also employs Mencken's curiously effective system of "shorthand"; that is, it summarizes and condenses various theories that other writers would spend pages talking about without ever really clarifying the matter in such a way that it would stick in the memory. Here is yet another example of how the manner is so tightly allied to the matter that paraphrase would almost surely distort to some extent. It is also evident from the following passage that Mencken was not one of those who held that a particular theory was the *only* true one.

> One group argues, partly by direct statement and partly by attacking all other groups, that the one defensible purpose of

the critic is to encourage the virtuous and oppose the sinful—
in brief, to police the fine arts and so hold them in tune with
the moral order of the world. Another group, repudiating this
constabulary function, argues hotly that the arts have nothing
to do with morality whatsoever—that their concern is solely
with pure beauty. A third group holds that the chief aspect of
a work of art, particularly in the field of literature, is its aspect
as psychological document—that if it doesn't help men to know
themselves it is nothing. A fourth group reduces the thing to
an exact science, and sets up standards that resemble algebraic
formulae—that is the group of metrists, of contrapuntists and
of those who gabble of light-waves. And so, in order, follow
groups five, six, seven, eight, nine, ten, each with its theory
and its proofs.

Against all these groups stood Major J. E. Spingarn, U.S.A.,
former "professor in rebellion" of Columbia University. Mencken,
who could not help praising a professor who was "at least magnificently unprofessorial," built his essay around Spingarn and his
theory, "for a professor must have a theory, as a dog must have
fleas." Spingarn felt that the critic's first and only duty was, as
Carlyle once put it, to find out "what the poet's aim really and
truly was, how the task he had to do stood before his eye, and
how far, with such materials as were afforded him, he has fulfilled
it." In paraphrasing the theory, Mencken asked his reader to substitute the word *artist* for Spingarn's *poet*, "or, if literature is in
question, substitute the Germanic word *Dichter*—that is, the artist
in words, the creator of beautiful letters, whether in verse or in
prose. Ibsen always called himself a *Digter*, not a *Dramatiker*, or
Skuespiller. So, I daresay, did Shakespeare." It is not the critic's
business to determine whether the work of art heeds Aristotle or
flouts Aristotle, nor can he pass judgment on its rhyme scheme, its
length and breadth, its iambics, its politics, its patriotism, its piety,
its psychological exactness, its good taste. The critic may remark
these things, but he may not protest about them; that is, "he may
not complain if the thing criticized fails to fit into a pigeon-hole.
Every sonnet, every drama, every novel is *sui generis:* it must stand
on its own bottom; it must be judged by its own inherent inten-
tions." Poets do not set out to write epics, pastorals, lyrics, and so
on; rather, to quote Spingarn, "they express *themselves, and this
expression is their only form.* There are not, therefore, only three

or ten or a hundred literary kinds; there are as many kinds as there are individual poets." Moreover, according to both Mencken and Spingarn, there can be no valid appeal *ad hominem*. Mencken opposed the vast majority of his contemporary American critics when he insisted, "The character and background of the poet are beside the mark; the poem itself is the thing. Oscar Wilde, weak and swine-like, yet wrote beautiful prose. To reject that prose on the ground that Wilde had filthy habits is as absurd as to reject *What Is Man?* on the ground that its theology is beyond the intelligence of the editor of the New York *Times*."

As Mencken pointed out, Spingarn had voiced "a doctrine borrowed from the Italian, Benedetto Croce, and by Croce filched from Goethe—a doctrine anything but new in the world, even in Goethe's time, but nevertheless long buried in forgetfulness." In paraphrasing the theory, he did not miss the opportunity to fire a salvo at the American critics of the opposing camp—critics who had attacked Mencken particularly and the radicals generally during the recently ended war with every weapon at their disposal, using, for example, the *ad hominem* argument against Mencken, who was, after all, of German blood and hence a rascal. Stuart Sherman's lengthy references to Mencken's genealogy were both venomous and childish. To be sure, Mencken had been anything but pacifistic in his comments on academic critics, especially those who sought to silence Dreiser. And now, with the war over, he could be more outspoken than was formerly possible. After pointing out that Spingarn's theory presupposed that the critic be "a civilized and tolerant man, hospitable to all intelligible ideas and capable of reading them as he runs," Mencken concluded that this was too much to ask of most practicing critics.

This is a demand that at once rules out nine-tenths of the grown-up sophomores who carry on the business of criticism in America. Their trouble is simply that they lack the intellectual resilience necessary for taking in ideas, and particularly new ideas. The only way they can ingest one is by transforming it into the nearest related formula—usually a harsh and devastating operation. This fact accounts for their chronic inability to understand all that is most personal and original and hence most forceful and significant in the emerging literature of our country. They can get down what has been digested and redigested, and so brought into forms that they know, and carefully labeled by predecessors of their own sort—but they exhibit alarm immediately they come into the presence of the extraordinary. Here we have an explanation of [William Lyon] Phelps's inability to comprehend the colossal phenomenon of Dreiser, and of [Percy H.] Boynton's childish nonsense about realism, and of Sherman's effort to apply the Espionage Act to the arts, and of [Paul Elmer] More's querulous enmity to romanticism, and of all the fatuous pigeon-holing that passes for criticism in their more solemn literary periodicals.

Running through all the criticism of "the dull fellows who combine criticism with tutoring," there was the dictum that a work of art must not vary from the neat grooves of orthodoxy. If the writer or painter or composer was what might be called a "right thinker," if he devoted himself "to advocating the transient platitudes in a sonorous manner," then he was deemed worthy of respect. The artist, according to the "pious academicians," was not a reporter or critic of life; he was a teacher. The artist must depict the world, not as it is, but rather as it ought to be. Art must lift up man and focus his eyes on the shining stars above. Such, according to Mencken (and even allowing for his obvious exaggeration I can find no reason for disputing his belief), was the dominant view in American criticism. The *dominant* view, mind you. But so far Mencken has said little of what criticism should do and how it could be done; rather, he has concentrated on the shortcomings of American criticism in general.

Although he was aware of various efforts on the part of the younger critics to break through the walls erected by the school of critical uplift, Mencken sadly concluded that American criticism was in a bad way. To begin with, the popular critics—that is, the moralists and uplifters—were supported by an American populace that was accustomed to puritanical restraints. "We are, in fact," he wrote, "a nation of evangelists; every third American devotes himself to improving and lifting up his fellow-citizens, usually by force; the messianic delusion is our national disease." Moreover, American literature of the period was bound to influence criticism to some extent, and that literature had, of course, been hamstrung by the critics. In other words, cause and effect were interchangeable. The writer who wished to depict life realistically has almost no chance of breaking through the formidable barrier of genteel critics to the protected reader.

"Here is a novel," says the artist. "Why didn't you write a tract?" roars the professor—and down the chute go novel and novelist. "This girl is pretty," says the painter. "But she has left off her undershirt," protests the head-master—and off goes the poor dauber's head. At its mildest, this balderdash takes the form of the late Hamilton Wright Mabie's "White List of Books"; at its worst, it is comstockery, an idiotic and abominable thing. Genuine criticism is as impossible to such inordinately narrow and cocksure men as music is to a man who is tone-deaf. The critic, to interpret his artist, even to understand his artist, must be able to get into the mind of his artist; he must feel and comprehend the vast pressure of the creative passion; as Major Spingarn says, "aesthetic judgment and artistic creation are instinct with the same vital life." This is why all the best criticism of the world has been written by men who have had within them, not only the reflective and analytical faculty of critics, but also the gusto of artists—Goethe, Carlyle, Lessing, Schlegel, Sainte-Beuve, and, to drop a story or two, Hazlitt, Hermann Bahr, Georg Brandes and James Huneker. Huneker, tackling *Also sprach Zarathustra*, revealed its content in illuminating flashes. But tackled by Paul Elmer More, it became no more than a dull student's exercise, ill-naturedly corrected.

The iconoclastic side of Mencken is again apparent: he is more concerned with ridiculing the critics of the ivory tower than he is with expressing his views on what criticism should do. As was often the case, he presented his thesis by indirection; that is, he first destroyed and then built anew on the razed site.

Although he was convinced that Spingarn's theory was far sounder and more stimulating than any of those cherished by other professors, Mencken saw that the "ingenious ex-professor, professorlike," injured his theory by claiming too much for it. "Having laid and hatched, so to speak, his somewhat stale but still highly nourishing egg, he begins to argue fatuously that the resultant flamingo is the whole mustering of the critical *Aves*." Actually, criticism falls a good deal short of an intuitive re-creation of beauty, and, on the other hand, it goes a great deal further than Spingarn would have us believe. Criticism must not only interpret in terms that are exact; it must also employ terms that are comprehensible to the reader, "else it will leave the original mystery as dark as before—and once interpretation comes in, paraphrases and transliteration come in." The recondite must be made plain; what is transcendental must be rendered in common modes of thought. Mencken then asked: "Well, what are morality, trochaics, hexameters, movements, historical principles, psychological maxims, the dramatic unities— what are all these save common modes of thinking, short cuts, rubber stamps, words of one syllable?" Moreover, Spingarn seemed to think that beauty was a sort of apparition *in vacuo,* whereas it actually has social, political, even moral implications. The critic who endeavors to segregate the work of art from the multifarious conditions under which it was produced, as, it must be clear, too many of the so-called New Critics today endeavor to do, forgets that art is essentially a reflection of some aspect of the workaday world. For example: "The Finale of Beethoven's C minor symphony is not only colossal as music; it is also colossal as revolt; it says something against something. Yet more, the springs of beauty are not within itself alone, nor even in genius alone, but often in things without. Brahms wrote his Deutsches Requiem, not only because he was a great artist, but also because he was a good German."

Mencken's highest praise was for Spingarn's advocacy of free speech in art with "no protective tariffs, and no *a priori* assumptions, and no testing of ideas by mere words." The true critic, like Huneker, begins in the same manner as does Spingarn, but always "with a due regard for the prejudices and imbecilities of the world." As Mencken remarked in a passage just quoted, the weakness of so highly impressionistic a theory is that it assumes the critic possesses an extremely high degree of taste and knowledge, indeed that he be a thoroughly competent artist himself; and even then no allowance is made for the reader who may require the aid of some sort of standardized critical vocabulary before he can fully comprehend the critic's evaluation. Mencken felt that, of all American critics, Poe came closest to realizing Spingarn's demand that the critic re-create the work of other artists, but Poe did not always restrict himself to the work of art; and besides being an artist, Poe was a man of the world, and what he said was apposite and instructive. The critic, indeed, *has* to be something of an instructor, though never a "birchman." Which is to say, the critic is always on the outside looking in at the work of art, endeavoring to explain or interpret its meaning to others on the outside. Furthermore, in his unyielding pronouncements, Spingarn was setting up new restrictions to replace the old; above all, he was depriving the critic of that pragmatic resiliency so necessary to his trade. Herein we see one of Mencken's greatest attributes as a critic.

> To denounce moralizing out of hand is to pronounce a moral judgment. To dispute the categories is to set up a new anti-categorical category. And to admire the work of Shakespeare is to be interested in his handling of blank verse, his social aspirations, his shot-gun marriage and his frequent concessions to the bombastic frenzy of his actors, and to have some curiosity about Mr. W. H. The really competent critic must be an empiricist. He must conduct his exploration with whatever means lie within the bounds of his personal limitation. He must produce his effects with whatever tools will work. If pills fail, he gets out his saw. If the saw won't cut, he seizes a club.

In the last analysis, Mencken is saying, criticism is written by humans, not machines; and the personal limitations must be taken into account. Moreover, the tools a critic uses will of necessity vary from occasion to occasion. At times only the club seems to have an effect, as Mencken was to prove in his assault on the genteel critics—an assault which had much to do with changing the direction of criticism in America. Today, when the club is out of fashion (a few critics still use it effectively, of course; for example, Donald Malcolm, Anthony West, Dwight Macdonald, and a few others), pills are used to produce the effects.

Finally, Mencken would have substituted the word "catalytic" for "creative" in Spingarn's title, which is to say that Mencken felt criticism was a catalyzer rather than a separate creation. (We shall see how he modifies this belief rather drastically in his "Footnote on Criticism.") It is the critic's business to provoke the reaction between the work of art and the spectator. The untutored observer often views the painting, reads the book, or hears the piece of music without its making an intelligible impression. If he were spontaneously sensitive to art, there would be no need for criticism. As it is, the critic, if he is a good one, can make the art live for the spectator and the spectator live for the art by acting as catalyst. "Out of the process come understanding, appreciation, intelligent enjoyment—and that is precisely what the artist tried to produce."

By the time Mencken came to write "Criticism of Criticism of Criticism," he had spent more than a decade propounding many of the ideas, with the few noted exceptions, that are to be found in Spingarn's essay. Spingarn went too far in his anarchistic revolt against the traditionalists, as he himself later admitted,[1] but his "romantic" attitude toward the "rules" of the critical trade opened avenues for both critic and artist that had been closed before. It is, of course, one thing to voice such open-minded and amoral theories; it is quite another to make them heard, and still another to get them accepted. Like the vast majority of theorists, Spingarn never wrote criticism; he was not a reviewer or critic of books at all, any more than the academicians today who discourse at length in the quarterlies on this or that aspect of criticism are critics. Until the theorist has provided concrete evidence that his theory is actually useful, he must remain in the anterooms of criticism, just as the critic must remain in the anteroom of art. It is easy enough to hatch theories; it is difficult to write good criticism. Such yeoman work is best performed by the journalistic critic; that is, by the professional writer who day after day presents his critical evaluations to the reading public. And if the journalist has, as did Mencken, a great gusto in living, an enthusiastic delight in literature, a fair sense of values, and, most rare and most important perhaps of all traits, an enormous talent for arranging words effectively, he can contribute to the making of his age.

As has been shown, Mencken met Spingarn only about halfway. That is, he agreed that criticism should not be the handmaiden of history, politics, morality (or theology), psychology (or any of the sciences), but was, properly speaking, a branch of aesthetics. Criticism, in brief, was an art. But he refused to go all the way with Spingarn in his insistence that it should be divorced from all these various enterprises or disciplines. Rather, it should take them all into consideration, or better, take whichever of the other branches of knowledge might be useful in specific instances of criticism. Mencken has been called, with some justice, one of the aesthetics, just as, with a degree of justice, he has been catalogued with the impressionists (all competent critics are impressionists to some degree). But it is necessary to remember that when he spoke of art, he spoke of that which reflected, interpreted, and "criticized" or offered some kind of judgment on life in its broadest implications. And it was thus perfectly logical for him to conclude that criticism (an art, remember) offered comment on art, which *was* life or experience dramatically revealed. How, then, he would ask, can the critic say that he is not going to concern himself with history, morals, the sciences, politics, and so forth, when by his very calling he *must* concern himself with all those human aspects?

Though I do not know what Mencken thought of the New Critics who came to power in the thirties and forties and whose influence is presently being conserved by the academies, it seems logical to assume that he would have considered their primary premise as an exercise in escapism. By refusing to judge art against the other aspects or materials of life—which that art attempted to depict—the New Critic commits the arch mistake of criticism. Though no New Critic has ever practiced precisely what he preaches, his preachments would doubtless cause Mencken to wonder if he were not engaged in some branch of metaphysics, rather than in the soundly rational art of criticism. I do know that Mencken severely chastised those Southern Agrarians in the nineteen-thirties (see his essay, "The South Astir," in *Virginia Quarterly Review* for January, 1935) who advocated cutting the South loose from northern industry and ideas and returning to the forty-acres-and-a-mule beliefs of their grandfathers. Mencken blasted such escapist thinking on the grounds that it was flatly impossible to return to the nineteenth century, for better or worse, and that even if it were possible it would have a deleterious effect on a South that was enough of a cultural Tibet already. Rather than concern themselves with attacking northern atheism and materialism, he asked them to pay more attention to cleaning up their own backyards. Need I remind the reader that the Agrarians were precisely those who later made up the core of the New Critics? Nor should I have to point out that a man who tries to escape the harsh realities of the present in the political and sociological realms (as did the Agrarians) will try to escape those same realities when he turns to literature. Moreover, the type of Christianity of many of the southerners certainly helps explain their disinclination to have any truck with the modern world of deterministic science.

II

In a letter dated August 30, 1925, to Ernest Boyd, Mencken remarked that he never had any interest in the numerous aesthetic theories that were prevalent in 1908, when he began his work on the *Smart Set*. The "aesthetic gabble" seemed to him "to be mainly

buncombe. I have, in fact, no respect for aesthetic theories. They
are always blowing up. More and more I incline to the notion that
every first-rate work of art, like very first-rate man, is *sui generis*.
When I hear a theory I suspect a quack." This same critical atheism
(or determinism) Mencken had developed at length in his "Footnote on Criticism" three years earlier.[2] To begin with, one must
understand the title of the essay: it is a "footnote," a peripheral
comment on the art of criticism, and not an analytic study of
literary criticism or any other particular type of critical writing. It
is concerned with the sort of man who makes a good critic, rather
than with criticism itself. Primarily, it comments on the motivating
power that sets man to writing as against indulging in some other
human enterprise; and secondarily, it is an attack on the sentimental belief that the critic is, or *should* be, interested in uplifting
the arts, the belief that "he writes because he is possessed by a passion to advance the enlightenment, to put down error and wrong,
to disseminate some specific doctrine: psychological, epistemological, historical, or aesthetic." Only bad critics were moved by any
such messianic desire. The best critics were moved by the motives
of the artist. "It is no more and no less than the simple desire to
function freely and beautifully, to give outward and objective form
to ideas that bubble inwardly and have a fascinating lure in them,
to get rid of them dramatically and make an articulate noise in
the world."

Writing as if he were no longer concerned with literary criticism,
Mencken remarked that "years ago," when he was writing about
Dreiser's work, people assumed that he was interested in furthering
the cause of Dreiser for one of two reasons: either he was devoted
to Dreiser's ideas and wished to propagate them, or else he "yearned
to lift up American literature." Actually, Mencken had, he insisted,
little interest in Dreiser's ideas, a statement that is quite true: the
two men were as different as are the head and the heart. But then
Mencken is here loading his argument. He always insisted that the
value of Dreiser's thought was nil; but he was certainly serious in
praising the novelist's ability to evoke an emotional involvement
from the reader, and that, as Mencken always said, was far more
important in art than its intellectual content. Going further,
Mencken stated that he was "wholly devoid of public spirit, and
[hadn't] the least lust to improve American literature; if it ever

came to what I regard as perfection my job would be gone."
Actually, his motive was much less philanthropic than that. "My
motive, well known to Mr. Dreiser himself and to every one else
who knew me as intimately as he did, was simply and solely to
sort out and give coherence to the ideas of Mr. Mencken, and to
put them into suave and ingratiating terms, and to discharge them
with a flourish, and maybe with a phrase of pretty song, into the
dense fog that blanketed the Republic." But then those ideas of
Mr. Mencken, who is here up to his old trick of shifting the pea
from cup to cup (now you see it, now you don't), were ideas *about*
Mr. Dreiser, not *about* Mr. Mencken. We are going in circles, and
all the while Mencken is trying to convince us that he is leading
us away from a belief that is somehow important: that is, the belief
that writers are devoted to some kind of Red Cross mission—a
belief held by overly idealistic youngsters, perhaps, but certainly
not by any writer of importance. (This is not to say, unfortunately,
that men have not got into print by *saying* that critics write in
order to further some cause or other. Politicians, of course, tell such
lies every day, even to the point of convincing themselves.)

Far from choosing freely to write criticism for any reason whatsoever, the individual is pretty much outside the domain of free
choice: "The critic's choice of criticism rather than of what is called
creative writing is chiefly a matter of temperament—perhaps, more
accurately of hormones—with accidents of education and environment to help." The critic is moved to write by the work of other
men; he is more a commentator than a creator; hence it is easy to
explain why the artist usually considers the critic a second-rate
writer, or rather the practitioner of an inferior art form. If the critic
"lacks the intellectual agility and enterprise needed to make the
leap from the work of art to the vast and mysterious complex of
phenomena behind it," he will always remain "no more than a
fugleman or policeman to his betters."

> But if a genuine artist is concealed within him—if his feelings
> are in any sense profound and original, and his capacity for
> self-expression is above the average of educated men—then he
> moves inevitably from the work of art to life itself, and begins
> to take on a dignity that he formerly lacked. It is impossible
> to think of a man of any actual force and originality, universally
> recognized as having those qualities, who spent his whole life
> appraising and describing the work of other men. Did Goethe,

or Carlyle, or Matthew Arnold, or Sainte-Beuve, or Macaulay, or even, to come down a few pegs, Lewes, or Lowell, or Hazlitt? Certainly not. The thing that becomes most obvious about the writings of all such men, once they are examined carefully, is that the critic is always being swallowed up by the creative artist—that what starts out as the review of a book, or a play, or other work of art, usually develops very quickly into an independent essay upon the theme of that work of art, or upon some theme that it suggests—in a word, that it becomes a fresh work of art, and only indirectly related to the one that suggested it. This fact, indeed, is so plain that it scarcely needs statement. What the pedagogues always object to in, for example, the *Quarterly* reviewers is that they forgot the books they were supposed to review, and wrote long papers—often, in fact, small books—expounding ideas suggested (or not suggested) by the books under review. Every critic who is worth reading falls inevitably into the same habit.

Mencken was right, of course. Great writers never stick to the task before them; invariably they are more interested in the subject of the book than in the book itself. Moreover, Emerson was right when he said that one must be an inventor to read well. What the pedagogues objected to in Mencken's day, they still object to today; that is, they object in theory to a critic's using the work of art as a mere springboard for the promulgation of his own ideas on the subject. Mencken was perhaps right when he called mere reviewing "a much inferior business"; but he should have added that, inferior or not, it was a most necessary business that had to be done by someone.

Writing book reviews was not a difficult business, Mencken believed, since the young man just out of college often made an excellent reviewer of books, and

> even decayed pedagogues often do it, as such graves of the intellect as the New York *Times* bear witness. But if he continues to do it, whether well or ill, it is a sign to all the world that his growth ceased when they made him *Artium Baccalaureus*. Gradually he becomes, whether in or out of the academic grove, a professor, which is to say, a man devoted to diluting and retailing the ideas of his superiors—not an artist, not even a bad artist, but almost the antithesis of an artist.

I find only one thing wrong with all this: the book reviews in the New York *Times* do *not* bear witness that reviewing is a simple business; on the contrary, those reviews often prove, it seems to me, by their very badness that reviewing is rather a difficult business—that is, if you assume that a review should also be a criticism. On the other hand, Mencken's remarks about the incompetence of the "professor" in the field of criticism are certainly valid. It would be simple enough for me to develop a long argument "proving" that the professor, by his very nature and training, will at best be no better than a mediocre critic. Suffice it to say that the best literary criticism being written today, just as in Mencken's day, is done by professionals living outside the academic walls. The artist differs from his fellows, Mencken continued, in that he is driven by an "impulse to self-expression," not in that he is necessarily superior intellectually. The ideas he expresses are rarely singular in that the nonwriter never thought of them; he is singular in the vigor of the impulse within him to give his ideas objective form. Only in the hallucinations of poets did the mute, inglorious Miltons exist.

Finally, "Footnote on Criticism," which is a kind of valedictory to that part of Mencken's career which was predominantly concerned with literary criticism, is an essay on the nature of truth. Or, more specifically, on the importance of "truth" to the artist and to the place posterity assigns him. Admitting that Carlyle "was surely no just and infallible judge," but was on the contrary "full of prejudices, biles, naïvetés, humors," Mencken added that he was, in spite of these shortcomings, still read, still "attended to." Macaulay, Sainte-Beuve, Arnold, and Goethe were little less free from such deficiencies; yet they, too, were remembered. "What saved Carlyle, Macaulay and company is as plain as day. They were first-rate artists. They could make the thing charming, and that is always a million times more important than making it true." And precisely here do we ascertain a "truth." Mencken was himself a case in point. He is remembered today, though a bit gingerly by many pedagogues, not because of any great truths that he unearthed—he employed in much of his literary criticism classical standards that are as old as Pericles' Athens; he said little about aesthetic theory that may be described as original—but for his ability to express himself in resounding phrases (only Emerson and Thoreau equaled him as phrase-makers) and convincing terms. Readers still turn, and with profit, to his essays on Dreiser, Howells, Wells, Shaw, Veblen, Nietzsche, Conrad, Bennett, and numerous lesser figures. Mencken did not deny the existence of provisional truths: "There is, year by year, a gradual accumulation of what may be called, provisionally, truths—there is a slow accretion of ideas that somehow manage to meet all practicable human tests, and so survive. But even so, it is risky to call them absolute truths." And a moment later, remarking on the provisional nature of truth: "The profoundest truths of the Middle Ages are now laughed at by schoolboys. The profoundest truths of democracy will be laughed at, a few centuries hence, even by school-teachers." What delight Justice Oliver Wendell Holmes, an ardent Mencken admirer, must have taken in this skeptical relativism!

Whereas Spingarn had attacked those critics who used moralistic standards in criticizing a work of art, Mencken attacked criticism proper in a vital area: its self-congratulatory pretensions of arriving at final answers. "Let us forget," Mencken fumed, "all the heavy effort to make a science of [criticism]; it is a fine art, or nothing." This statement might be used as the subtitle to the as yet uncollected literary criticism of H. L. Mencken. Hear his argument before the critical bar:

> If the critic, retiring to his cell to concoct his treatise upon a book or play or what-not, produces a piece of writing that shows sound structure, and brilliant color, and the flash of new and persuasive ideas, and civilized manners, and the charm of an uncommon personality in free function, then he has given something to the world that is worth having, and sufficiently justified his existence. Is Carlyle's "Frederick" true? Who cares? As well ask if the Parthenon is true, or the C Minor Symphony, or "Wiener Blut." Let the critic who is an artist leave such necropsies to professors of aesthetics, who can no more determine the truth than he can, and will infallibly make it unpleasant and a bore.

So convinced was he that criticism was indistinguishable from skepticism, he forswore any effort to make converts of his readers. This is more than a little odd, though, when we remember that he placed persuasiveness very high on the list of qualities a critic should have. Since he was unable to imagine any aesthetic idea or theory as being "palpably and incontrovertibly sound," he could see no sense in what passed for "constructive" criticism. If a man were an artist, he would simply refuse to be told by the critic how he should create his art. Using his own experience with critics (and they devoted more time to criticizing Mencken than to any other critic before or since his day in America) who reviewed his books at great length, Mencken admitted to having learned nothing whatever from those who offered him suggestions as to how he might write better books. (He freely accepted and appreciated help in writing his language volumes, but the suggestions in that case concerned factual errors and had nothing to do with his ideas.) His arrogance, galling though it may be, is still the arrogance of the true artist. Though he refused to listen to those who asked him to adopt a different style, to use fewer German words or slang expressions, or to do something else that would be totally foreign to him, he did admit to having benefited from destructive criticism.

> A hearty slating always does me good, particularly if it be well written. It begins by enlisting my professional respect; it ends by making me examine my ideas coldly in the privacy of my chamber. Not, of course, that I usually revise them, but I at least examine them. If I decide to hold fast to them, they are all the dearer to me thereafter, and I expound them with a new passion and plausibility. If, on the contrary, I discern holes in them I shelve them in a *pianissimo* manner, and set about hatching new ones to take their place. But constructive criticism irritates me. I do not object to being denounced, but I can't abide being schoolmastered, especially by men I regard as imbeciles.

One remembers Huck Finn's remark that a hiding always done him good and cheered him up.

This equanimity before the censures of critics was not just derring-do or bluff on Mencken's part, as the publication of *Menckeniana, a Schimpflexikon* (1928) readily proves. What other author in American history has had the audacity or the cunning to publish a book that contains hundreds of the most scalding attacks, neatly indexed under twenty-three chapter headings, upon his person, his beliefs, and every aspect of his work? Ernest Boyd concluded his delightful review of the book (in the *Independent* for January 28, 1928) by remarking that this was the first time, so far as he knew, that an author succeeded in making his enemies earn royalties for him.

Mencken felt that the critic's willingness to forget friendships and view the book before him objectively made him a kind of natural enemy of the artist. A *reviewer* will normally confine himself to the modest task of interpreting the work before him—and thereby win, oftentimes, the approval of the artist. But the *critic*, Mencken believed, is always moved by an impulse that carries him beyond mere reviewing; he goes beyond interpretation, which, after all, is rather like the sort of thing the instructor does with a class of undergraduates. The danger of just interpreting the work of art lies in the fact that the interpretation tends to prevent the critic from judging the work, that is, testing its validity against standards. As Mencken pointed out in the earlier essay, this was the greatest weakness of Spingarn's theory. The impressionistic critic, like Spingarn and his descendants, will usually stop at interpretation; the judicial critic will evaluate or judge. Usually, of course, a critic does both to some degree. In distinguishing between reviewing and criticizing, Mencken again separated what he termed "pedagogy" from art.

Mencken believed that the critical war of the period in which he was writing did at least two things: "On the one hand, it exposes all the cruder fallacies to hostile examination, and so disposes of many of them. And on the other hand, it melodramatizes the business of the critic, and so convinces thousands of bystanders, otherwise quite inert, that criticism is an amusing and instructive art, and that the problems it deals with are important. What men will fight for seems to be worth looking into." Such a belief seems foreign to criticism today, when judicial criticism is rarely practiced save in a few trade magazines. The worst failing of academic criticism, which, once again, has almost replaced professional criticism, is its concentration on analysis at the expense of judging. This concern for analysis has resulted in an overconcentration on those writers who are most concerned with technique. The very bulk of the criticism devoted to analyzing the fiction of Henry James, for example, has caused many to overestimate that work—certainly not a difficult thing to do. In concentrating on the "manner" of James, critics have overlooked the more important question of his "matter." We should be concerned with the "how" of art, but not at the expense of the "what." The fact that James's "people" are "gutted of the common stuff that fills characters in other books, and ourselves," as E. M. Forster told us, and have neither bowels nor sexual organs, as Somerset Maugham told us, seems to matter little to those who are intent on underlining James's passion for form—that is, his passion for art for art's sake. In like manner, an overestimate of T. S. Eliot's poetry has resulted from the excessive attention paid to his symbolism. It is also a general practice among academic critics, who spend most of their time re-evaluating past literature, to discuss, say, the novels of Fenimore Cooper in such a way that the reader may conclude that those novels are worth reading, whereas they are hardly readable; or discuss the poetry of D. H. Lawrence in terms that might lead one to suspect that Lawrence and Keats were poets of kindred ability. Such critical blindness occurs when the critic is unable to judge the work of art against "the vast and mysterious complex of phenomena behind it."

If Mencken sought to justify the job of the critic in "Criticism of Criticism of Criticism," he seemed to deprive him of the rank of first-class citizen in the world of letters in the essay written three years later. Rather than despair of the practice of criticism, as so many good critics have done, he dialectically "proved" that the best critics were unable, since they were creative artists, to stick to the task of criticizing *just* the work of art and that they eventually abandoned criticism for other types of writing which allowed them the free play of their creative ability. This was not the same thing as saying that criticism was impossible or unworthy; it is still necessary, though not of lordly stature. But there is still an obvious contradiction here when Mencken states, in effect, that the best "critics" cannot force themselves to practice criticism per se. By "critic" Mencken seems to mean "personality," or at least "artist" (if criticism is an art, then it is practiced by artists). In one sense he was right: the critic who restricts himself to interpretation and analysis of the work of art is not remembered; nor is he, Mencken would say, an artist. He is swallowed up by the art he criticizes; he is nothing more than a handmaiden to the artist. Still, that man does perform a praiseworthy service in that he helps the reader (or viewer or listener) to understand, appreciate, and enjoy the work of art—as Mencken said in the earlier essay, written before he decided to give up literary criticism as his major occupation.

It is not surprising, considering Mencken's low estimate of *book* criticism, that so little literary criticism is found in the *Chrestomathy*, in which are included what he considered his most representative out-of-print essays. There is only one essay on a book (*An*

American Tragedy) and only a few (outstanding are those on Twain, Howells, Bierce, Lardner, Huneker, and Conrad) on authors, under the chapter heading "Literati." The entire section composes no more than 5 per cent of the volume. Mencken was doubtless right in assuming that his book criticism was dated and was thus not worthy of inclusion among the writing for which he wished to be remembered. But that is true of almost all book criticism. It is of interest to the specialist only; that is, once it has lost its sense of immediacy. To view that special area of Mencken, one must go through the files of the *Smart Set*, particularly those *before* the nineteen-twenties, the period when Mencken reached the zenith of his power as a critic of ideas and institutions. Those who missed reading the *early* literary criticism missed reading the best that Mencken was ever to write and the best that was written by an American of his day.

CHAPTER SEVEN

Götterdämmerung

MENCKEN is credited, and rightly so, with having aided a large number of the younger writers of his day. Moreover, the writers he praised between 1900 and 1925 are, almost without exception, still "living" today. To be sure, in his later years Mencken refused to take any credit for having helped aspiring artists, dismissing the often repeated remark that he was to some extent responsible for their eventual success. In a recorded conversation made for the Library of Congress (he was asked several times to make the record before consenting, being reluctant to take part in any project sanctioned by the federal government), Mencken insisted that any writer, who was really a writer, whom he had praised or otherwise helped during his years as a literary critic would have made himself known even had Mencken never existed. This is not just modesty (and Mencken was surprisingly modest on many such occasions), but is more the product of his concept of determinism. Though he was at least partially correct in his view, there were many writers whom he influenced and whose writings bear out the theory that a man of power, though a product of forces, is nonetheless a maker himself. He greatly influenced Dreiser and Lewis, for example, in their choice of subject matter. And F. Scott Fitzgerald composed much of his fiction *for* Mencken's approval. In his preface to the Modern Library edition of *The Great Gatsby*, Fitzgerald credited Mencken with having created in the nineteen-twenties a favorable climate for fiction. In the nineteen-thirties, when Mencken had subsided, no one had taken his place, and young talents (he cited Nathanael West and Vincent McHugh) were expiring from lack of a stage to act on.

Though Mencken's criticism of individual writers was influential and often profound, I am convinced that his greatest service (if that is the correct word to use) to the national letters was the creation of that "favorable climate" which Fitzgerald remarked. And that climate was one of Sturm und Drang, of freshness, of experimentation, of freedom. It was also an *American* climate. Commenting on the state of American criticism in 1919, Vincent O'Sullivan wrote that our critics, generally speaking, were often learned, well-behaved, prudent, not at all eccentric; in short, men who had reputations for decorum to keep up. Their criticism was not easily distinguishable from that of other nations. "The worst thing about [American academic criticism] is that it is vacuous by dint of respectability. Its bland impersonal presentations, sometimes haughty, urbane at times, often irritable and always dogmatic, have absolutely no effect on the poets and novelists of the United States. Some of them may read it, some of them may even believe it. But influence them it does not. It couldn't. It is too lifeless." The critics of the genteel period and the academicians of the present, O'Sullivan believed, were "products of European, and chiefly English, culture, who have continued the European tests on the American body, even as Henry James did so mistakenly." But among all these rather dull and completely ineffectual schoolmasters was one critic who was obviously alive and who was influential. His name was H. L. Mencken. "He may provoke animosity, he may rouse protestations even vehement, but he is read, he is attended to. With foundations perhaps solider than any solemn professor of them all, he is not solemn. He is not bored: whether or not he approves of the American welter, it does not bore him. He attacks his material with gusto. A criticism by him is as absorbing as a well-planned short story. Just as much art goes into it."[1] O'Sullivan went on to comment on the extreme American flavor of Mencken's style ("He is as peculiarly American as pumpkin-pie"), which, amusingly enough, was precisely what irritated the academics of the period—and still, I fear, causes pedagogic eyebrows to rise uneasily.

Before a vigorous new growth may appear, in literature as in horticulture, the deadwood which suffocates the new must be removed. More than any other American writer, Mencken was responsible for the destruction of the brambles and refuse that choked American writers. Not at all paradoxically, it was Mencken's assault on the old that helped usher in the new. When he denounced American literature, he made it clear that he was denouncing not just American writers, who were in large part results, but the American people in general and certain national ideas in particular. Literature is not created in a vacuum, nor does it exist in a vacuum. Rather it is the creation of artists who are in large part the expression of a culture; and Mencken was always more interested in culture in the broad sense than in culture (or, as he called it, *Kultur*) in the narrow sense. Nathan clearly was more interested in *cultured* things than in American civilization. He and Mencken never saw eye to eye in this. Shakespeare, Mencken would have said, was a man of his age as well as a man of the ages. In other words, the artist is both cause and effect. To produce the right effects, of course, one must be conscious of causes. To diagnose the ills of the literary body, one must examine the history of influences on that body. This Mencken did in "The National Letters," which appeared in its revised form in 1920.

Unlike many of his contemporaries before World War I, Mencken could find no evidence of an American renaissance in letters. In the literature of the nineteen-twenties, he found much to praise, but in the complacency and optimism of the literary historians and critics of the first two decades of the century, he found only an indifference to common sense. Examining the causes for the optimism, he found them invalid when not downright ludicrous. Benjamin De Casseres wrote that Mencken's hundred-page indictment of American culture disproved Burke's belief that it was impossible to indict a whole people. Indeed, not only was the essay an indictment of a people; it was a barbecue à la Torquemada. De Casseres called it "the solidest and most completely murderous piece of criticism that has been penned since God put down in his diary, 'Tomorrow I shall drown the whole human race with the exception of Noah.'"[2]

Mencken began the critique by looking briefly at the "Prophets and Their Visions" ("It is convenient to begin, like the gentlemen of God, with a glance at a text or two"). The first text was Emer-

son's "The American Scholar," delivered before the Phi Beta Kappa
Society at Cambridge on August 31, 1837. Emerson had already
published *Nature,* had made the acquaintance of Landor and Carlyle, and was at the time rather well known in his own land. The
address was hailed as the intellectual declaration of independence
of the American people, "and that judgment, amiably passed on by
three generations of pedagogues, still survives in the literature
books." Mencken then quoted the following brief passage from the
opening paragraph of the "declaration": "Our day of dependence,
our long apprenticeship to the learning of other lands, draws to a
close. . . . Events, actions arise, that must be sung, that will sing
themselves. Who can doubt that poetry will revive and lead in a
new age, as the star in the constellation Harp, which now flames in
our zenith, astronomers announce, shall one day be the pole-star
for a thousand years?"

Thirty-four years later another prophet, Walt Whitman, "put
into his gnarled and gasping prose" another prophecy even more
farfetched than Emerson's. In his *Democratic Vistas,* from which
Mencken took the following quotation, Whitman had a vision of

> a class of native authors, literatuses, far different, far higher in
> grade, than any yet known, sacerdotal, modern, fit to cope with
> our occasions, lands, permeating the whole mass of American
> morality, taste, belief, breathing into it a new breath of life, giv-
> ing it decision, affecting politics far more than the popular su-
> perficial suffrage, with results inside and underneath the elec-
> tions of Presidents or Congress—radiating, begetting appropriate
> teachers, schools, manners, and, as its grandest result, accom-
> plishing (what neither the schools nor the churches and their
> clergy have hitherto accomplished, and without which this na-
> tion will no more stand, permanently, soundly, than a house will
> stand without a substratum), a religious and moral character
> beneath the political and intellectual bases of the States.

It would have been difficult for Mencken to have found in Whitman a passage whose steaming rhetoric more perfectly bespoke the
naïve and sentimental optimism of nineteenth-century America. Out
of the vision came the prophecy—nay, certainty—that America was
on the verge of producing an original literature far above that of
all other lands in all other previous times. What an amazing contrast *The Education of Henry Adams* provides to *Democratic Vis-*

tas! The opposite poles of pessimism and optimism; the hard head and the soft heart.

After examining various other texts of like tenor that appeared both before 1837 and after 1871, Mencken remarked that these visions were almost entirely the work of imagination, with very little evidence to support them. America has not seen (or at least had not at the time Mencken wrote) any such "new and greater literatus order" as that announced by Whitman. Reading Whitman today (and his prose is read by Whitman scholars only), one is amazed at just how badly wrong a man could be in his predictions. For example, the great artists in America, as elsewhere, have not been advocates and teachers of democracy; on the contrary, they have been, almost without exception, violent critics of the democratic spirit. "Democracy has not liked the artist, and the artist has not liked democracy, for culture in the narrow sense of the word has always been aristocratic, and the disappearance of aristocracy meant that the artist was left stranded."[3] This might have been written by Mencken, rather than by Eric Bentley. Among the great writers, Bentley continued, whose work "implies dislike not only of what democracy actually is, but of what democracy is even in aspiration" are Marcel Proust, Thomas Mann, James Joyce, Rainer Maria Rilke, W. B. Yeats, and T. S. Eliot. Many writers—at least the good ones—have found little to praise in American culture or democracy, and many of them have strongly objected to their homeland. One remembers Melville, Henry James, Henry Adams, Willa Cather, Edith Wharton, Thomas Wolfe, William Faulkner, Ernest Hemingway, E. A. Robinson, Conrad Aiken, Robinson Jeffers, Sinclair Lewis, Ezra Pound, Eugene O'Neill, and John Dos Passos (both in his liberal and his conservative stages).

Mencken could say with impunity that our literature, despite several false starts that promised much, was chiefly remarkable, in 1920 as before, for its respectable mediocrity. "Its typical great man, in our own time, has been Howells, as its typical great man a generation ago was Lowell, and two generations ago, Irving. Viewed largely, its salient character appears as a sort of timorous flaccidity, an amiable hollowness." Each prophet began with a discussion of what is lacking in our literature and then proceeded to herald a new dawn. Emerson began by lamenting almost precisely what Whitman lamented years later and what Van Wyck Brooks was still lamenting at the beginning of the nineteen-twenties. The optimists were forever in the unenviable position of saying No to what was and Yes to what was not. They simply translated Clough into prose:

> And not by eastern windows only,
>   When daylight comes, comes in the light;
> In front the sun climbs slow, how slowly,
>   But westward, look, the land is bright!

In viewing the current scene, *circa* 1920, Mencken found much more to lament than to praise. After dividing our literature into three layers, "each inordinately doughy and uninspiring—each almost without flavor or savor," he was hard put to say, with much critical plausibility, which layer deserved to be called the upper. For decorum's sake, the choice was fixed upon that which met with the approval of the academic critics, which is to say, the "correct" works of the survivors of New England *Kultur*: the fiction of Howells, Judge Grant, Alice Brown, and company; the academic poetry of George Woodberry and Robert U. Johnson; the tea-party essays of Rev. Samuel Crothers, Miss Repplier, and cohorts; and the "solemn, highly judicial, coroner's inquest criticism of More, Brownell, Babbitt and their imitators"—all of them writers now resting in the graveyard of deceased gods, or, even worse, remembered only as the lifeless ghosts inhabiting graduate seminars. Mencken said nice things about their "manner," but in all their works he detected the "faint perfume of college-town society." There was no relation whatsoever between the "literature as an academic exercise for talented grammarians" and the fascinating phenomena of American life.

Mencken felt that the New Englander, with all his talk of moral purpose, of uplifting the American, was almost the opposite of the true artist. Art to him was "a temptation, a seduction, a Lorelei, and the Good Man may safely have traffic with it only when it is broken to moral uses—in other words, when its innocence is pumped out of it, and it is purged of gusto. It is precisely this gusto that one misses in all the work of the New England school, and in all the work of the formal schools that derive from it." Mencken felt that Henry van Dyke was an excellent specimen of the whole clan. He came about as close as any of his fellows to being a genuine artist. He had a hand for pretty verses. He wielded a facile rhetoric. He even showed, "in indiscreet moments," a touch of imagination. "But all the while he remains a sound Presbyterian first and an artist second, which is just as comfortable as trying to be a Presbyterian first and a chorus girl second. To such a man it must inevitably appear that a Molière, a Goethe or a Shakespeare was more than a little bawdy."

Just as in poetry, the novel, and the essay, the criticism that supported "this decaying caste of literary Brahmins" was less concerned with making a purely aesthetic judgment upon an aesthetic question than it was with formulating ethical criteria. The whole body of William Lyon Phelps's "we churchgoers" criticism—to Mencken "the most catholic and tolerant, it may be said in passing, that the faculty can show"—consisted chiefly of "a plea for correctness, and particularly for moral correctness; he never gets very far from 'the axiom of the moral law.'" Mencken was a good deal more severe with Phelps's academic cohorts:

> Brownell argues eloquently for standards that would bind an imaginative author as tightly as a Sunday-school superintendent is bound by the Ten Commandments and the Mann Act. Sherman tries to save Shakespeare for the right-thinking by proving that he was an Iowa Methodist—a member of his local Chamber of Commerce, a contemner of Reds, an advocate of democracy and the League of Nations, a patriotic dollar-a-year-man during the Armada scare. Elmer More devotes himself, year in and year out, to denouncing the Romantic movement, i.e., the effort to emancipate the artist from formulae and categories, and so make him free to dance with arms and legs. And Babbitt, to make an end, gives over his days and his nights to deploring Rousseau's anarchistic abrogation of "the veto power" over the imagination, leading to such "wrongness" in both art and life that it threatens "to wreck civilization." In brief, the alarms of schoolmasters.

These critics seldom dealt with contemporary literature, except to condemn it. Mencken wondered what sort of picture of American life was conjured up by foreigners who read such men. "How can such a foreigner, moving in those damp, asthmatic mists, imagine such phenomena as Roosevelt, Billy Sunday, Bryan, the Becker case, the I.W.W., Newport, Palm Beach, the University of Chicago, Chicago itself—the whole gross, glittering, excessively dynamic, infinitely grotesque, incredibly stupendous drama of American life?"[4]

To illustrate his remark that the professors seldom noticed contemporary writers, Mencken cited More's Shelburne Essays. There was no essay on Howells, certainly the most widely known man of his age, or on the novelist Winston Churchill, or on Edith Wharton. More evidently thought American literature expired with Longfellow. Mencken quoted More on the practices of academic critics who wrote for the *Nation,* that is, the *Nation* in its "pre-Bolshevik" days.[5] More wrote that he "soon learned that it was virtually impossible to get fair consideration for a book written by a scholar not connected with a university from a reviewer so connected." Mencken felt that such class consciousness should not apply to artists, "who are admittedly inferior to professors." Even among the critics who escaped the "schoolmastering frenzy," there was a decided penchant for the "culture" of the provincial schoolmarm. Had not Clayton Hamilton, vice-president of the National Institute of Arts and Letters, proposed certain tests for anyone who aspired to write dramatic criticism? Mencken gleefully quoted the tests:

    1. Have you ever stood bareheaded in the nave of Amiens?
    2. Have you ever climbed to the Acropolis by moonlight?
    3. Have you ever walked with whispers into the hushed presence of the Frari Madonna of Bellini?

To Mencken nothing could "more brilliantly evoke an image of the eternal Miss Birch, blue veil flying and Baedeker in hand, plodding along faithfully through the interminable corridors and catacombs of the Louvre, the while bands are playing across the river, and young bucks in three-gallon hats are sparking the gals, and the Jews and harlots uphold the tradition of French *hig leef* at Longchamps, and American deacons are frisked and debauched up on martyrs' hill."

On the bottom layer of the National Letters, and at the opposite extreme from the so-called upper layer, was the literature of Greenwich Village. By Greenwich Village, Mencken meant the more advanced wing in letters, "whatever the scene of its solemn declarations of independence and forlorn hopes." There was Miss Amy Lowell, "a fully-equipped and automobile Greenwich Village, domiciled in Boston amid the crumbling gravestones of the New England *intelligentsia,* but often in waspish joy-ride through the hinterland." There was Vachel Lindsay with his pilgrim's staff. The senior member of the Village group was *Poetry: A Magazine of Verse,* located in Chicago. Wherever there was a Little Theater and a couple of local Synges and Chekhovs to supply its stage, there was the Greenwich Village movement. What lay beneath the movement and gave it impetus was the natural revolt of youth against the "pedagogical Prussianism of the professors." If the oppression was extreme, then so, too, was the rebellion.

Imagine a sentimental young man of the provinces, awaking one morning to the somewhat startling discovery that he is full of the divine afflatus, and nominated by the hierarchy of hell to enrich the literature of his fatherland. He seeks counsel and aid. He finds, on consulting the official treatises on that literature, that its greatest poet was Longfellow. He is warned, reading More and Babbitt, that the literatus who lets feeling get into his compositions is a psychic fornicator, and under German influences. He has formal notice from Sherman that Puritanism is the lawful philosophy of the country, and that any dissent from it is treason. He gets the news, plowing through the New York *Times Book Review,* the *Nation* (so far to the left in its politics, but hugging the right so desperately in letters!), the *Bookman,* the *Atlantic* and the rest, that the salient artists of the living generation are such masters as Robert Underwood Johnson, Owen Wister, James Lane Allen, George E. Woodberry, Hamlin Garland, William Roscoe Thayer and Augustus Thomas, with polite bows to Margaret Deland, Mary Johnston and Ellen Glasgow. It slowly dawns upon him that Robert W. Chambers is an academician and Theodore Dreiser isn't, that Brian Hooker is and George Sterling isn't, that Henry Sydnor Harrison is and James Branch Cabell isn't, that "Chimmie Fadden" Townsend is and Sherwood Anderson isn't.

Is it any wonder that such a young fellow, after one or two sniffs of the prep-school fog, swings so vastly backward that one finds him presently in corduroy trousers and a velvet jacket, hammering furiously upon a pine table in a Macdougal street cellar, his mind full of malicious animal magnetism against even so amiable an old maid as Howells, and his discourse full of insane hair-splittings about *vers libre,* futurism, spectrism, vorticism, *Expressionismus, heliogabalisme*? The thing, in truth, is in the course of nature. The Spaniards who were outraged by the Palmerism[6] of Torquemada did not become members of the Church of England; they became atheists. The American colonists, in revolt against a bad king, did not set up a good King; they set up a democracy, and so gave every honest man a chance to become a rogue on his own account. Thus the young literatus, emerging from the vacuum of Ohio or Arkansas.[7]

Mencken felt that the Villagers were, more often than not, mere pretenders. They spent their time discussing art rather than creating it. There was also a tendency among the young rebels to overemphasize the importance of form or technique: "Half the wars in the Village are over form; content is taken for granted." The extreme leftists often descended to meaningless gibberish as a last defiance to intellectualism. This was the era of Dada and the "mindless" stream of consciousness, an age of experimentation and folly (as well as greatness) that Malcolm Cowley so vividly portrayed in *Exile's Return* (1934). As an editor of the *Smart Set*, by then the leading literary magazine in America, Mencken was in a position to read most of what was being produced by the Villagers. "Probably nine-tenths of the stuff written in the dark dens and alleys south of the arch comes to my desk soon or late, and I go through all of it faithfully. It is, in the overwhelming main, jejune and imitative." Seldom was there even personality in it; all the Villagers seemed to write alike. As one writer in *Poetry*, the best of the *avant-garde* magazines according to Mencken, put it: "Unless one is an expert in some detective method, one is at a loss to assign correctly the ownership of much free verse—that is, if one plays fairly and refuses to look at the signature until one has ventured a guess. It is difficult, for instance, to know whether Miss Lowell is writing Mr. Bynner's verse, or whether he is writing hers." In drama the Village fared somewhat better. Eugene O'Neill had written some of his one-acters there; Rita Wellman and Zoë Akins had also produced work of high quality. Mencken could not give all the credit to the movement, however, for these "mere acts of God." The best dramatic pieces showed no sign of revolt; they were simply first-rate work "done miraculously in a third-rate land."

But if the revolt was sterile of direct results, Mencken felt that at least it offered evidence of something not to be disregarded: "the gradual formulation of a challenge to the accepted canons in letters and to the accepted canon lawyers." The young rebels were at least alive, and some of them were making an honest effort to create something new. Certainly Mencken preferred the Villager to "the young tutor who launches into letters with imitations of his seminary chief's imitations of Agnes Repplier's imitations of Charles Lamb." What is more, life in the Village was more conducive to artistic creation than was life in the average American town.

Even the shy and somewhat stagey carnality that characterizes the Village has its high symbolism and its profound uses. It proves that, despite repressions unmatched in civilization in modern times, there is still a sturdy animality in American youth, and hence good health. The poet hugging his Sonia in a Washington square beanery, and so giving notice to all his world that he is a devil of a fellow, is at least a better man than the emasculated stripling in a Y.M.C.A. gospel-mill, pumped dry of all his natural appetites and the vacuum filled with double-entry bookkeeping, business economics and autoeroticism. In so foul a nest of imprisoned and fermenting sex as the United States, plain fornication becomes a mark of relative decency.[8]

The Greenwich Village complex took a dreadful beating from Mencken in the years when youth was revolting for the sake of revolt, when any oddity could become a fad overnight. For one thing, Mencken never shared the bohemian's belief that art throve in poverty. Such a belief was held usually by those who had failed at acquiring economic freedom; they then took refuge in the childish notion that there was something honorable about poverty per se. "Poverty may be an unescapable misfortune, but that no more makes it honorable than a cocked eye is made honorable by the same cause. Do I advocate, then, the ceaseless, senseless hogging of money? I do not. All I advocate—and praise as virtuous—is the hogging of enough to provide security and ease."[9] If the best art was produced by men who were free from the oppressive wants of the body, then one of the artist's first duties was to make efforts to achieve that tranquility for himself. Shakespeare, Beethoven, Wagner, Brahms, Ibsen, and Balzac were a few of the artists Mencken mentioned who attempted to obtain security. Goethe, Schopenhauer, Schumann, and Mendelssohn were born wealthy. Joseph Conrad, Richard Strauss, and Anatole France were three artists of Mencken's own time who made conscious, and successful, efforts to avoid physical need. The most salient example of an American artist since Mencken's day making efforts to achieve the freedom that comes with financial solvency is Faulkner. His rather frequent, but always brief, forays into the Philistine night of Hollywood provided him with the opportunity to create in Mississippi a body of work that stands above that of any other writer of his time. He also wrote for the *Saturday Evening Post*, considered a crime by many, particularly by those unable to barter their wares in that fat market.

Finally, there is *Sanctuary,* which Faulkner claimed to have written solely for money, but which is, nonetheless, a far better novel than he would have us believe.

Though he scorned the idea that the artist grew fat on hunger (a nice paradox, which, like most paradoxes, is flatly absurd), Mencken did believe that the artist profited from ideological warfare; he grew fat on the conflict with other artists. To be complacent is to be insentient; when artists create utopian colonies in order to work and create in an atmosphere of "togetherness," they are, as artists, in a moribund state of being. Some six years after his essay on "The National Letters," Mencken summed up his opinion of Greenwich Village:

> As one who poked many heavy jocosities at it while it lasted, I hope I may now say with good grace that I believe Greenwich Village did a good service to all the fine arts in this great land, and left a valuable legacy behind it. True enough, its own heroes were nearly all duds, and most of them have been forgotten, but it at least broke ground, it at least stirred up the animals. When it began to issue smoke and flame, the youth of the country were still under the hoof of the schoolma'm; when it blew up at last they were in full revolt. Was it Greenwich Village or Yale University that cleared the way for Cabell? Was it the Village or the Philharmonic Society that made a place for Stravinsky? Was it the Village or the trustees of the Metropolitan Museum that first whooped for Cézanne? That whooping, of course, did not stop with Cézanne, or Stravinsky, or Cabell. There were whoops almost as loud for Sascha Gilhooly, who painted sunsets with a shaving brush, and for Raoul Goetz, who wrote quartettes for automobile horns and dentist's drills, and for Bruce J. Katzenstein, whose poetry was all figures and exclamation points. But all that excess did no harm. The false prophets changed from day to day. The real ones remained.[10]

Both Mencken's strictures and praise of the Village are pretty much substantiated by Allen Churchill's *The Improper Bohemians* (1959), a delightful informal history of the heyday, 1912–1930, of the place. On the last page of the book, Churchill states that the Village "is still a state of mind through which numerous members of the younger generations feel they must pass."

Having examined the upper and lower layers, Mencken turned his gaze to the middle layer, "the thickest and perhaps the most significant of the three." The writers in this group were the most popular; they produced "the literature that pays like a bucket-shop or a soap-factory, and is thus thoroughly American." The worst of this literature, Mencken remarked, reached such depths of banality that it would be difficult to match it in any other country. In the "inspirational" and patriotic essays of Dr. Frank Crane, Orison Swett Marden, Porter Emerson Browne, Gerald Stanley Lee, E. S. Martin, Ella Wheeler Wilcox, and Rev. Dr. Newell Dwight Hillis; in the novels of Harold Bell Wright, Eleanor H. Porter, and Gene Stratton Porter; and in the prose and verse that filled the cheap fiction magazines—there was a native quality as unmistakable as that of Mother's Day, Billy Sundayism, or Rotary. "It is the natural outpouring of a naïve and yet half barbarous people, full of delight in a few childish and inaccurate ideas." But much of the literature of the middle layer—"for example, the work of Mrs. Rinehart, and that of Corra Harris, Gouverneur Morris, Harold MacGrath and the late O. Henry"—showed technical excellence and even a sort of civilized sophistication. Moreover, this literature constantly graduated writers to a higher level; for example, Booth Tarkington, Zona Gale, Ring Lardner, and Montague Glass. (At the time this essay was written, Sinclair Lewis was on the verge of "graduation," *Main Street* appearing a few months later.) Mencken also reminded his readers that Mark Twain was a graduate of this school.

There were, of course, more writers who compromised their high aims to share in the profits of "popular" literature than there were writers who began by publishing in the mass circulation magazines and graduated to better things. Mencken listed a number of these renegades: for example, Henry Milner Rideout, Jack London, Owen Johnson, Hamlin Garland, Will Levington Comfort, Stephen French Whitman, James Hopper, Harry Leon Wilson—most of whom are now completely forgotten. There was a general tendency to blame the *Saturday Evening Post* for ruining able writers, but Mencken felt this was simply "blaming the bull for the sins of all the cows." Compared to such magazines as *Cosmopolitan, Hearst's, McClure's,* the *Metropolitan,* and the women's magazines, the *Post* was not at all bad. In its pages could be found the work of several authors of very solid talent, notably Glass, Lardner, and E. W. Howe. It had been hospitable to such men as Dreiser and Joseph Hergesheimer, and it had avoided "the Barnum-like exploitation of such native bosh-mongers as Crane, Hillis and Ella Wheeler Wilcox, and of such exotic mountebanks as D'Annunzio, Hall Caine and Maeterlinck." Actually, the *Post* was, Mencken felt, much better than either Greenvich Village or the Cambridge campus was willing to admit. "It is the largest of the literary Hog Islands, but it is by no means the worst." A more harmful influence than the *Post*, according to Mencken, was Hollywood, then beginning its most dazzling era as an art form.

Thus Mencken on the state of American literature in 1920. In the remaining sixty pages of his essay, he endeavored to diagnose the ills, to point out the causes for the failure of America to produce a body of works comparable to that of other Western nations. He felt obliged to examine the background of the artist in America, to comment on the civilization that produced him. Generally speaking, the American is an optimist, and he is essentially interested in becoming a "success." Hence, the literature of the American tends to reflect this national attitude. (It might be argued, though, that peoples of other nations are also interested in such "success.") The average American wants to see the hero of a novel in conflict with external forces, making his way to the top of the ladder, attaining power and wealth. The reflective man has no interest in such enterprises. As has been shown before, Mencken felt the superior man's struggle in the world was not with "policemen, rivals in love, German spies, radicals and tornadoes, but with the obscure, atavistic impulses within him—the impulses, weaknesses and limitations that war with his notion of what life should be." And usually this man succumbs to the forces within and without which beset him. His aspiration is almost infinitely above his achievement. "The result is that we see him sliding downhill—his ideals breaking up, his hope petering out, his character in decay. Character in decay is thus the theme of the great bulk of superior fiction." Here, as elsewhere, Mencken supported his generalizations with elaborate specifics; from his wide reading he could draw overwhelming evidence to back his arguments. He believed, for example, that the best American short stories were not to be mentioned in the same breath with Conrad's *Heart of Darkness* or *Youth*, or Andreev's *Silence*, or Sudermann's *Das Sterbelied*, or the least considerable tale of Anatole France.

After commenting at length on the apathy toward, or misunderstanding of, Hawthorne, Emerson, Poe, and Whitman in their own day, Mencken attempted to isolate the reasons for American artists' feeling like aliens in their own land. The major cause was clear enough: America has produced no civilized aristocracy, "secure in its position, animated by an intelligent curiosity, skeptical of all facile generalizations, superior to the sentimentality of the mob, and delighting in the battle of ideas for its own sake." Mencken realized, fortunately, the necessity of making clear what he meant by the term "aristocracy." A public "fed upon democratic fustian" would naturally associate wealth with the term and would have visions of "stockbrokers' wives lolling obscenely in opera boxes, or of haughty Englishmen slaughtering whole generations of grouse in an inordinate and incomprehensible manner, or of Junkers with tight waists elbowing American schoolmarms off the sidewalks of German beer towns, or of perfumed Italians coming over to work their abominable magic upon the daughters of breakfast-food and bathtub kings." According to Mencken, the yellow press was in part responsible for this misconception so deeply buried in the mass mind. The so-called leaders of society in large cities were sometimes called aristocrats, just as the peerage of England was often mistaken for the gentry. Americans cherished their misconception of what an aristocracy was because they cherished the nebulous belief in equality. Indeed, "the inferior man needs an aristocracy to demonstrate, not only his mere equality, but also his actual superiority." To Mencken the spurious American aristocracy was no more than a snobbish clique composed of the most timorous sort of conformists. Anyone aspiring to enter this childish domain must abase himself in all sorts of ways, and after gaining entry into fashionable society he must remain timorous or lose the position he had gained.

He must exhibit exactly the right social habits, appetites and prejudices, public and private. He must harbor exactly the right political enthusiasms and indignations. He must have a hearty taste for exactly the right sports. His attitude toward the fine arts must be properly tolerant and yet not a shade too eager. He must read and like exactly the right books, pamphlets and public journals. He must put up at the right hotels when he travels. His wife must patronize the right milliners. He himself must stick to the right haberdashery. He must live in the right neighborhood. He must even embrace the right doctrines of religion. It would ruin him, for all opera box and society column purposes, to set up a plea for justice to the Bolsheviki, or even for ordinary decency. It would ruin him equally to wear celluloid collars, or to move to Union Hill, N.J., or to serve ham and cabbage at his table. And it would ruin him, too, to drink coffee from his saucer, or to marry a chambermaid with a gold tooth, or to join the Seventh Day Adventists. Within the boundaries of his curious order he is worse fettered than a monk in a cell.[11]

This segment of society, still very much a part of our civilization, has been vividly depicted in such novels of John O'Hara as *Appointment in Samarra, Butterfield 8, A Rage to Live,* and *Ten North Frederick.*

Obviously, such a civilization could in no way promote a native literature, except insofar as it furnished writers with subject matter. The intellectual aristocracy that Mencken advocated, which was very similar to Jefferson's concept of a "natural" aristocracy, was almost the diametrical opposite of the American plutocracy. For example, Mencken believed that a true aristocracy would never punish eccentricity by expulsion; on the contrary, it would throw a mantle of protection about it to safeguard it from the suspicions and resentments of the lower orders of men. Aristocracy was nothing if it was not autonomous, curious, venturesome, courageous, and everything if it was. "It is the custodian of the qualities that make for change and experiment; it is the class that organizes danger to the service of the race; it pays for its high prerogatives by standing in the forefront of the fray." The makings of such an aristocracy were visible in the later eighteenth century, but with the passing of the Jeffersons, Washingtons, Adamses, and others the promise died. And after the advent of Jacksonianism, there has been nothing even remotely resembling such a class in America. Only a craven plutocracy has been produced. In describing this order, Menken allowed his general good humor to become somewhat corrupted by what Nietzsche called moral indignation. It may be necessary to inform the reader that Mencken was not exaggerating in the least when he wrote of the "Big Red Scare." Not even the insane McCarthyism of post–World War II days compares with the hysteria of the two or three years immediately following World War I. Mencken's comments on the plutocracy still ring true a half-century later.

Imagine a horde of peasants incredibly enriched and with

almost infinite power thust into their hands, and you will have a fair picture of its habitual state of mind. It shows all the stigmata of inferiority—moral certainty, cruelty, suspicion of ideas, fear. Never did it function more revealingly than in the late *progrom* against the so-called Reds, i.e., against humorless idealists who, like Andrew Jackson, took the platitudes of democracy seriously. The machinery brought to bear upon these feeble and scattered fanatics would have almost sufficed to repel an invasion by the united powers of Europe. They were hunted out of their sweat-shops and coffee-houses as if they were so many Carranzas or Ludendorffs, dragged to jail to the tooting of horns, arraigned before quaking judges on unintelligible charges, condemned to deportation without the slightest chance to defend themselves, torn from their dependent families, herded into prison-ships, and then finally dumped in a snow waste, to be rescued and fed by the Bolsheviki. And what was the theory at the bottom of all these astounding proceedings? So far as it can be reduced to comprehensible terms it was much less a theory than a fear—a shivering, idiotic, discreditable fear of a mere banshee—an overpowering, paralyzing dread that some extra-eloquent Red, permitted to emit his balderdash unwhipped, might eventually convert a couple of courageous men, and that the courageous men, filled with indignation against the plutocracy, might take the highroad, burn down a nail-factory or two, and slit the throat of some virtuous profiteer.[12]

The major difference between the plutocracy at the top of American culture and the "vast mass of undifferentiated human blanks at the bottom" was a difference in the amount of wealth and power possessed by each group. They were almost the same in kind; the ruling emotion of both was fear, "the one permanent emotion of the inferior man, as of all the simpler mammals." This man, for example, will have no objection to kaiserism or Communism or fascism or any other "ism" so long as he is unafraid. The average man today bears no grudge against fascist Spain or Communistic Yugoslavia. The inferior man—that is, the man who is neither courageous, intelligent, nor honest—derives his notions, social, political, aesthetic, ethical, from the newspapers. From that source he gets support for his elemental illusions. From the newspaper Homo boobiens draws "fuel for his simple moral passion, his congenital suspicion of heresy, his dread of the unknown. And behind the newspaper stands the plutocracy, ignorant, unimaginative and timorous."

Thus the top and bottom layers of American society. To be sure, the plutocracy possessed one of the necessary elements of an aristocracy: truculent egoism. But one searched in vain for intelligence, "ease and surety of manner," enterprise and curiosity. "Where, above all, is courage, and in particular, moral courage—the capacity for independent thinking, for difficult problems, for what Nietzsche called the joys of the labyrinth?" In pointing out the ills of American civilization, Mencken was saying almost precisely what is being said today by the intellectuals, but with one major difference. Contemporary critics of conformity, complacency, and "other directedness" are not so forthright in maintaining that democracy has played a leading part in the surrender of man to the mass. Mencken was one of that small but vocal group that condemned the leveling process inherent in democracy. If nothing else, he was forthright:

> It is precisely here, of all civilized countries, that eccentricity in demeanor and opinion has come to bear the heaviest penalties. The whole drift of our law is toward the absolute prohibition of all ideas that diverge in the slightest from the accepted platitudes, and behind that drift of law there is a far more potent force of growing custom, and under that custom there is a national philosophy which erects conformity into the noblest of virtues and free functioning of personality into a capital crime against society.[13]

A third group in America, squeezed between the plutocracy on one side and the mob on the other, was the intelligentsia. In this group were men of enormous learning and diligence, most of them college or university professors, who exerted a strong influence on public opinion. "They dominate the weeklies of opinion; they are to the fore in every review; they write nine-tenths of the serious books of the country; they begin to invade the newspapers; they instruct and exhort the yokelry from the stump; they have even begun to penetrate into the government." Indeed, everywhere one turned there was a professor. "A professor was until lately sovereign of the country, and pope of the state church." Certainly, the opportunities for the pedagogues had been enormous. Their achievements, Mencken felt, were somewhat less gaudy.

Because of the "impenetrable operations of fate," Mencken had early in life assumed the "rather thankless duties of a specialist in the ways of pedagogues, a sort of professor of professors." Admittedly, the job had got him enemies.

> I have been accused of carrying on a defamatory *jehad* against virtuous and laborious men; I have even been charged with doing it in the interest of the Wilhelmstrasse, the White Slave Trust and the ghost of Friedrich Wilhelm Nietzsche. Nothing could be more absurd. All my instincts are on the side of the professors. I esteem a man who devotes himself to a subject with hard diligence; I esteem even more a man who puts poverty and a shelf of books above profiteering and evenings of jazz; I am naturally monkish.[14]

Although predisposed to side with the professors (after all, he descended from a long line of German professors), his researches had provided him with materials not altogether flattering to the *Gelehrten.*

> What I have found, in brief, is that pedagogy turned to general public uses is almost as timid and flatulent as journalism—that the professor, menaced by the timid dogmatism of the plutocracy above him and the incurable suspiciousness of the mob beneath him, is almost invariably inclined to seek his own security in a mellifluous inanity—that, far from being a courageous spokesman of ideas and an apostle of their free dissemination, in politics, in the fine arts, in practical ethics, he comes close to being the most prudent and skittish of all men concerned with them—in brief, that he yields to the prevailing correctness of thought in all departments, north, east, south and west, and is, in fact, the chief exponent among us of the democratic doctrine that heresy is not only a mistake, but also a crime.

As will be apparent when I discuss Mencken's battle with the academicians, the accusations made against him—particularly those made by Stuart Sherman—were, in fact, as wild as Mencken would have us believe. He was hated and feared more than any other American of his day by the average university teacher. Still, one suspects that Mencken was not altogether fair in expecting academicians to be any other than timid men. Imagine a professor who was as outspoken as Mencken! He would have been cashiered instanter. Moreover, Mencken had no respect for martyrs, so, to be logical, he should not have expected professors to be unprofessorial.

To prove his thesis that the pedagogue was anything but "a courageous spokesman of ideas and an apostle of their free dissemination" was easy enough. He only needed to point to the recent war. During time of war the worst fears and prejudices of the ignorant and emotional man naturally come to the fore, but a time of strife and frenzied action should show more clearly than ever the inward metal of the superior man. What actually happened was that the professors acted, not like intelligent men, but like mob masters. "They constituted themselves, not a restraining influence upon the mob run wild, but the loudest spokesmen of its worst imbecilities. They fed it with bogus history, bogus philosophy, bogus idealism, bogus heroics." During the war Mencken accumulated, with the aid of "three clipping-bureaux," a very large collection of "academic arguments, expositions and pronunciamentos" for "the instruction and horror of posterity." (In several places he mentioned his intention to publish this "edifying" collection, but he never did so.) During the war, demands were made that the study of the German language and literature be prohibited by law, German science was denounced as "negligible and fraudulent," and, among other things, it was proved "that the American Revolution was the result of a foul plot hatched in the Wilhelmstrasse of the time." As "one of the few Americans who [had] actually read the proclamations of the German professors," Mencken denied that the enemy professors had ever indulged in any such rabble-rousing.

> No German professor essayed to prove that the Seven Years' War was caused by Downing Street. No German professor argued that the study of English would corrupt the soul. No German professor denounced Darwin as an ignoramus and Lister as a scoundrel. Nor was anything of the sort done, so far as I know, by any French professor. Nor even by any reputable English professor. All such honorable efforts on behalf of correct thought in wartime were monopolized by American professors. And if the fact is disputed, then I threaten upon some future day, when the stealthy yearning to forget has arisen, to print my proofs in parallel columns—the most esteemed extravagances of the German professors in one column and the corresponding masterpieces of the American professors in the other.[15]

Within four years after the war ended and two years after the publication of "The National Letters," the overwhelming majority of literate Americans had forgotten that Germany was once the monster of their imaginings. Indeed, most American writers, I may safely generalize, were by that time convinced that America should never have gone into the war, and many felt the nation doubly erred by going in on the wrong side. When George F. Babbitt learned of this, he was for an instant shocked; but then, the sort of thing that shocked Babbitt was precisely what was generally accepted in more learned circles. By the time Dos Passos was saying (in *U.S.A.*) America went the wrong way in 1917, there was hardly anyone to say him nay. Mencken concluded this section on the professors by remarking that there were a few self-respecting men who maintained their dignity throughout, "A small minority, hard beset and tested by the fire!"

The American artist was, indeed, saddled with an intolerable burden. In need of support, he could find none. The mob was too suspicious of all ideas ever to offer him aid; the plutocracy was devoted to maintaining the intellectual status quo; the intelligentsia lacked either the courage or the strength to go beyond mere "correctness." The man who devotes his life to creating works of the imagination—that is, the man who devotes all his strength and energy to struggling with problems that are essentially delicate and baffling and pregnant with doubt—such a man does not ask for recognition as a reward for his industry; but he certainly does need sympathetic friends, "a necessary help to his industry." The understanding and friendship offered the artist by other artists were in most cases not enough. "Sympathy must be more than the mere fellow-feeling of other craftsmen; it must come, in large part, out of a connoisseurship that is beyond the bald trade interest; it must have its roots in the intellectual curiosity of an aristocracy of taste." Poe had been forced to find consolation among his inferiors, just as Twain had been forced to conceal his most profound beliefs from the public. And Dreiser and Cabell, in 1920, were subjected to incessant attacks by malignant stupidity. The "moral certainty of the mob" had its powerful spokesman in the form of comstockery, but precious few voices were raised by the opposition.

Not only was the American artist oppressed at home; he had to wait for the foreign seal of approval before he could hope to gain recognition in his own land. Poe, for example, entered the American Valhalla through the back door; that is, he was first discovered in Europe and then accepted in America.

It was Baudelaire's French translation of the prose tales and Mallarmé's translation of the poems that brought Poe to Valhalla. The former, first printed in 1856, founded the Poe cult in France, and during the two decades following it flourished amazingly, and gradually extended to England and Germany. It was one of the well-springs, in fact, of the whole so-called decadent movement. If Baudelaire, the father of that movement, "cultivated hysteria with delight and terror," he was simply doing what Poe had done before him. Both, reacting against the false concept of beauty as a mere handmaiden of logical ideas, sought its springs in those deep feelings and inner experiences which lie beyond the range of ideas and are to be interpreted only as intuitions.[16]

Mencken reiterated Poe's complaint that the United States was nothing more than a literary colony of Great Britain. To Mencken, America was "almost as much an English colonial possession, intellectually and spiritually, as it was on July 3, 1776." And no one was more aware of this than the British, who knew how to "use" President Wilson to the best advantage. Even the American's "recurrent attacks of Anglophobia are no more than Freudian evidences of his inferiority complex. He howls in order to still his inner sense of inequality, as he howls against imaginary enemies in order to convince himself that he is brave and against despotisms in order to prove that he is free." The abject aping of English ways and the bowing down to English taste were to Mencken clear signs of the inferiority of our criticism. The works of Frank Harris, for example, had never been kindly received by any American critics. And when in 1914 he said a number of unkind things about the English, among whom he had lived since the early eighteen-eighties, he was immediately taken to task by the Anglomaniacs. As Mencken put it: the American arbiters of taste "called a special meeting of the American Academy of Arts and Letters, sang 'God Save the King,' kissed the Union Jack, and put Harris into Coventry." And there he remained until 1921 when

> the English, with characteristic lack of delicacy, played a ghastly trick upon all those dutiful and well-meaning colonists. That is to say, they suddenly forgave Harris his criminal refusal to take their war buncombe seriously, exhumed him from his long solitude among the Anglo-Ashkenazim, and began praising him in rich, hearty terms as a literary gentleman of the first water, and even as the chief adornment of American letters!

When the English reviews of *Contemporary Portraits: Second Series* lauded Harris to the skies, the American critics were aghast:

One imagines the painful sensation in the New York *Times* office, the dismayed groups around far-flung campus pumps, the special meetings of the Princeton, N.J., and Urbana, Ill., American Legions, the secret conference between the National Institute of Arts and Letters and the Ku Klux Klan. But though there was tall talk by hot heads, nothing could be done. Say "Wo!" and the dutiful Jackass turns to the right; say "Gee!" and he turns to the left. It is too much, of course, to ask him to cheer as well as turn—but he nevertheless turns. Since 1921 I have heard no more whispers against Harris from professors and Vigilantes.[17]

Since, according to Mencken, the world of letters, like all other "worlds," was composed primarily of lesser men, the lack of a confident and egoistic intellectual viewpoint in America made itself all the more evident. Neither Poe nor Whitman made the slightest concession to the English taste or authority of his time, nor did either of them yield to "the maudlin echoes of English notions that passed for ideas in the United States"; but they were rare men indeed. It should be noted that Mencken is not here attacking the English (though at a later date he disparaged the English in his praise of American literature), but rather the obsequiousness of Americans, the vast bulk of whom took the easy way out by courting English favor. "On the one hand, we have Fenimore Cooper first making a cringing bow for English favor, and then, on being kicked out, joining the mob against sense; he wrote books so bad that even the Americans of 1830 admired them. On the other hand, we have Henry James, a deserter made by despair; one so depressed by the tacky company at the American first table that he preferred to sit at the second table of the English." And then we have the amalgamation of these two tendencies in Mark Twain, "at one moment striving his hardest for the English *imprimatur,* and childishly delighted by every favorable gesture; at the next, returning to the native mob as its premier clown—monkey-shining at banquets, cavorting in the newspapers, shrinking poltroonishly from his own ideas, obscenely eager to give no offense." Mencken considered Twain a far greater artist than either Poe or Whitman, but a good deal lower as a man. He makes it clear in this section of his diagnosis that he considered the American worship of England a serious weakness. It is evident that Mencken, the great enemy of chauvinism, was himself so completely American that he could not bear his fellows looking to England for guidance.

In concluding "The National Letters," Mencken insisted that he had no remedy to offer; he refused to place himself in the unenviable position of an Emerson or a Whitman. He admitted that the obstacles standing in "the way of the development of a distinctly American culture, grounded upon a truly egoistic nationalism and supported by a native aristocracy," may, after all, prove insurmountable. Puritanism may be too deeply imbedded in the national consciousness ever to be completely eradicated. Although professing to offer no remedy for the cerebral paralysis in America, he felt that a general skepticism was the first step to combating the Puritan childishness, the nature of which must now be discussed. As an antidote to Puritanism, which depends upon faith for its impetus, Mencken offered the self-reliance of individualism and libertarianism. Skepticism, by its very nature, makes necessary a large amount of self-reliance, just as faith demands reliance on something or someone outside the self. To prove that hope will not down, Mencken pointed to the skepticism that was already beginning to show itself "in the iconoclastic political realism of Harold Stearns, Waldo Frank and company, in the groping questions of Dreiser, Cabell and Anderson, in the operatic rebellions of the Village." The skepticism of Stearns and Frank, it might be added, was short-lived, since both men succumbed to political idealism of the left in the nineteen-thirties and wrote disparagingly of the preceding decade. Mencken believed that great literature was chiefly a "product of doubting and inquiring minds in revolt against the immovable certainties of the nation." He concluded his inquiry with the faint, glimmering hope that on some dim tomorrow the molders of taste in America would be challenged by more than a few solitary iconoclasts. There was then no way of knowing that within the next ten years the skeptical attitude would become almost universal in the world of art and that America, artistically speaking, would reach its highest point. While it is now fashionable to condemn skepticism as "old-fashioned" or even "shallow," the fact remains that out of the rebellious twenties came a literature that for the first time placed us on a level with other leading nations.

CHAPTER EIGHT

The American Hydra

B<small>ROADLY</small> speaking, Mencken performed two major services for the national letters: he led the attack on Puritanism, which had crippled the artist in America for generations; and he gave great aid to a large number of the best writers America has produced. Before a new house can be built, it is necessary to clear the ground of all debris. Before the young slave can be freed, it is necessary to convince his master that freedom is its own excuse for being; and when the master cannot be convinced, as is oftentimes the case, he should be hanged by his own rope, or at least rendered helpless. And then the freedman should be closely watched.

Down to the nineteen-twenties in America, the "master" of the arts had things pretty much his way. He was powerful; he was confident; he was popular. He was the proud descendant of Puritanism in its narrowest sense. He still objected violently to anything that smacked of heresy; especially did he object to the modern-day Maypole dancers. He represented the "moral viewpoint," the "closed vision," the "narrow outlook"—call it what you will. This ogre haunting the dreams of honest writers had over the years taken many shapes in the daylight world of actuality. In the first two decades of this century, the Puritanical restrictions were upheld in art by a class of men—the academicians—and by a philosophy— humanism. Moreover, the stronghold of Puritanism in the social realm had moved from New England to the South. Mencken's criticism of the professor, of the humanist, and of the South is of one cloth.

The founding fathers of New England came to America to estab-
lish one particular type of freedom: the freedom to enforce their
own narrow beliefs without any deviations.[1] Indeed, one of the first
things the college student learns in a course on early American
literature or history is that the concept of the Pilgrims which he
acquired from high school must be radically revised. It is really an
example of *un*learning. In Europe the Puritans had been persecuted
largely because they were public nuisances, malcontents unable or
unwilling to live and let live, similar in many ways to the God-crazy
Anabaptists who were wont to run through the streets naked and
howling to the invisible powers and principalities of the air. Only
in a land uninhabited by civilized man could the Puritan hope to
set up his peculiar kingdom of God. In America he had to contend
only with the Indian, who was an easy prey for the sharp-trading,
vindictive Puritan.

Mencken was one of the first, and certainly the most influential,
of those who finally succeeded in correcting our warped view of
Puritanism. If today we take for granted his historical analysis of
our forefathers, as we take for granted T. H. Huxley's defense and
elucidation of biological evolution, we must still remember that he,
like Huxley, performed an invaluable service to education. In his
criticism for December, 1921, Mencken took to task those historians
who credited the Puritans with the invention of most of the liberal
institutions and ideas, such as they were, in America. "There is not
a single right of the citizen of today, from free speech to equal suf-
frage and from religious freedom to trial by jury, that [the Puri-
tans] did not oppose with all their ferocious might." Actually, as
Mencken pointed out, it was the non-Puritan immigrants to New
England who were responsible for overthrowing the Puritan and
setting up free institutions in the country.

> To [the anti-Puritans] we owe everything of worth that has ever
> come out of New England. They converted the sour gather-
> ing of hell-crazy deacons into the town-meeting; they converted
> the old pens for torturing little children into public-schools;
> they set up free speech, free assemblage, a free press, trial by
> jury, equality before the law, religious freedom, and manhood
> suffrage; they separated church and state; they broke down the
> old theology and substituted the rationalism that was to come to
> flower in New England's Golden Age. The Puritans were abso-

lutely against all of these things. They no more gave them to the Republic than they gave it Franklin or Emerson. What they gave it was something quite different: the shivering dread of the free individual that is still the curse of American civilization. They gave it canned patriotism, comstockery, intolerance of political heresy, Prohibition. They gave it Wilsonism, Burlesonism, and the Ku Klux Klan.[2]

The main ideas of Mencken on Puritanism are found in "Puritanism as a Literary Force," one of the major documents of American criticism. Aside from its value as a penetrating analysis of the debilitating effects of Puritanism on art, the essay served as a spark to ignite the most bitterly waged critical war of the century. At the time of its publication (in *A Book of Prefaces* [1917]; the other three essays in the volume are on Conrad, Dreiser, and Huneker) Mencken was at the height of his powers as a literary critic. He was thirty-seven years old and not yet disenchanted with the profession of book criticism. Moreover, *A Book of Prefaces* was his first important volume of criticism (not counting the book on Nietzsche, which was primarily exposition). And it stands today, along with various essays in the *Prejudices,* as the best writing he was ever to do in that particular area. Indeed, within ten years after it appeared, Mencken had given up criticism of belles-lettres except for occasional pieces and comments that continued to see print until his death in 1956.

Inevitably, the reigning America First critics fell on *A Book of Prefaces* like angels on the Antichrist. Never before in America had a writer directed such a blast against an American sacred cow. And to publish such an un-American essay just when the nation was making the world safe for democracy was more than any right-thinking man could stand. The reception of *Prefaces*—which had a small sale in 1917, but enjoyed a wide audience when reissued in 1924—is a good gauge of Mencken's popularity. Only a few rebels could stomach him during the war (Sergeant Edmund Wilson, for example, read and reread the book, which convinced him more than any other single work that literary criticism was a worth-while profession); after the return of the conquering armies, a whole generation accepted the Menckenian theses as gospel.

In the opening pages of "Puritanism as a Literary Force," Mencken made it clear that Puritanism as a theological doctrine was pretty much exploded: "That primitive demonology still survives in the barbaric doctrines of the Methodists and Baptists, particularly in the South; but it has been ameliorated, even there, by a growing sense of the divine grace, and so the old God of Plymouth Rock, as practically conceived, is now scarcely worse than the average jail warden or Italian padrone."[3] But as an ethical concept, Puritanism lived on in all its fury. To Mencken, the American still described all value judgments, even those of aesthetics, in terms of right and wrong. It was only natural that such "moral obsession" should strongly color our literature. In the histories of all other nations there have been periods of what Mencken called "moral innocence—periods in which a naif *joie de vivre* has broken through all concepts of duty and responsibility, and the wonder and glory of the universe have been hymned with unashamed zest." But in America no such breathing spells have lightened the almost intolerable burdens of man. For proof of this continued moralism, one need only glance at the critical articles in the newspapers and literary weeklies—that is, at those of the period before and during World War I. "A novel or a play is judged among us, not by its dignity or conception, its artistic honesty, its perfection of workmanship, but almost entirely by its orthodoxy of doctrine, its platitudinousness, its usefulness as a moral tract. A digest of the reviews of such a book as Ibsen's *Hedda Gabler* would make astounding reading for a Continental European." Had not most of the critics of Dreiser's *The Titan* indignantly denounced the morals of Frank Cowperwood, the novel's central character? "That [Cowperwood] was superbly imagined and magnificently depicted, that he stood out from the book in all the flashing vigour of life, that his creation was an artistic achievement of a very high and difficult order—these facts seem to have made no impression upon the reviewers whatever. They were Puritans writing for Puritans, and all they could see in Cowperwood was an anti-Puritan, and in his creator another."[4]

When one encounters an American humorist of high rank, Mencken said, he finds further evidence of the Puritan mind. Aside from Ambrose Bierce, actually a "wit" and not at all well known, there have been few scurvy fellows of the Fielding-Sterne-Smollett variety. Mencken believed that our great humorists "have had to take protective colouration, whether willingly or unwillingly, from the prevailing ethical foliage, and so one finds them levelling their darts, not at the stupidities of the Puritan majority, but at the evidences of lessening stupidity in the anti-Puritan minority." Rather than do battle against, they have done battle for, Philistinism; and Philistinism is just another name for Puritanism. An exception might easily have been found in the person of George Ade, whose "fables" could hardly be said to support Philistinism. But then Ade was a singular case; besides, he did not offer much as a witness to the prosecution, and Mencken was intent on prosecuting. Mencken saw his favorite American artist, Mark Twain, as a perfect example of the American whose nationality hung about his neck like a millstone. "In the presence of all beauty of man's creation—in brief, of what we roughly call art, whatever its form—the voice of Mark Twain was the voice of the Philistine."

In tracing the development of Puritanism in America, Mencken found two main streams of influence. First, there was the force from without; that is, the influence of the original Puritans, who brought to the New World a philosophy of the utmost clarity, positiveness, and inclusiveness. In a letter to Gamaliel Bradford dated October 24, 1924, Mencken wrote that he had no great objections to the original Puritans' philosophy; what he objected to was that philosophy's "perversion by Methodists, Rotarians and other such vermin." Needless to say, his essay of seven years before contradicts his friendly letter.

The eighteenth century saw the passing of the Puritans as a powerful body of lawmakers. Deism undermined the old theology; epistemological studies replaced metaphysics. The proper study of mankind was thought to be man. Skepticism was all but universal among the learned of Europe, and Americans still imported their ideas wholesale from the mother countries. Both political and theological ideas were imported from France, where Voltaire, Diderot, d'Alembert, and the Encyclopedists were giving an entirely new direction to world philosophy. Mencken noted that even in New England, the last stronghold of the old Puritanism, this European influence was felt: "there was a gradual letting down of Calvinism to the softness of Unitarianism, and that change was presently to flower in the vague temporizing of Transcendentalism." This decline of Puritanism proper was not, however, an unalloyed blessing. For as Puritanism "declined in virulence and took deceptive new forms, there was a compensating growth of its brother, Philistinism, and by the first quarter of the nineteenth century, the distrust of beauty, and of the joy that is its object, was as firmly established throughout the land as it had ever been in New England." With the passing of the Adamses and the Jeffersons, Mencken remarked, the nation was quickly turned over to the tradesmen and the peasants. There was, he maintained, but one major difference between American peasants and those of other nations: the American peasant was listened to; he possessed power. (There is, of course, no such thing as a peasant in America today—only social unfortunates.) With the election of Andrew Jackson, Philistinism became the national philosophy. Jackson did what had not been done before: "he carried the mob's distrust of good taste even into the field of conduct; he was the first to put the rewards of conformity above the dictates of common decency; he founded a whole hierarchy of Philistine messiahs, the roaring of which still belabours the ear." The chief concern of Americans ever since the official triumph of mobocracy has been politics; what is more, politics tended to absorb the rancorous certainty of the fading religious ideas; the game of politics had turned itself into a holy war.

> The custom of connecting purely political doctrines with pietistic concepts of an inflammable nature, then firmly set up by skilful persuaders of the mob, has never quite died out in the United States. There has not been a presidential contest since Jackson's day without its Armageddons, its marching of Christian soldiers, its crosses of gold, its crowns of thorns. The most successful American politicians, beginning with anti-slavery agitators, have been those most adept at twisting the ancient gauds and shibboleths of Puritanism to partisan uses. Every campaign that we have seen for eighty years has been, on each side, a pursuit of bugaboos, a denunciation of heresies, a snouting up of immoralities.[5]

The pervasiveness of Puritan ethics (not, remember, theology) placed all purely aesthetic concerns in limbo. Mencken stated that with the exception of Whitman there was hardly a major writer who used the materials of his own age for subject matter. Algernon Tassin's *The Magazine in America* (1916) supported his thesis that the literature of the ante-bellum period was almost completely divorced from life as men were then living it. Only in such "crude politico-puritan tracts" as *Uncle Tom's Cabin* was there any attempt made to interpret, or even to represent, the culture of the time.

(The fact that Mrs. Stowe was chastised in her own day for her "realistic" novels only supports Mencken's contention.) Later, the culture found historians, and in at least one work—*Huckleberry Finn*—it was depicted with the highest art, but Twain's magnum opus was a rare exception. The nineteenth-century novelists did not even sentimentalize the here and now in the manner of Mencken's contemporaries. The best minds of that period were engaged in either business or politics. The few competent men of the period who were artists almost without exception forsook the present for the nonpolitical, nonsocial realms of Arcadia or El Dorado. It is evident that much of the material in "Puritanism as a Literary Force" was condensed in the later essay on "The National Letters." For example:

> Fenimore Cooper filled his romances, not with the people about him, but with the Indians beyond the sky-line, and made them half-fabulous to boot. Irving told fairy tales about the forgotten Knickerbockers; Hawthorne turned backward to the Puritans of Plymouth Rock; Longfellow to the Acadians and the prehistoric Indians; Emerson took flight from earth altogether; even Poe sought refuge in a land of fantasy. It was only the frank second-raters—e.g., Whittier and Lowell—who ventured to turn to the life around them, and the banality of the result is a sufficient indication of the crudeness of the current taste, and the mean position assigned to the art of letters. This was pre-eminently the era of the moral tale, the Sunday-school book.[6]

In his little book on Hawthorne, Henry James complained that American life was lacking in a complexity of themes and types to be employed by the creative artist. In one of the famous passages of this biography, James compiled a long list of things that had supplied European artists with subject matter, but were missing from the American scene. There was in America a conspicuous absence of a sovereign, a court, personal loyalty, an aristocracy, a church, a clergy, an army, a diplomatic service, country houses, parsonages, thatched cottages, ivied ruins, cathedrals, abbeys, and "little Norman churches" (James's list is profoundly snobbish, not to say slightly amusing). There were no great universities or public schools; there were no literature, no museums, no pictures, no political society, no sporting class. Horrifyingly enough, there was not even an Epsom or an Ascot! Cooper (and Irving before him) lamented much the same thing years before James: "There are no annals

for the historian; no follies (beyond the most vulgar and commonplace) for the satirist; no manners for the dramatist; no obscure
fictions for the writer of romance; no gross and hardy offenses
against decorum for the moralists; nor any of the rich artificial
auxiliaries of poetry." One can—indeed, must—object to these objections. Wherever there are people there certainly will be follies
for the satirist, "obscure fictions," and "hardy offenses against
decorum." And there were more American citizens in Cooper's day
than there were Greeks in the age of Pericles. It is also probable
that these Americans were just as heroic and cowardly, just as good
and bad, just as simple and complex as were the people in, say,
Russia or Norway or Germany. At least so the immense body of
literature on the period which is being written today would have us
believe. People and their customs are all the subject matter the
artist needs. His problem is one of choosing, not one of finding. In
his essay on "The Poet," Emerson had complained that America had
produced no genius to exploit "our incomparable materials":

> Banks and tariffs, the newspaper and caucus, Methodism and
> Unitarianism, are flat and dull to dull people, but rest on the
> same foundations of wonder as the town of Troy and the temple
> of Delphi, and are as swiftly passing away. Our log-rolling, our
> stumps and their politics, our fisheries, our Negroes and Indians,
> our boats and our repudiations, the wrath of rogues and the
> pusillanimity of honest men, the northern trade, the southern
> planting, the western clearing, Oregon and Texas, are yet unsung.

James's complaint is even more shallow and "precious" than
Cooper's. To be sure, there was little in America conducive to his
own obsession with an effete and desiccated segment of the upper
crust of society (and often English society, at that), but there is,
let us hope, more between heaven and hell than is depicted in
James's very limited and narrow creations. It is too much to expect
either Cooper or James (and I choose them as examples only) to see
the effects of Puritanism. For one thing, they were too close to the
period to see clearly the causes behind the effects; and for another,
they were not at all exempt from the forces about which Mencken
wrote. The belief that America of the nineteenth century offered no
material for the artist is simply ludicrous.

In the seventies and eighties, with the appearance of such men
as James, Howells, and Twain (Mencken also listed Bret Harte,

even though he never considered him even a good second-rate artist), a better day seemed to be dawning. These writers gave promise of turning away from the past to the teeming and colorful life that lay about them. The promise, however, was not fulfilled.

> Mark Twain, after *The Gilded Age*, slipped back into romanticism tempered by Philistinism, and was presently in the era before the Civil War, and finally in the Middle Ages, and even beyond. Harte, a brilliant technician, had displayed his whole stock when he had displayed his technique: his stories were not even superficially true to the life they presumed to depict; one searched them in vain for an interpretation of it; they were simply idle tales. As for Howells and James, both quickly showed that timorousness and reticence which are the distinguishing marks of the Puritan, even in his most intellectual incarnations. The American scene that they depicted with such meticulous care was chiefly peopled with marionettes.[7]

The writers who imitated the "artful emptiness" of Howells and James appeared to be composing parodies on their masters. To read them—Frances Hodgson Burnett, Mary E. Wilkins Freeman, F. Hopkinson Smith, Alice Brown, James Lane Allen, Sarah Orne Jewett, among others—was, Mencken wrote, "to undergo an experience that is almost terrible." And yet these were the writers that college professors were upholding as leading artists. Mencken used F. L. Pattee's *A History of American Literature Since 1870* (1915), "one of the latest and undoubtedly one of the least unintelligent of these books," as an example of the professorial attitude. Mencken, incidentally, had a number of kind things to say about Pattee's book when he reviewed it in his November, 1916, criticism, entitled "Professors at the Bat." Also, an essay by Pattee, entitled "Call for a Literary Historian," appeared in the June, 1924, issue of the *American Mercury*. In that essay, Pattee simply restated what Mencken had been saying for years; to wit, that our literature was in great need of numerous books to replace those that had been written by the genteel critics and scholars. Mencken thought that Carl Van Doren's *The American Novel* (1921) was a definite, advance in the much-needed reassessment of our literary past. In his review of that book, he praised Van Doren for the emphasis he placed on such little-remembered but important novels as John W. DeForest's *Miss Ravenel's Conversion from Secession to Loyalty*, Joseph Kirkland's *Zury*, Henry Adams' *Democracy*, and E. W.

Howe's *The Story of a Country Town*: "all of them marked distinct advances in the practice of the novelist's art among us, and are hence of far more importance to the literary historian than such universally read works as *Ben Hur, Graustark* and *Richard Carvel*."[8]

The force from within was, in essence, a force of "conditioning." The American tended to view all the workings of God, fate, man, and nature as exemplifications of a moral order or structure or pattern, just as his forebears had done. The rebel—that is, the writer who made an earnest attempt to depict his surroundings realistically rather than romantically or sentimentally—had had little influence on the main stream of American literature. Such writers as Hamlin Garland began as realists, but soon saw a rosy light and devoted themselves to safer enterprises; Garland ended his days by composing books on spiritualism, or, as Mencken put it, by "chasing spooks." (Garland, as well as Howells, refused to sign the Dreiser Protest, a petition objecting to the ban placed on *The "Genius."*) In the early days of the twentieth century, there had been a few realists—for example, Ambrose Bierce, Frank Norris, Stephen Crane, David Graham Phillips, Henry Fuller, Upton Sinclair—but their rebellion was apparently ineffectual.

> The normal, the typical American book of today is as fully a remouthing of old husks as the normal book of Griswold's day. The whole atmosphere of our literature, in William James' phrase, is "mawkish and dishwatery." Books are still judged among us, not by their form and organization as works of art, their accuracy and vividness as representations of life, their validity and perspicacity as interpretations of it, but by their conformity to the national prejudices, their accordance with set standards of niceness and propriety. The thing irrevocably demanded is a "sane" book; the ideal is a "clean," an "inspiring," a "glad" book.[9]

In addition to the impulse from within, there was a pervasive Puritan influence from without. No examination of the history and present condition of American letters, Mencken believed, could have any value at all unless it took into account the influence and operation of this external Puritan force. Supported by the almost incredibly large body of American laws, this power resided in the inherited traits of Puritanism, which were evident in the "conviction of the pervasiveness of sin, of the supreme importance of moral correctness, of the need of savage and inquisitorial laws." The history of the nation, Mencken said, might be outlined by the awakenings and reawakenings of moral earnestness. The spiritual eagerness that was the basis for the original Puritan's moral obsession had not always retained its white heat, but the fires of moral endeavor had never gone out in America. Mencken remarked that the theocracy of the New England colonies had scarcely been replaced by the libertarianism of a godless Crown when there came the Great Awakening of 1734, "with its orgies of homiletics and its restoration of talmudism to the first place among polite sciences." The boob-bumping of Jonathan Edwards' *Sinners in the Hands of an Angry God* stands as a testament to that holy resurrection of Almighty Sin.

During the Revolution, politics superseded theology as the national pastime, and there was a brief period of relative quiet. But no sooner had the Republic emerged from the throes of adolescence than "a missionary army took to the field again, and before long the Asbury revival was paling that of Whitefield, Wesley and Jonathan Edwards, not only in its hortatory violence but also in the length of its lists of slain." From Bishop Asbury down to the present day, that is, to World War I, the country was rocked periodically by furious attacks on the devil. On the one hand, the holy *Putsch*

> took a purely theological form with a hundred new and fantastic creeds as its fruits; on the other hand, it crystallized into the hysterical temperance movement of the 30's and 40's, which penetrated to the very floor of Congress and put "dry" laws upon the statute-books of ten States; and on the third hand, as it were, it established a prudery in speech and thought from which we are yet but half delivered. Such ancient and innocent words as "bitch" and "bastard" disappeared from the American language; Bartlett tells us, indeed, in his *Dictionary of Americanisms*,[10] that even "bull" was softened to "male cow." This was the Golden Age of euphemism, as it was of euphuism; the worst inventions of the English mid-Victorians were adopted and improved. The word "woman" became a term of opprobrium, verging close upon downright libel; legs became the inimitable "limbs"; the stomach began to run from the "bosom" to the pelvic arch; pantaloons faded into "unmentionables"; the newspapers spun their parts of speech into such gossamer webs as "a statutory offence," "a house of questionable repute" and "an interesting condition." And meanwhile the Good Templars and Sons of Temperance swarmed in the land like a plague of

celestial locusts. There was not a hamlet without its uniformed
phalanx, its affecting exhibit of reformed drunkards.[11]

Mencken argued that the Civil War itself was primarily a result
of the agitations of antislavery preachers. He admitted that to many
historians the antislavery feeling had economic origins, but he
insisted, probably correctly, that the war was largely the result of
ecstatically moral pleas. Elsewhere, he attributed the Negro's bondage in the South today to the fact that the war was won by the
North. Before the surrender at Appomattox, there was little hatred
of the Negro in the South. Also, the Negro would most certainly
have been made a freedman before the end of the nineteenth
century anyway, and without the resulting hostility between the
races. The Union victory, as Mencken stated, simply deprived the
best southerners of any say in national and regional affairs, and
placed the lower orders—the scalawags, carpetbaggers, freed slaves,
and poor white trash—in the saddle. The Negro, of course, was
soon disfranchised again, but the power remained in the hands of
incompetent whites.

The Puritan of the days between the Revolution and the Civil
War was, according to Mencken, different from the Ur-Puritan
and neo-Puritan of the post-bellum period. The distinguishing mark
of the original Puritanism, at least after it had attained to the
stature of a national philosophy, was its appeal to the individual
conscience, its exclusive concern with the elect, its strong flavor
of self-accusing. Certainly the Abolitionists were less concerned
with punishing slaveowners than they were with ridding themselves
of "their sneaking sense of responsibility, the fear that they themselves were flouting the fire by letting slavery go on." The Aboli-
tionist was willing, in most cases, to compensate the slaveowner
for his property. The difference between the new Puritanism with
its astoundingly ferocious and uncompromising vice crusading and
the Puritanism of the eighteen-forties was of great degree, if not
of kind: "In brief, a difference between *re*nunciation and *de*nunciation, asceticism and Mohammedanism, the hair shirt and the
flaming sword." After going through a number of stages and fads,
neo-Puritanism found its apex in comstockery. And in comstockery
there was a frank harking back to the primitive spirit.

The original Puritan of the bleak New England coast was not
content to flay his own wayward carcass: full satisfaction did

not sit upon him until he had jailed a Quaker. That is to say, the sinner who excited his highest zeal and passion was not so much himself as his neighbor; to borrow a term from psycho-pathology, he was less the masochist than the sadist. And it is that very peculiarity which sets off his descendant of today from the ameliorated Puritan of the era between the Revolution and the Civil War. The new Puritanism is not ascetic, but militant. Its aim is not to lift up saints but to knock down sinners. Its supreme manifestation is the vice crusade, an armed pursuit of helpless outcasts by the whole military and naval forces of the Republic. Its supreme hero is Comstock Himself, with his pious boast that the sinners he jailed during his astounding career, if gathered into one penitential party, would have filled a train of sixty-one coaches, allowing sixty to the coach.[12]

While avoiding the jargon and the overemphasis on sex that mar the typical Freudian criticism, Mencken here is using a "tool" obviously borrowed from the laboratory of psychoanalysis. Though his harsh treatment of amateurs in the field has caused many to assume that Mencken was an anti-Freudian, it is clear that he appreciated the work being done in Vienna. Moreover, his admiration for Havelock Ellis dated back to the earliest days on the *Smart Set*. In "The Genealogy of Etiquette," which first appeared in the September, 1915, *Smart Set* and was later included in *Prejudices: First Series*, Mencken wrote, with something like a flash of divine insight:

Even so ingenious and competent an investigator as Prof. Dr. Sigmund Freud, who has told us a lot that is of the first importance about the materials and machinery of thought, has also told us a lot that is trivial and dubious. The essential doctrines of Freudism [*sic*], no doubt, come close to the truth, but many of Freud's remoter deductions are far more brilliant than sound, and most of the professed Freudians, both American and European, have grease-paint on their noses and bladders in their hands and are otherwise quite indistinguishable from evangelists, corn-doctors and circus clowns.

In a long essay on the new interest in psychoanalysis, entitled "Rattling the Subconscious" (*Smart Set*, September, 1918), Mencken praised the work of numerous men in the field. After remarking that the early announcements of Freud appeared to be extravagant, it became evident on further study that his fundamental ideas were sound, especially as they were developed and modified by Adler, Jung, Ferenczi, Bjerre, Brill, Ernest Jones, and "scores of other widely dispersed investigators." These men had made intelligible for the first time the process of thought: "It responds to causation; it is finally stripped of supernaturalism; it is seen to be determined by the same natural laws that govern all other phenomena in space and time. And so seen, it gives us a new understanding of the forces which move us in the world, and shows us the true genesis and character of our ideas, and enormously strengthens our grip upon reality." Not only was Mencken familiar with the psychoanalytical studies of the time, but he was, we must assume, influenced by them.

In accounting for the wholesale ethical transvaluation that came after the Civil War, Mencken pointed to the Golden Calf; in short, Puritanism became bellicose and tyrannical when it became rich. History shows that a wealthy people are never prone to soul-searching. The solvent citizen is less likely to find fault with himself than with those about him; indeed, he has more time and energy to devote to the enterprise of examining the happy rascal across the street. The Puritan of America was, generally speaking, spiritually humble down to the Civil War because he was poor; he subscribed to a *Sklavenmoral*. But after the Civil War prosperity replaced poverty; and from prosperity came a new morality, to wit, the *Herrenmoral*. Great fortunes were made during the conflict, and even greater wealth followed during the years of the robber barons. Nor was this new prosperity limited to a few capitalists only; the common laborer and the farmer were better off than ever before.

The first effect of prosperity was, as always, a universal cockiness, a delight in all things American, the giddy feeling that success has no limits. "The American became a sort of braggart playboy of the western world, enormously sure of himself and ludicrously contemptuous of all other men." Mencken observed that religion, which is always dependent upon its popularity for survival, naturally began to lose its inward direction and take on the qualities of a business enterprise. The revivals of the eighteen-seventies were similar to those of a half-century before, except that the converts at the later date were more interested in serving than in repenting. The American Puritan was less concerned with saving his own soul than in passing salvation on to others, especially to those reluctant individuals who hung back and resisted the power of divine grace. It became apparent to the more forward-looking ecclesiastics that the rescue of the unsaved could be converted into a big business. All that was needed was organization. Out of this unabashed industrialization of religion came a new force, one that still exerts great influence on American society. "Piety was cunningly disguised as basketball, billiards and squash; the sinner was lured to grace with Turkish baths, lectures on foreign travel, and free instructions in stenography, rhetoric and double-entry book-keeping." Religion lost its old contemplative nature and became an enterprise for the public-relations man, the bookkeeper, and the extrovert. In short, religion was "modernized." What was true at the time Mencken wrote this essay is, as a pragmatist would say, even more true in the nineteen-sixties.

After giving the necessary background material, Mencken then devoted a lengthy section of his essay to the workings and accomplishments of Anthony Comstock and his associates. The various laws, state and national, which Comstock got passed offer the contemporary reader a sorry spectacle of the vice crusader's power. As a public figure, Old Anthony was as well known as P. T. Barnum or John L. Sullivan. He had disciples in every large city who were just as eager for blood as he was. Since there were few American writers brash enough to challenge the inquisitors, Comstock and company were forced to turn to foreign works. Rabelais and the *Decameron* were naturally banned (they are still being banned in various American cities today); Zola, Balzac, and Daudet were driven under the counters; Hardy's *Jude the Obscure* and Harold Frederic's *The Damnation of Theron Ware* were also among the victims. These are but leading examples of the purge. In fact, Comstock got 2,682 convictions out of 3,646 prosecutions and is credited by his official biographer with having destroyed 50 tons of books, 28,682 pounds of stereotype plates, 16,900 photographic negatives, and 3,984,063 photographs. That such a Herod's record could have been compiled was largely a result of the postal laws, for which, of course, Comstock was responsible in the first place. The very vagueness of the law was of great convenience to the prosecutors. That a novel like George du Maurier's *Trilby*, could have been widely condemned as "lewd," "obscene," and "lascivi-

ous" is next to incredible. It merely provides further proof that
Swift's *Gulliver's Travels* is a good deal closer to reality than it is
to fantasy.

> It is held in the leading cases that anything is obscene which
> may excite "impure thoughts" in "the minds . . . of persons that
> are susceptible to impure thoughts,"[13] or which "tends to de-
> prave the minds" of any who, because they are "young and
> inexperienced," are "open to such influences"[14]—in brief, that
> anything is obscene that is not fit to be handed to a child just
> learning to read, or that may imaginably stimulate the lubricity
> of the most foul-minded. It is held further that words that are
> perfectly innocent in themselves—"words, abstractly considered,
> [that] may be free from vulgarism"—may yet be assumed, by
> a friendly jury, to be likely to "arouse a libidinous passion . . .
> in the mind of a modest woman." (I quote exactly! The court
> failed to define "modest woman.")[15] Yet further, it is held that
> any book is obscene "which is unbecoming, immodest. . . ."[16]
> Obviously, this last decision throws open the door to endless
> imbecilities, for its definition merely begs the question, and so
> makes a reasonable solution ten times harder. It is in such mazes
> that the Comstocks safely lurk. Almost any printed allusion to
> sex may be argued against as unbecoming in a moral republic,
> and once it is unbecoming it is also obscene.[17]

Mencken then cited numerous cases to show that the defendant
was helpless in proving his innocence against any of a whole host
of charges of immorality. Besides, Dr. Johnson was obviously right
when he stated that no man would want to go on trial, even if
possessed of absolute proof of his innocence. Obviously, neither
author nor publisher ever knew what might pass the watchful eyes
of the self-appointed smuthounds and defenders of decency. Competent work invariably was banned, while the frankly prurient and
vulgar went unmolested. Though our staunchest advocate of free
speech, Mencken was indignantly amazed that the serious work of
an Auguste Forel or a Havelock Ellis should be barred from the
mails while the countless volumes of "sex hygiene" by filthy-minded
clergymen and "smutty old maids" were circulated by the million
and without challenge.

It was no wonder, Mencken wrote, that American literature down
to World War I was primarily remarkable for its artificiality. He
compared our fiction to eighteenth-century poetry; it was just as conventional and artificial, just as far removed from reality. In America,

and probably only here, could an obvious piece of reporting like Upton Sinclair's *The Jungle* create a sensation, or Dreiser's *Jennie Gerhardt* evoke such astonishment and rage. As an editor of the *Smart Set*, Mencken was fully aware of the dangers lying in the path of any publisher who attempted to give his readers quality writing. Since his magazine was frankly addressed to a sophisticated minority, sold for a relatively high price, and contained no pictures or other baits for the childish, Mencken assumed that "its readers are not sex-curious and itching adolescents, just as my colleague of the *Atlantic Monthly* may assume reasonably that his readers are not Italian immigrants." Nevertheless, he was constantly forced to keep the comstocks in mind while reading a manuscript sent him by an author. According to Ben Hecht, Mencken warned his contributors to keep clothes on their female characters at all times. Mencken was a man marked by the Puritan elements in the country, and he knew it.[18] But he certainly possessed nothing resembling a martyr complex. As he wrote Dreiser in 1921, the joy of living in America "does not lie in playing chopping-block for the sanctified, but in outraging them and getting away with it. To this enterprise I address myself. Some day they may fetch me, but it will be a hard sweat."

Although our literature was policed and picketed by a small band of comstocks, the fact remains that the American people offered little resistance; they were perfectly willing to be led by their noses like so many cattle. The American was "school-mastered out of gusto, out of joy, out of innocence." He could in no way understand William Blake's belief that "the lust of the goat is also to the glory of God." When the comstocks examined *The "Genius"* to determine its harmful effect on immature female readers, they tacitly admitted, Mencken wrote, that "to be curious is to be lewd; to know is to yield to fornication." The medieval doctrine that woman is depraved was, and, for that matter, still is, widely accepted in our own century. The right-thinking man must do all he can to save her from her innate depravity. "The 'locks of chastity' rust in the Cluny Museum: in place of them we have comstockery."

CHAPTER NINE

A Trinity: The Prof. Drs.,
The Humanists, and Dixie

Mencken believed that so long as writers are forbidden to experiment with new methods and attempt to interpret their chosen segment of life freely, realistically, truthfully, just so long will the various arts remain conventional and immature. That the ingrown and inbred Puritanism in America has exerted a tremendous effect on American literature from its beginning is beyond dispute. Also, it is evident that puritanical restrictions have been the product of a small minority. The melancholy fact that criticism can exert great influence on a literature is nowhere more evident than in America before and during World War I.

The belief that great ages of literary creativity are preceded by a sound body of criticism is patently false. The unending talk one hears today about the role of criticism is written, at least in large part, by critics of criticism intent on justifying their somewhat shaky existence. In *The Armed Vision* (1948) Stanley Edgar Hyman succeeded better than most in proving how magnificently dull this sort of thing can be. These spokesmen of the critical faculty do not address themselves to artists or to readers per se; rather, they address their jehads to other critics of criticism or, more practically, to the heads of their English departments in charge of promotions.

On the other hand, criticism, especially journalistic criticism, can and often does perform yeomen service for literature. The critic who aids the serious writer to find a sympathetic audience not only does a service for the individual writer; he also helps future writers. The good critic (to continue my criticism of criticism) must be a liberal in matters of art, or, better, a libertarian. He must allow and even encourage the artist to experiment. Above all else, he must *not* ride a theory which in any way confines the artist to a set pattern. For all theories, it must be remembered, are but a step removed from the pigeonhole—the infernal pit into which all bad critics place works of art.

In *A Book of Prefaces*, Mencken endeavored to do at least two things: he wished to promote three extraordinarily free artists (Conrad, Huneker, and Dreiser), and he wished to liberate other artists from the narrow conventions which oppressed them in America. The last desire could be fulfilled only insofar as the reading public (the 2 or 3 per cent of the population) was made accessible to the artist. The writer must, of course, also be given the opportunity to display his wares; and the writer must be given a relatively fair notice by the critics. This is not to say that a book cannot succeed without the aid of favorable criticism. Pornography is popular, especially in highly "moral" nations, no matter whether it is even reviewed at all. But adult readers tend to buy the books or see the plays or view the paintings that find favor with the reigning critics. And the vast majority of literary critics between 1900 and 1920 were intent on preserving the Puritan tradition in letters.

I

It is perhaps only natural that the Puritan tradition should have been strongly supported by academic critics, for the teacher is by nature a preserver of the past, not a harbinger of the future, and most certainly not a creator. It is no wonder that the college professor has been blind to the truly important work of his contemporaries, for he labors under an almost insurmountable handicap: that is, he attempts to criticize literature, which is simply an intelligent expression or depiction or criticism of life, when he is himself by character and profession divorced from life. The average professor has spent his life in school in the study of books and ideas; and more often than not, these books and ideas are far removed from the bases of all works of art. He is rarely a well-read man in the sense that his reading has been broad. If he teaches English literature, he reads just enough of that literature to give a very restricted course in some area of the subject. Indeed, a professor who wishes to "keep up" in the literature being published in his speciality has little time for reading outside that chosen field. Edmund Wilson startled no intelligent reader when he wrote (in the *New Yorker*, May 24, 1958) that professors of American literature relish the dry bones of T. S. Eliot because Eliot wrote very little and what he did write is vague and hence open for all kinds of interpretation; on the other hand, the books and articles *on* Eliot constitute a formidable body of work. The professor talks about fewer and fewer books at greater and greater length and in a far more specialized way than ever before. The reading public is not always aware of this and is hence susceptible to professorial criticism, but the artist in America, almost without exception, has been privy to the fact. The best American novelists of this century —that is, Dreiser, Lewis, Dos Passos, Fitzgerald, Hemingway, Wolfe, Faulkner—have been almost savagely contemptuous of college people in general and academic critics in particular.

Up to 1920 Mencken periodically lambasted the pedagogues who divided their time between tutoring and passing judgments on contemporary literature. After that date the academic critics were pretty effectively stripped of their influence, and Mencken's remarks became less acerb, even though he remained the target of academic ire through the nineteen-twenties. It is noteworthy that Mencken never attacked the weak and harmless; his ammunition was reserved for big game only. He began an early criticism on Mark Twain, entitled "The Greatest of American Writers," by asking: "How long does it take a new idea to gain lodgment in the professorial mind? The irreverent ignoramus may be tempted to answer six days and six nights, or just as long as it took to manufacture and people the world; but any such answer would be a gross and obvious understatement." He went on to say that exactly twenty-five years after the publication of *Huckleberry Finn*, a Prof. Dr., William Lyon Phelps, got around to making the first trembling admission that Twain was a greater artist than Oliver Wendell Holmes. "After all, the sun *do* move! After all, there is yet hope!"

Mencken's battle with the pedants reached a high point during World War I. In those days of patriotic fervor, when the Bill of

Rights had been officially revoked, the academicians brought a new and powerful weapon to play upon Mencken: the charge of un-Americanism. The publication of *A Book of Prefaces* provided them with a perfect point of reference. Mencken had written a long essay analyzing the inimical influence of Puritanism on our literature; the professors answered by attacking not only the book but the author personally. Of the several score notices the book received, only three were favorable. Leading the forces of what Ernest Boyd called the Ku Klux Kritics was Professor Stuart Pratt Sherman, of the University of Illinois. Sherman, an admirer and former student of Irving Babbitt at Harvard, gave notice that Mencken was the main trouble with America in general when he wrote a savage review of *Prefaces* for the *Nation*, then under the editorship of Paul Elmer More. Employing what he hoped would pass as Swiftian irony, Sherman began his review thus:

Mr. Mencken is not at all satisfied with life or literature in America, for he is a lover of the beautiful. We have nowadays no beautiful literature in this country, with the possible exception of Mr. Dreiser's novels; nor do we seem in a fair way to produce anything aesthetically gratifying. Probably the root of our difficulty is that, with the exception of Mr. Huneker, Otto Heller, Ludwig Lewisohn, Mr. Untermeyer, G. S. Viereck, the author of "Der Kampf um deutsche Kultur in Amerika," and a few other choice souls, we have no critics who, understanding what beauty is, serenely and purely love it. Devoid of aesthetic sense, our native "Anglo-Saxon" historians cannot even guess what ails our native literature. For a competent historical account of our national anaesthesis one should turn, Mr. Mencken assures us, to a translation from some foreign tongue—we cannot guess which—by Dr. Leon Kellner. Thus one readily perceives that Mr. Mencken's introductions to Conrad, Dreiser, and Huneker and his discourse on "Puritanism as a Literary Force" are of the first importance to all listeners for the soft breath and finer spirit of letters.

Though a lover of the beautiful, Mr. Mencken is not a German. He was born in Baltimore, September 12, 1880. That fact should silence the silly people who have suggested that he and Dreiser are secret agents of the Wilhelmstrasse, "told off to inject subtle doses of *Kultur* into a naif and pious people." Furthermore, Mr. Mencken is, with George Jean Nathan, editor of that staunchly American receptacle for *belles-lettres*, the *Smart Set*. He does indeed rather ostentatiously litter his pages with German words and phrases—*unglaublich, Stammvater, Sklaven-*

moral, Kultur, Biertische, Kaffeklatsch, die ewige Wiederkunft, Wille zur Macht . . . u.s.w. He is a member of the Germania Mannerchor, and he manages to work the names of most of the German musicians into his first three discourses. His favorite philosopher happens to be Nietzsche, whose beauties he has expounded in two books—first the "philosophy," then the "gist" of it. He perhaps a little flauntingly dangles before us the seductive names of Wedekind, Schnitzler, Bierbaum, Schoenberg, and Korngold. He exhibits a certain Teutonic gusto in tracing the "Pilsner motive" through the work of Mr. Huneker. His publisher is indeed Mr. Knopf. But Mr. Knopf disarms anti-German prejudice by informing us that Mr. Mencken is of "mixed blood—Saxon, Bavarian, Hessian, Irish, and English"; or, as Mr. Mencken himself puts it, with his unfailing good taste, he is a "mongrel." One cannot, therefore, understand exactly why Mr. Knopf thinks it valuable to announce that Mr. Mencken "was in Berlin when relations between Germany and the United States were broken off"; nor why he adds, "Since then he has done no newspaper work save a few occasional articles." Surely there can have been no external interference with Mr. Mencken's purely aesthetic ministry to the American people.[1]

The review continues in the same way, ending with even more snide remarks about the "European" culture which Mr. Mencken prefers to his own native one.

Sherman's essay was reprinted in the New York *Tribune* under the headline WHAT H. L. MENCKEN'S "KULTUR" IS DOING TO AMERICAN LITERATURE. The national press chorused the battle cry, and Mencken found himself everywhere denounced as an enemy alien seeking to undermine Sherman's dictum that "Beauty has a heart of service." Burton Rascoe stood almost alone when he lauded the *Prefaces* in his book section, "Fanfare," in the Chicago *Tribune*. Thankful for any aid he could enlist, Mencken wrote Rascoe: "As George Cohan says, I thank you; my family thanks you; my valet, Rudolph, thanks you; my Bierbruder, George Nathan, thanks you; my pastor thanks you; my brother, Wolfgang, thanks you; my chauffeur, Etienne, thanks you; my secretary, Miss Goldberg, thanks you; my accompanist, Signor Sforzando, thanks you." Rascoe followed his review by blasting Sherman and his ilk, but he was only one man, little read outside Chicago.

One would like to praise Sherman for one thing, anyway: he was at least forthright; there was never any doubt where his sympathies lay. But it is difficult to praise a man for these traits when the object of his assault was outnumbered a hundred to one. It takes little courage to attack a man who is clearly out of step with the overwhelming majority of his fellows. Although Sherman has been lauded for his willingness to step manfully into the fray, I find little in his behavior that would justify such praise. Scenting the possibility of making a name by slaying the dragon Mencken, Sherman followed his review with other attacks—equally vicious, equally chauvinistic, equally absurd.

An almost archetypal Prof. Dr. of the Puritan species,[2] and hence worthy of examination, Sherman began as a humanist (of the More-Babbitt-Foerster variety), as is evidenced in his first collection of essays, *On Contemporary Literature* (1917). His first book, also published in 1917, was *Matthew Arnold: How to Know Him*. His text for the book of essays: "The great revolutionary task of the nineteenth century thinkers was to put man into nature. The great task of twentieth century thinkers is to get him out again." Thus Dreiser was anathema, "the vulgarest voice yet heard in American literature," and almost as bad were Wells, George Moore, and John Millington Synge. Mark Twain was also dismissed because he did not help us to realize "our best selves."

From humanism Sherman moved to an extreme nationalism in *Americans* (1922). In that stage he felt that the two chief traditions in America were Puritanism and Anglo-Saxondom. Unlike Mencken, Sherman considered the Puritan to be an iconoclast; Puritanism, to him, was "a formative spirit, an urgent and exploring and creative spirit." He insisted that critics with "foreign" names (like Mencken and Huneker and Lewisohn, for example) who praised Scandinavian, German, or Russian writers could not be expected to hear any profound murmurings of ancestral voices or to experience any mysterious inflowing in meditating over such names as Bradford or Emerson or Lincoln or Thoreau. Actually, Sherman was an extreme chauvinist as early as the beginning of World War I.

Always anxious to provoke Mencken to answer him directly, person-to-person, Sherman entitled his first essay in *Americans*, "Mr. Mencken, the Jeune Fille, and the New Spirit in Letters."[3] Sherman castigated the Jeune Fille, who lacked proper respect for the "classical period" of American literature, that is, the New

England writers. She read mountains (would that Sherman were right!) of foreign literature in preference to her own, though she did approve of such barbarians as Mark Twain, Edgar Lee Masters, Sherwood Anderson, and Theodore Dreiser. After discussing her tastes, with lascivious asides on the trimness of her ankles (a Freudian would delight in the essay's unwitting revelations of its author), he had Mencken enter "at a hard gallop, spattered with mud" and "high in oath." From this preliminary, he went on to review *Prejudices: Third Series*. Evidently an abstainer and proud of it, Sherman made a few mock-sympathetic remarks about Mencken's agony over Prohibition. He then paid a few half-hearted compliments to Mencken's style, but concluded that "Mr. Mencken has no heart." Mencken was also described as the author of a work on the American language, "over-ambitiously designed as a wedge to split asunder the two great English-speaking peoples"! Sherman was not, of course, the first to attack Mencken on the grounds that his language studies were nothing more than evidences of his Anglophobia (a few such idiots are still extant). The materials on that one aspect of his work would make a nice volume. It was all right for Professor Higgins in Shaw's *Pygmalion* to remark that *Americans* had not spoken English for years, but for Mencken to prove the point systematically was not at all to the liking of American schoolmarms. Ironically, the pedagogue was perfectly willing to have his countrymen chastised for their not speaking the King's English, but he objected violently to hearing their language discussed as a thing-in-itself, in no sense inferior because it did not abide by English rules. The Sherman essay ends when Francis Hackett, fresh from his labors for the *New Republic*, enters and asks Mencken to go to dinner. They leave, jauntily exploding the reputations of their betters as they go.

In his *Smart Set* criticism for March, 1923, entitled "Adventures Among Books," Mencken acknowledged the tribute Sherman paid him. At the same time he noticed a book by another professor, *Sidelights on American Literature* (1922) by F. L. Pattee. Admitting that both books placed a burden on him as a critic, since he was the villain of both works, he first addressed Professor Pattee's book, which contained, surprisingly enough, a polite chastisement.

In fact, [Pattee] is often *too* polite—for example, when he reprints long extracts from my juvenile verse, perhaps the worst piffle ever written in America before the New Poetry Movement began, and argues solemnly that it has some merit. If it has, then there is also merit in the state papers of the Hon. W. G. Harding. But it is my later prose that concerns Dr. Pattee most seriously. What he finds in it chiefly is a waste of God-sent talents—a fine gift for ingratiating utterance degraded to the uses of anarchy and atheism. His hope is that increasing years may bring me back to the good, the true and the beautiful. Who, indeed, can tell: Some die of diabetes; some die of growing good. The professor is an earnest man, and he shakes me not a little. But he would have shaken me a great deal more had he not grounded his case against me (see his page 77) upon a note on criticism that was written, not by me, but by Colleague Nathan. You will find it in *The World in Falseface*, page 39, #93. Need I add that I dissent from its doctrine absolutely, and regard it with even more abhorrence than Dr. Pattee does?

After paying temperate praise to the rest of Pattee's book, he then turned to *Americans*. In his devastating review of Sherman's central thesis, Mencken places Sherman in an impossible position: he is made to appear not hateful but simply absurd, and hence incapable of answering. The impulsive anger which marred some of his earlier writings on those who attacked him and Dreiser, among others, for their "un-Americanism" is absent from this review. He does in effect what the mature Lord Byron did in *The Vision of Judgment*: he leaves his opponent hanging by puppet's strings, dancing ludicrously in the breeze. First, an effort was made, in the most innocently objective manner, to determine the precise nature of Sherman's ailment.

Just what ails Prof. Dr. Sherman it is rather difficult to determine. During the war it was easy to recognize him as a patriot driven to a desperate and heroic resistance by the Kaiser's plot to destroy Christianity, conquer Europe and enslave the United States. Like many another brave pedagogue of the time he was moved by this threat to throw down his rattan and mount the stump. The historian will find an eloquent record of his sweatings for democracy in one of the publications of the Creel Press Bureau, by title, "American and Allied Ideals." This brochure, which was distributed to the conscripts of the Republic before the battle of Chateau-Thierry, to heat up their

blood, is now somewhat rare, but fortunately it is not copy-
righted, and so I may reprint it later on, with a gloss. But all
that, as I say, was in war-time, and Sherman followed a large
and clearly visible star. Now, however, with the ideals of the
Allies in a somewhat indifferent state of repair, it is hard to
make out precisely what he is in favor of, and what he is
against. On the one hand he lays down the Ku Klux doctrine
that no American who is not 100 per cent Anglo-Saxon can ever
hope to write anything worth reading and on the other hand
he praises the late Andrew Carnegie, who was no more an
Anglo-Saxon than Abraham Cahan is, and reads a severe lesson
to Paul Elmer More, who is the very archetype of the species.
The truth about Dr. Sherman, I fear, is not to be sought in
logical and evidential directions. It lies deeper, to wit, among
the emotions, or, as Prof. Dr. Freud would say, in the unconscious. What afflicts him, no doubt, is what afflicts many another
Americano of his peculiar traditions and limitations: the uneasy
feeling that something is slipping from under him. The new
literature of the Republic, both in prose and in verse, tends
more and more to be written by fellows bearing such ghastly
names as Ginsberg, Gohlinghorst, Casey, Mitnick and Massaccio.
To put down these barbarians by purely critical means becomes increasingly difficult, for the scoundrels begin to practise criticism themselves, and some of them show a lamentable
pugnacity. Well, then, let us put them down by force. Call out
the American Legion! Telephone the nearest Imperial Wizard!
Set the band to playing "The Star-Spangled Banner"!

Sherman probably longed secretly, Mencken suspected, for the
days of the Creel Press Bureau, "when the easy way to get rid of
a poet who wrote against the Anglican Holy Ghost was to allege
that his grandfather was a Bavarian." But now that such methods
were ineffective, he was left high and dry, and his books showed
inconsistency and uncertainty. Only two courses were left before
him, "if he would avoid exhausting himself by chasing his own
tail." He could on the one hand join the Ku Klux Klan openly and
perhaps become its Literary Grand Cyclops or Imperial Kritik,
or, on the other hand, he could quietly make peace with the enemy.
Sherman had, as Mencken points out, already begun praising
Sinclair Lewis and Ludwig Lewisohn. If he undertook a peaceful
penetration, however, he would be swallowed up. And if he went
the Klan route he would simply get himself laughed at. Finally,
Mencken spoofed the charge that he was himself

the Grand Cyclops of a vast horde of extremely toothsome but unhappily antinomian young gals from the foreign missions and mail order belt, descending upon New York in perfumed swarms to hear me defame Jonathan Edwards, the *Stammvater* of Billy Sunday and Paul Elmer More. Ah, that it were true—but the facts are the facts! No such sweet ones ever appear; I have yet to see a single ankle of the kind the professor so lasciviously describes; all the actual arrivals are overweight and of a certain age.

Mencken wrote off Sherman's allusions as "Freudian nonsense." The other essays he found "correct" and harmless enough.

In *The Genius of America* (1923), Sherman attempted to answer Spingarn's principle that literary criticism is not concerned with moral truth or democracy. Sherman felt that every American schoolboy, if he understood Spingarn's supersubtle Italian criticism, would feel it to be false to the history of beauty in America! It was not long after he moved to New York (where, according to his friend Carl Van Doren, he was surprised to find that some young people were still raising families in the old-fashioned legal way) that he flopped to the opposite side of the fence and began eulogistically hymning the realists that Mencken had helped make popular—especially Sinclair Lewis, on whom he composed a small book. It was embarrassing, and probably amusing in a diabolical way, to Mencken to watch his old antagonist point out the sheer genius of Lewis. Though he could not, of course, refute all he had said about Dreiser and Mencken, among others, Sherman soon came to the belief that Dreiser was one of the giants. What is more, a note of timid admiration began to creep into his still frequent discourses on Mencken (in one place he compared him to Heine), and he made it known that he would like to bury the hatchet with the Baltimore Sage. At a large New York party given by B. W. Huebsch in honor of Sherwood Anderson, Sherman and Mencken came together for the first and only time. Carl Van Doren asked Sherman, who had but recently moved to New York to head the New York *Tribune* book section, if he would like to be introduced to Mencken. Sherman consented and eagerly crossed the room to shake Mencken's hand. Knowing that Mencken was, as Van Wyck Brooks put it, the personification of good nature, everyone assumed that he would readily forgive and forget the attacks of Sherman

during and after the war. But he refused to acknowledge the out-
stretched hand of Sherman, refused even to look at the man, and
remarked: "I'd rather pass into heaven without the pleasure of
his acquaintance. He is a dirty fighter." Brooks recalled this as the
only instance he knew of in which Mencken was unforgiving.

Mencken's refusal ever to answer Sherman's charges of un-
Americanism and vulgarity is understandable: first, given Sherman's
definitions, the charges were not without valid basis; and second,
he knew that Sherman was begging for a personal battle so as to
gain more recognition. When he engaged in literary wars, Mencken
wished his opposition to at least use weapons that were not invented by the mob. He wrote Van Doren (September 1, 1936)
concerning the latter's account in *Three Worlds* of the Sherman-
Mencken feud:

> My objection to Sherman was not that he denounced *me* as
> pro-German. As a matter of fact, I was on the best of terms with
> various men who had done the same thing. Until the United
> States got into the war and free speech was cut off, I was writing
> politics in the Baltimore *Evening Sun* almost daily, and my
> arguments in favor of the Germans were certainly not pianis-
> simo. It seemed to me, therefore, to be quite fair for anybody
> to denounce me for what I had done. My objection was to
> Sherman's denunciation of *Dreiser*. Dreiser had written nothing
> about politics, and was hardly interested in the subject. The
> accusation that he was pro-German was made without adequate
> evidence and had the obvious effect of greatly damaging him
> at a time when he surely had enough other troubles. It seemed
> to me that in the heat of controversy Sherman hit below the
> belt, and that's the reason I refused to have anything to do with
> him. But I certainly never complained about what he wrote
> about *me*. As a matter of fact, I have always made it a point
> to take such things lightly. And, as I have said, I got on very
> well with some of the patriots who belabored me violently
> during the war. I should add, of course, that as soon as my
> hands were free I did my best to cave in their literary skulls.[4]

This explanation may be accepted at face value, since Mencken
was certainly accustomed to being waylaid by well-nigh the whole
American press and the vast majority of the older critics.

As William Van O'Connor wrote: Sherman never grew; he just
changed. One minute a moralist, then a spokesman for Uplift,
devoted Rotarian, the disciple of Cleanliness, Health, Swift Mobil-

ity, Publicity, and Athletics, and finally, last scene of all, "hard-bitten," pseudobroad-minded literary editor. He was, in brief, a second-rate man who wrote second-rate criticism.[5]

Never one to deny that the college professor had his uses, Mencken admitted that he was one of God's creatures and performed certain onerous, but essential, duties in the antechambers of beautiful letters. First, it was his duty to ground unwilling schoolboys in the rudiments of knowledge and taste. Secondarily, it was his job

> to do the shovel and broom work of literary exploration—to count up the weak and strong endings in *Paradise Lost*, to guess at the meaning of the typographical errors in Shakespeare, to bowdlerize Hannah More for sucklings, to establish the date of *Tamburlaine*, to prove that Edgar Allan Poe was a tee-totaler and a Presbyterian, to list all the differences between F_1 and F_2, to edit high-school editions of *Tales of a Traveler*, *Die Jungfrau von Orleans* and *La Mort de Pompée*.[6]

Mencken almost perfectly defined professorial "criticism" in a remark he made in his essay on Nathan in *Prejudices: First Series*: "The professor is nothing if not a maker of card-indexes; he must classify or be damned."

But it was not the professor's business to sit in judgment on contemporary literature, for that job required qualities which he did not have—indeed could not have and still hold his job. Those qualities—an eager intellectual curiosity, a quick hospitality to ideas, a delight in novelty and heresy—are precisely those that the professor lacked. He was hired by God-fearing and excessively solvent old gentlemen who sit on college boards, not to search out the new and dangerous, but to defend the old and safe. He was not asked to inflame his students with novel doctrines, but to make them accept docilely the ideas that have been approved as harmless. And his advance in the pedagogic profession was in ratio to his fidelity to the program.

As an instance of what happens to the professor who wanders from the beaten path, there is the case of economics professor Scott Nearing, a socialist who was cashiered from the University of Pennsylvania in 1915 for divulging his heinous beliefs. Mencken, incidentally, greatly admired Nearing. Although Nearing was a socialist and an idealist, Mencken defended him against those who dismissed his output as vapid dreamwork. Certainly he was a better man than the college presidents who refused him the chance to speak on their campuses. "His virtues are completely civilized ones; he is brave, independent, unselfish, urbane and enlightened. If I had a son growing up I'd want him to meet Nearing, though the whole body of doctrine that Nearing preaches seems to me false. There is something even more valuable to civilization than wisdom, and that is character. Nearing has it."

There were numerous professors whom Mencken admired for vastly different reasons from those which brought praise to Nearing. The charge that he was flatly antiacademic is without basis in fact. He had long been an admirer of Georg Brandes (Ernest Boyd first heard of Mencken from Brandes, who, in Denmark, was reading the American iconoclast and finding in him a kindred spirit). He also greatly admired Gilbert Murray and, naturally, many of the European philologists, especially Otto Jespersen. But it was the American professor who primarily interested him, and when he found one that deserved praise he made the fact known. He began his criticism for July, 1919, by listing the volumes he was reviewing for the month, pointing out that several of the best ones were by professors. He was especially impressed by John Livingston Lowes's *Convention and Revolt in Poetry*. The thought that a college professor could write so well sent him, as he put it, into his praying chamber to ask forgiveness for his oft repeated generalization that American professors were dull fellows. He was amazed to learn that Dr. Lowes sat in a chair at Harvard, and asked him to hide his book under the bed. "If it ever gets about that a man so intelligent is on the faculty there will be calls for a general court-martial and the abatement of the outrage." There is in all this a tone that is almost mellow, at least compared to the comments he made on professors only two years before in *A Book of Prefaces*. There he objected violently to the academic remoteness in American criticism.

> The American critic of beautiful letters, in his common in-carnation, is no more than a talented sophomore, or, at best, a somewhat absurd professor. He suffers from a palpable lack of solid preparation; he has no background of moving and illuminating experience behind him; his soul has not sufficiently adventured among masterpieces, nor among men. Imagine a

Taine or a Sainte-Beuve or a Macaulay—man of the world, veteran of philosophies, "lord of life"—and you imagine his complete antithesis.

The American manifestation of the critic knew only the fossil literature taught in colleges. Before the academician presumed to "teach" a work, it had to be dead. Worst of all, he appeared to be totally ignorant of what went forward in other lands.

To Mencken, critics of former days had been little better. Emerson, though "a diligent drinker from German spigots," was always an amateur in literary criticism. Lowell was even worse; all that remains of him is a somewhat smoky pleasantness. Poe was certainly the most penetrating critic of his day, far more original than either Emerson or Lowell; and yet he was, according to Mencken, enormously ignorant of good books, and he was never free from a congenital vulgarity of taste, so painfully visible in the strutting of his style. Nevertheless, Mencken felt that Poe earned as a critic much of the excess praise he got as a romancer and a poet. Though he never thought very highly of Poe's poetry or short stories, Mencken considered him second only to Mark Twain as a literary figure or force. In 1911 he objected to critics who compared Poe to Leonid Andreev. The realism of Andreev, especially *The Seven Who Were Hanged*, was far superior, Mencken believed, to the best of Poe's tales. "Poe was a romanticist—and romance, like a warm bath, is a thing to be enjoyed and forgotten. But Andreev is a realist—and realism sticks." Mencken never had admired the gothic prose of Poe's stories. In his June, 1909, criticism he stated that Poe's influence on the style of southern writers had been a curse. "I have no doubt that [Poe] sat up many a night trying to think of some cataclysmic variation of the too simple phrase, 'He said.' The writers of the South, brought up at the Poe altar, too often borrow his bass drum and gold lace. The result is a vast excess of parts of speech, a surfeit of polysyllables, an appalling flapping of wings." Having lived all his life within a mile of Poe's tomb, Mencken admitted to having been "hopelessly infected with the loathsome bacilli." In an effort to cure himself, he had swallowed enormous doses of Huxley and others, but the taint remained: "If I try to write, 'The dog bit a negro,' I find myself swallowed up by, 'A terrified Afro-American was partially ingested by the sinister dachshund.' It is a horrible affliction, believe me, and only by eternal vigilance and heroic physicking may one get even temporary relief."

Actually, Mencken was a good deal more interested in Poe the man than in Poe the artist. Reviewing Joseph Wood Krutch's *Edgar Allan Poe: A Study in Genius* (1926), he clearly showed that his interest was more psychological, or pathological, than literary. Agreeing with Krutch's thesis (Krutch did with Poe much the same thing that Brooks had done with Twain a few years before), Mencken remarked that it was impossible to separate the man from the work: "The man simply poured himself into his writings. They have only the remotest sort of contact with anything external to his own singular personality. They are full of the strange horrors that beset him; there is little in them else." The review justifies, at least in part, those who felt that Mencken was in many ways like Poe, both in his assets and in his weaknesses. Numerous writers—like Edmund Wilson, Vincent O'Sullivan, Carl Van Doren, Percy Boynton—have compared the two critics, some by way of pointing out Mencken's greatness, others to exemplify his shortcomings. In this particular review, Mencken is at his worst when he remarks that Poe's "criticism, for all its acumen, is couched mainly in bombast." It would be impossible to divorce style and content more completely. He continues:

> His poetry is popular in proportion as it justifies Emerson's sneer: to wit, that it consists of jingles. But Poe himself remains. There is something titanic in his tragedy. It breaks through his ornate and rococo sentences; it overwhelms his nonsensical theories and idle pedantries; it gives an austere dignity to even his worst jingles. It will always bring a crowd to his booth— a crowd fascinated and yet a bit uneasy. There have been far greater artists, but there have been few more glamorous men.[7]

This is excellent prose, but one wonders what the "something titanic" is; Mencken leaves too much unsaid here to be very convincing. Still, his often repeated remark that Poe's criticism was superior to his other writings can hardly be denied. According to Mencken, because Poe wanted people to admire him as a linguist, a scientist, and a philosopher, when he was none of them, his genuine worth as a critic has been overlooked. A better reason is that criticism is the least memorable of all the arts. I am convinced, for one, that T. S. Eliot's criticism is superior to his poetry; I am further convinced, however, that Eliot will be remembered as a poet long after his criticism is forgotten.

After the nineteen-twenties brought an unprecedented popularity to Mencken (he was generally regarded as the most influential man of letters America ever produced), there was no longer a need to bemoan the presence of the Prof. Drs. in the field of criticism. They had lost their old power to the journalistic critics who either stemmed from or actually followed Mencken or Ezra Pound, who was himself influenced by Mencken. A few of the leading critics were Carl Van Doren, Van Wyck Brooks, Ben Hecht, Edmund Wilson, Ernest Boyd, Burton Rascoe, Ludwig Lewisohn, Francis Hackett. Wilson, for example, wrote in 1943 that by the time he came upon the literary scene, *circa* 1919, the battle for freedom in the arts had been won: "I was myself a beneficiary of the work that had been done by Mencken and others."[8] In this period Mencken himself had all but given up literary criticism; he was interested in other matters. In one of his more skeptical moments, he reminisced:

> During the decade 1910–1920 I was chiefly engaged in literary controversies, and so my politics were aside from the issue. But when the great wave of idealism engulfed the United States in 1917, I was at once bawled out as a German spy, and open demands were made that my purely aesthetic heresies be put down by the *Polizei*. One of my opponents, in those days, was an eminent college professor [Stuart Sherman], now unhappily deceased. He not only attempted to dispose of my literary judgments by arguing that they were inspired by the Kaiser; he even made the same charge against the works of the writers I was currently whooping up. And so did many of his learned colleagues. It was not easy to meet this onslaught by logical devices; logic, in those days, was completely adjourned, along with the Bill of Rights. Moreover, there was considerable plausibility in the general charge. So I attempted no defense; it is, indeed, against my nature to take the defensive. Instead, I launched into an elaborate effort to prove that all college professors, regardless of their politics, were hollow and preposterous asses, and to this business I brought up all the ancient and horrifying devices of the art of rhetoric.[9]

The joke, as it turned out, was on the professors. After 1918 it was no longer damaging to associate Mencken with the Hohenzollerns.

The worst thing about the controversy was that it went too far. Never one to flay a dead horse, Mencken ceased to revile the Prof. Drs. once the war mania had quieted. Various other controversialists, however, took up the jehad, and in a short while the battle raged from coast to coast. As Mencken put it:

> It got far beyond anything I had myself dreamed of. Indignant publicists, quite unknown to me, began grouping all professors with chiropractors, congressmen, and spiritualists as quacks. In dozens of colleges large and small, north, east, south, and west, the students began holding meetings and flinging insults at their tutors. Scores of college papers, for flouting them in contumacious terms, had to be suppressed. In several great institutions of learning the thing actually reached the form of physical assault.[10]

When the smoke cleared from the battlements, the professor, once a highly respected man, found himself a sort of questionable character. Mencken agreed that in many cases the Prof. Dr. was a lightweight. (Who could forget Shaw's famous, though unfair, remark: "Those who can, do; those who can't, teach"?) But there were many innocents who suffered in the war, which was not of their making. As he sympathized, Mencken also mocked: "Many an honest and God fearing professor, laboriously striving to ram his dismal nonsense into the progeny of Babbitts, is bombarded with ribald spitballs as a result of a controversy which began outside his ken and speedily got far beyond the issue between the original combatants." It is noteworthy that Mencken enlisted articles from several of these "honest and God fearing" professors for the *American Mercury,* which was widely read by university teachers and was to a large extent tailored to fit academic tastes (see M. K. Singleton's *H. L. Mencken and the American Mercury Adventure* [1962]). Especially did he solicit the professors for articles on the physical and natural sciences, architecture, music, painting, literary history, history, philology, sociology, and anthropology.[11] But for the English teacher, Mencken never had much respect—that is, as a class or general group. In *The American Language* he examined at length the antipathy of the typical native teacher of English for American, which the pedagogue considered as nothing more than an unseemly corruption of English. After paying tribute to Noah Webster for protesting against this pedantry, which "continues to be cherished among the rank and file of American pedagogues, from the kinder-garten up to the graduate school," Mencken remarked: "In the American colleges and high-schools there is no faculty so weak as the English faculty. It is the common catch-all for aspirants to the birch who are too lazy or too feeble in intelligence to acquire any sort of exact knowledge, and the professional incompetence of its typical ornament is matched only by his hollow cocksureness." Unfortunately, as the best (and only the best) English teachers will admit, there is a great deal of truth in this indictment.

Although he ardently loved controversy, Mencken was not at all sure that it succeeded in unearthing many new truths. To begin with, verbal warfare tended to allow the contestants too much fighting room. The historic battle between Huxley and Wilberforce, for example, began with Huxley trying to prove that Darwin's *Origin of Species* was a sound book and ended with Bishop Wilber-force trying to prove that Huxley's grandfather was a gorilla.

II

The timorousness of the Prof. Dr. and the self-righteousness of the Puritan are nowhere more evident than in the abortive attempts of the New Humanists to set up moral criteria for literature and life. First of all, one must not confuse the New Humanists (who con-sidered themselves classicists) with the historical humanism which warred so effectively with medieval scholasticism and became the moving spirit of the Renaissance in the fourteenth century. Where the Middle Ages placed immense emphasis on asceticism and the philosophy that life was a mere training period for citizenship in the City of God built in the world of spirit, humanism emphasized man's life in this world. Art was deemed beautiful by the humanists in proportion to its exactness in depicting man. As the humanists tended toward paganism in philosophy and art, the power of the Catholic Church dwindled. And society became more and more urban as capitalism replaced feudalism. The humanists, to quote George Santayana, "believed in the sufficient natural goodness of mankind, a goodness humanized by frank sensuality and a wink at all amiable vices." They were, according to Santayana, much nearer the revolutionaries of today—that is, the radicals of the first decades of the twentieth century—than they were to the merely academic people who continue thrashing little boys into reading Latin verses.

It seems evident, indeed, from the beliefs of the New Humanists that they were much closer to scholastic thought than to classicism. Whereas the humanists of yore were rebels, the New Humanists were not just conservatives, but outright reactionaries. Whereas the former immersed themselves in the splendor and welter of life, the latter shrank from life as from a scrofulous disease, usually retreating behind academic walls to indulge their timid souls in hair-shirt asceticism. Rabelais was the epitome of humanism; Paul Elmer More and Irving Babbitt were the guiding lights of New Humanism. They were related in much the same sense that black and white are related.

Actually, there are several different sects of humanism, as there are of most -*isms*. There is the scientific humanism of John Dewey and Julian Huxley and Corliss Lamont. There is also a Christian humanism, similar in many respects to the humanism of Babbitt and More, but differing in that it grounds its philosophy on Christ rather than on "the best that has been thought and said in the world." The most noteworthy exponent of this branch is Jacques Maritain, who discusses his beliefs at length in *True Humanism*. A third order is proletarian humanism, which is based on the writings of Marx and Lenin—a branch which was most vocal in the nineteen-thirties but has maintained silence of late either for lack of recruits or governmental restrictions. Precise classification is always risky, of course. For one thing, the classified individual is almost sure to complain that his uniqueness has suffered injury. "Probably a crab," William James once remarked, "would be filled with a sense of outrage if he could hear us class it without ado or apology as a crustacean, and thus dispose of it. 'I am no such thing,' it would say; 'I am *myself, myself* alone.'"

New Humanism found roots in the writings of W. C. Brownell, long-time literary adviser to the Scribner firm (1888–1928), who formulated the principles of the conservatives as early as 1900. Brownell rarely concerned himself with living literature; rather, he was a critic of critics and, foremost, an aesthetician. Insisting that all great literature was the result of rigid rules and standards, he believed no aesthetic valid which did not stand on the Christian ethic of character, the Platonic doctrine of form, and the Aristotelian reliance upon reason. He was, in many ways, the diametrical opposite of Joel Spingarn, the nihilist of aestheticians. These two men simply went to extremes in opposite directions, in much the same manner as Peter and Jack in Swift's *A Tale of a Tub*.

Although Brownell gave humanism much of its philosophy of negation, it remained for More and Babbitt to lay down in their periodic attempts at definition (the New Humanists spent a great deal of their energy trying to define themselves) the few vague principles of the order. The two younger men first met at Harvard in 1892, when they constituted Professor Charles R. Lanman's class in Sanskrit for a semester. Babbitt insisted all his life that the chief ills of the world were a result of naturalism and its sentimental cousin Romanticism. The only way out of the labyrinth into which modern life had fallen was a return to classicism, which would make humanity distinct from both nature and God. Nor should God and nature be thought of as one. The pantheistic tendencies of the romantics were just as much in error as were the naturalists who confused, or *fused,* man with nature. In brief, Babbitt preached a type of Calvinism very similar to that of the seventeenth-century Puritans. The Renaissance humanists, according to Babbitt, had correctly separated man from God (an oversimplification if not an untruth, since the scholastics before them had most certainly never said that God was within man but had believed instead that God was a separate entity), but they had then committed the error of identifying Him with nature. Bacon was one of the primary offenders insofar as he was a founder of naturalism; Rousseau was even worse, for he was the father of Romanticism. One may wonder what effect, if any, Darwin and his disciples had in this debate over man's place in the universe. The God-*and*-nature-*and*-man advocates found it expedient to ignore the facts of biological evolution, of course. There can be no doubt, however, that Babbitt scorned the best American writers of the twenties—including Lewis, Dreiser, O'Neill, Dos Passos— because of their naturalistic identification of man with his surroundings. Babbitt could not consider the writers after the genteel tradition at all decorous, and, as he put it: "Decorum is supreme for the humanist even as humility takes precedence over all other virtues in the eyes of the Christian."

In "The Critic and American Life," an essay which appeared in the February, 1928, issue of the *Forum,* Babbitt began by quoting the *Encyclopaedia Britannica* that Mencken was "the greatest critical force in America." He then quoted from Mencken's "Footnote on

Criticism" ("The critic is first and last simply trying to express himself . . ."), insisting that Mencken had not understood the meaning of "criticism," which was nothing more than the setting of standards. After remarking that we need more "discrimination" and less "creation" in America today, Babbitt brings in Socrates on his side, concluding: "It is, therefore, unfortunate that at a time like the present, which plainly calls for a Socrates, we should instead have got a Mencken." Babbitt then attacks Mencken's beliefs on democracy, going on to equate, quite wrongly, Nietzschean hardness with "an opportunity to live temperamentally" (and Nietzsche revolves agonizingly in his grave).

> As a matter of fact, if one sees in the escape from traditional controls merely an opportunity to live temperamentally, it would seem advantageous to pass promptly from the idealistic to the Nietzschean phase, sparing oneself as many as possible of the intermediary disillusions. It is at all events undeniable that the rise of Menckenism has been marked by a certain collapse of romantic idealism in the political field and elsewhere.

So, Babbitt says, Mencken was not all bad after all: he had helped bring about the collapse of the romantic dark tower. Also evident in the quotation above is the murkiness of Babbitt's thought. "Idealism" is good, but "romantic" idealism is bad. Considering Babbitt's vague use of the language, one should not be surprised that he attracted disciples—for a brief time. Objecting to what he called "naturalistic realism," as distinguished from both "humanistic realism" and "religious realism" (whatever that means), Babbitt assailed the intent and purpose, as he understood them to be, of the novels of Lewis, Dreiser, Anderson, Sandburg, Stephen Crane, and Dos Passos (*Manhattan Transfer* was depicted as an extreme example of "cluttered incoherency"). Finally, all the bad American artists were just following in the wake of European—particularly French—writers of a generation before. "Mr. Dreiser reminds one of Zola and his school. The technique of Mr. Dos Passos recalls that of the Goncourts. Our experimenters in free verse have followed in the wake not merely of Walt Whitman but of the French symbolists, and so on." Babbitt was correct, of course, in assuming that American writers of the period were under French influence, but whether that was altogether bad has not been established with much certainty.

It is noteworthy that Mencken did not answer this attack; he seldom answered his many critics—directly, at any rate. Rather it was a member of the Mencken party, Howard Mumford Jones, who broke lances with the Humanist. In "Professor Babbitt Cross-Examined," Jones began by refusing to place on Mencken, as Babbitt had done, all the blame for the errors of his followers (Babbitt held Mencken responsible for Anderson, Dreiser, and Lewis, among others). Objecting to Babbitt's vague and "romantic" use of terms, Jones accused Babbitt of indulging himself in the very thing he sought to combat. He pointed out the illogical nature of Babbitt's remarks on contemporary Americans, on Puritans, on Christian teachings, and so on. He also showed how Babbitt failed to see the close resemblance between the gloom of Sophocles (a good guy) and the gloom of Dreiser (a bad guy). Mencken, incidentally, had remarked that particular resemblance ten years before in *A Book of Prefaces*. Moreover, like most contemners of the present and idolaters of the past, Babbitt had allowed his sentimentality to overwhelm his intellect.

> Mr. Babbitt is as much of a day-dreamer as Jean-Jacques Rousseau. He wants to return to Buddha and the *bhong* tree, to Socrates and the ilex, not as these things were, but as he romantically imagines them to have been. Like the Romanticist, he dreams of a mankind released from the bonds of deterministic naturalism, idling away the happy hours in eloquent discourse of the eternal verities. He is as sentimental as Bernardin de St. Pierre.[12]

It was, so felt the New Humanist, through the "will to refrain" that man acquired happiness. Also, virtue was made to reside exclusively in the exercise of this "will" or abnegation. Only the ascetic could be blind to the fact that it is also possible to be virtuous and happy by exercising some will that is the opposite of the will to refrain. Indeed, if virtue is to have any meaning at all, that meaning must come from and be based on *acting*. For all that the abstainers might say to the contrary, morality is dynamic in nature, never static. It is unthinkable that "good" and "evil" may be discerned in stasis, where there is no action. The equating of virtue with abstinence has the ludicrous smack of the Sunday-school lesson. To defend the indefensible, Babbitt enlisted the names of numerous historical figures who simply would not fit the mold; for example, Aristotle and Sophocles. He even went so far as to insist that the highly tempestuous, passionate Antigone was a model of the will to refrain and was a true-blue Humanist![13]

The same rigid Calvinism that led Babbitt to scorn the starving prostitute as a bastard offspring of Rousseau led his friend More to defend the Colorado strikebreakers in 1914 on the ground that property rights, to the civilized man, were more important than the right to life. More based much of his philosophy on a nebulous concept which he called the "inner check." (About the only difference between the "will to refrain" and the "inner check" is a difference in *tone:* the former has a philosophical smack; the latter, a psychological ring. Both phrases have a moralistic meaning of a Thoushalt-not variety.) All life, to More, existed in the two realms of pure grace and pure evil. The good man, naturally enough, will always answer an uncompromising No to all manifestations of evil. Hardly a revolutionary doctrine! Good is still better than bad—or at least should be. And, one might add, the gleaming platitude still finds its place in the writings of moralists. An extreme ascetic, almost a hermit, More resembled nothing so much as a medieval monk. He was a thoroughgoing Platonist, always seeking design in the universe, firmly believing in the existence of absolute truths, and always endeavoring, as he put it, "to walk humbly with God, never doubting, whatever befall, that His will is good, and that His law is right." The nature of His will and law remains somewhat obscure.

More, again like Babbitt, refused to acknowledge any literature that identified man with nature, as most of the great literature in the Western world since the time of the Greek tragedians has either implicitly or explicitly done. Modern literature was especially repulsive to him. James Joyce was anathema, just as were the three Americans—Poe, Whitman, and Henry James—who were, according to More, the fathers of the naturalistic movement in this country. In *The Demon of the Absolute* he described Dos Passos' *Manhattan Transfer* (something of a whipping boy for the traditionalists) as "an explosion in a cesspool," never even dreaming that Dos Passos was condemning many of the same social conditions that More had always condemned. Edmund Wilson, one of the severest critics of the Humanists, stated that if Dos Passos had been a second-rate eighteenth-century essayist or the most obscure New England poet (of the seventeenth century), More would have read him sympathetically and thoroughly. As it was, he condemned without having read, or at least understood, Dos Passos. It seems to me that More was the sort of man who loved scholarship but hated literature— certainly not an uncommon breed of man. He also objected strongly to the heresies he found in Alfred North Whitehead's *Science and the Modern World*. Whitehead, it appears, failed to make the necessary distinction between "man" and "thing" in his philosophy —a distinction that all Humanists make.

More's most salient objections to modern literature may be found in his essay "The Modern Current in American Literature," which appeared in the *Forum* for January, 1928, a month before Babbitt's "The Critic and American Life" was published in that journal. More begins by admitting that the subject of his essay forbids him to write about the accomplished literary artists—Edith Wharton, E. A. Robinson, and Robert Frost—since these writers "are not at once both modern and American, in the sense of those who are asking us to sign a new Declaration of Independence in letters." He admits that "Mr. Frost rather shocked us at first by the audacity of his style, [but] it was soon discovered that in spirit he had not escaped from the New England tradition of Miss Jewett and Mrs. Freeman"! Had Frost "escaped," he would, one must assume, be unworthy of consideration.

More, who had by this time evidently read some contemporary literature, divided the "moderns" into two groups: the aesthetics and the realists. Amy Lowell was the leader of the former group, having borrowed her poetic form from Whitman and her practice of "imagism" from the French. Among living aesthetes, James Branch Cabell was best known. Although happy to see Cabell take arms against the realists, More was disturbed by the novelist's interpretation of what "ought to be." Cabell felt that "good" and "evil" were simply aesthetic conventions of romantic origin and further felt that moralism was definitely subsidiary to beauty. More objected that this makes "a divorce between the true in life and the beautiful in art which must spell death to any serious emotion in literature." The realists, unlike Miss Lowell and Cabell, are all uneducated people, principally from the midwestern states. "One of them, indeed, Sinclair Lewis, coming out of Sauk Centre, Minnesota, has a degree from Yale University; but intellectually he is perhaps the crudest member of the group, cruder, for instance, than Theodore Dreiser who got most of his education in the streets of Chicago and from the free libraries of this and that town, or than Sherwood Anderson who apparently owes his acquaintance with the alphabet to the grace of God." Beneath criticism is the man who sneers at the artist who lacks a college degree. In speaking of Dreiser, Masters, Lewis, Anderson, and some others, More descended to name-calling that was frankly petty and puerile; the *ad hominem* argument seldom becomes so fatuous as it did in More's "moral," "Christian," and "aristocratic" blast. (More could never be considered a true aristocrat, according to Mencken's definition of the term—and his definition is the best I know of—because More was hostile to innovations and considered free inquiry unbecoming if not immoral.) It is amusing that while he condemned Anderson's concern with sex, More quoted approvingly Plato's condemnation of the sexual appetites, not realizing, I suppose, that Plato's homosexuality probably accounts in large part for his hatred of normal sexual relationships. It is a well-known fact, after all, that sexual perverts are often highly puritanical; indeed, a loathing for the "filth" of heterosexual love is frequently given by psychoanalysts as a cause for inversion.

In his essay, More paid tribute to Babbitt, just as Babbitt always complimented More. More also praised five or six others—all college professors—and paid homage to W. C. Brownell, a New Yorker whose existence proved "that something intellectually fine can come out of our Babylon on the Hudson." More lamented that professors did not have wider audiences and that universities were often apathetic toward what was going on at the time—a rather strange remark to come from a man who seemed to be oblivious to what went on in his own day, at least until in the late nineteen-twenties, when he began condemning the leading writers of the period. Meanwhile, in the absence of leadership from the universities, "the critical ideas of the immature and ignorant are formed by brawling vulgarians like H. L. Mencken, who in stentorian tones champions any crude product of modernism which appeals to their own half-educated taste."

Actually, Mencken never really came to grips with the Humanists in the sense that he battled other offspring of Puritanism. By the time they were making much stir in the world of letters, he had all but given up literary criticism. He did, however, attend to the opening pleas and protests of the gloomy professors (almost all New Humanists, from beginning to end of their brief incarnation, have been college professors or else, as Mencken said, the "colicky sophomores who admire them"). The only Humanist who ventured outside the cloistered walls was Stuart Sherman, and no sooner was he beyond the gates than he refused to go back in again. Sherman's defection from Humanism undoubtedly added to the pessimism of More and Babbitt, for in him they saw a knight in shining armor. Although he disagreed with almost all of More's basic ideas, Mencken always rather admired the man's learning, narrow though it was, and his steadfastness in holding to his rigid beliefs. Indeed, he tried to provoke More into coming out of his cave, but to no avail. More spoke of Mencken briefly and acidly, referring to him as "the wolf," but he could not be enticed into the vulgar world which Mencken delightfully inhabited. Reviewing More's *With the Wits* in 1920, Mencken pointed out that the book was typical scholarship: correct and virtuous, but deadly dull. Like most scholars, More spent too much time collecting information and too little time digesting it.

> His essays on Pope, Swift and Lady Mary Wortley Montagu say absolutely nothing new. In his essay on Aphra Behn, the Elinor Glyn of the seventeeth century, he wastes a lot of space debating with an English pundit the question whether La Behn ever actually visited Surinam and whether her father was ever actually governor of that colony, as she herself used to maintain. Both More and his antagonist base their arguments upon intuition, word-juggling and the doctrine of probabilities. It seems to have occurred to neither of them to inspect the colonial records of Surinam, probably easily accessible in London. There is no sign that either has ever made the attempt. A good deal of so-called scholarship, especially in England, is grounded upon just such stupidity. It is simply medieval text-chewing. It gets nowhere, and is not even amusing.
>
> But More himself is, to me at least, a very interesting man. He is a perfect specimen of the civilized Puritan—pulled in the one direction by the lascivious lures of the bozart, and in the other direction by his inherited fears of beauty. One finds him, on the one hand, getting a sneaking sort of joy out of Beaumont and Fletcher, Swift and even La Behn; one finds him, on the other hand, full of moral indignation against such fellows as Oscar Wilde and Lionel Johnson. He actually argues, in all seriousness, that Wilde was a product of German influences![14]

In his reviews of More's books, Mencken chided the highly sophisticated professor for his consistent refusal either to learn anything or to forget anything. More fought and refought the battle

174 H. L. MENCKEN, LITERARY CRITIC

between the classicists and the romanticists, certainly a fruitless waste of energy, year in and year out, just as he warred against all systems of flux—pragmatism, science, rationalism, naturalism. To that enterprise, as his numerous books bear testament, he brought a vast amount of learning and the diligence of a German professor. But of the literature of his own century, he seemed to know nothing and to care less. And this man was for years editor of the *Nation*. "So far as his books offer any evidence, he has never heard of Dreiser and the Dreiser following, or of Amy Lowell and her janissaries, or old George Bernard Shaw, or of any of the new novelists in England, or even of Joseph Conrad, Thomas Hardy or George Moore, or even, God help us all, of Ibsen."[15] At the time Mencken wrote this, in 1921, More had shown no evidence of being aware of the great changes taking place in world literature; but a few years later More made it clear that precisely the writers Mencken mentioned were those whom he most detested. In his *A New England Group* (1921), More did make two rather interesting admissions: first, he admitted that Nietzsche, whom he had formally damned a few years before, was actually not so bad after all. As Mencken put it: "Now he salutes and almost embraces the brute." (A good insight into More's mind may be had from reading his little book on Nietzsche, published in 1912, and his long article on T. H. Huxley, which appeared in *The Drift of Romanticism*, published in 1913. Interestingly enough, More also included the Nietzsche "book" in *The Drift of Romanticism*. That volume, which is perhaps the best single statement of his major ideas, ends with a long essay on dualism in modern philosophy.) Mencken "forgave" More for not having understood Nietzsche before and remarked the similarities in the two men's thought: they were both conservatives, both ascetics, both believers in the Be-hard philosophy; and yet diametrically opposite, Mencken might have added, in that the German Antichrist forever faced life and shouted Yea! while More turned away from life and murmured Nay.

The second admission, which Mencken gleefully pounced on, was More's interest in the spook-chasing of the aged publisher and novelist Henry Holt. Though a bit cautious, More nevertheless was impressed by the astounding evidence of the mediums and considered Holt's quest one of high dignity. Mencken did not think this credulity at all strange. After all, did not Jonathan Edwards believe in witches, and was he not, to quote More, "the greatest theologian and philosopher yet produced in this country"?

> Assuming that man has an immortal soul—a gaseous part that resists both the metabolism of the worm and the hot coals of the crematory—isn't it reasonable to assume further that this soul may occasionally long to tread its old paths on the earth, and that, so longing, it may make the attempt? The first assumption is certainly one that no defender of the New England enlightenment can reject. Jonathan Edwards not only believed in witches; he also believed in souls, and in spooks to boot. Thus it is not surprising to find More disinclined to flout the last-named.[16]

As the Shelburne Essays were published, Mencken read them and noted that nothing new was to be found in any of them. Hell might bubble and Rome fall, but More would remain aloof in his ivory tower, completely deaf to the roars of the Goths and Huns at the gates below. More distrusted democracy as much as Mencken did, but for different reasons. To More democracy meant that the mob man would possess too much freedom, when he needed more restraint, order, discipline. As Ludwig Lewisohn remarked, More wanted the populace to be obedient and go to church on Sunday, whereas Mencken was willing to let the boobs get drunk on Saturday night. More was a medievalist who insisted that freedom allowed the rabble to become dangerous; Mencken was a libertarian who insisted that every man had the right to be his own ass—so long, of course, as his brays did not keep the man next door awake. Mencken summed up the Morean gospel:

> Year after year he simply iterates and reiterates his misty protests, seldom changing so much as a word. Between his first volume and his last there is not the difference between Gog and Magog. Steadily, ploddingly, vaguely, he continues to preach the gloomy gospel of tightness and restraint. He was against "the electric thrill of freer feeling" when he began, and he will be against it on that last gray day—I hope it long post-dates my own hanging—when the ultimate embalmer sneaks upon him with velvet tread, and they haul down the flag to half-staff at Princeton, and the readers of the New York *Evening Journal* note that an obscure somebody named Paul E. More is dead.[17]

Humanism in America has never succeeded in spreading beyond the groves of academe, and for good reasons. It is eminently pedagogical in nature; it is totally reactionary; it denies any relationship between art and life; it endeavors to police the emotions in the manner of a Calvinistic deacon. Certainly one may still hear of the Humanists, but to do so he must first register in a graduate seminar in a large university. Which is to say, he will hear of Humanism from the historians; it is a fossil to be studied in the laboratory. For a brief period, however, at the close of the nineteen-twenties, the Humanists made enough of a stir to issue a symposium, *Humanism and America* (1930), which moved the young liberals to reply with *The Critique of Humanism* (1930) and George Santayana with *The Genteel Tradition at Bay* (1931). It is revealing of Mencken's decline as a critical force that he was not asked to take part in the counterattack, even though he was still the critic most frequently taken to task by the Humanists. Mencken did, however, review both the collections, praising the *Critique* and satirizing the Humanist tome. Rather than paraphrase Mencken's *American Mercury* review, entitled "Pedagogues A-Flutter," I include it entire:

> This collection of essays is a manifesto for a movement called, by its proponents, Humanism, "which," so Dr. Foerster says in his preface, "is rapidly becoming a word to conjure with." It is not, it appears, a new movement, but goes back, like Free-masonry, to a remote and hoary antiquity, and has been supported, at one time or another, "by persons as various as Homer, Phideas, Plato, Aristotle, Confucius, Buddha, Jesus, Paul, Virgil, Horace, Dante, Shakespeare, Milton, Goethe; more recently, by Matthew Arnold in England and Emerson and Lowell in America." But at the moment, lacking any such whales, it is in the hands of a group of American pedagogues, of whom the imperial wizard is Prof. Irving Babbitt of Harvard, the grand goblin Prof. Paul Elmer More of Princeton, and the supreme sinister kligraph Prof. Foerster himself. The present pronunciamento embraces fifteen essays, three of them by the learned men I have just named and the rest by various lesser initiates, including eight more professors, an advanced poet, two college boys, and the author of *Waldo Frank: a Study.*
>
> In so large a collection there is necessarily some difference of opinion, both as to what is wrong with the world and what ought to be done about it. Prof. More seems to be most disturbed by Dr. A. N. Whitehead's somewhat ribald speculations about the nature of God and by the transcendental prose printed in the magazine called *transition.* His brother, Prof. Louis Trenchard More, denounces Whitehead too, but is also against Einstein and Planck, not to mention John B. Watson. Prof. G. R. Elliott of Amherst rages against "softening God's laws" and pleads for "a

rediscovery of their severity"; he believes that "the two most potent and distinguished personalities . . . that have so far appeared in the English literature of the Twentieth Century" are the late Baron Friedrich von Hügel and Prof. Babbitt. Prof. Thompson prints an earnest essay on the nature of tragedy: it would get him an A in any course in Freshman English. Prof. Robert Shafer of the University of Cincinnati compares Dreiser to Aeschylus and proves that Aeschylus was the better when it came to asserting "his faith that Moral Law uncompromisingly governs the life of man." Prof. Harry H. Clark of Wisconsin shows that the only recent American novel worth a hoot is Dorothy Canfield's *The Brimming Cup,* and argues that the only way to get better ones is for "our interpreters of literature in college and university" to put their heads together, and show the boys "the unerring congruency to human nature demanded of great art." And so on down to Mr. Gorham B. Munson, author of the monograph on Waldo Frank, who first shows that criticism is in a sad state in America, and then "takes the risk"—his own words—"of nominating Matthew Arnold as having the build of a great critic." Alas, Mr. Munson is modest!

All this, I fear will strike the reader of these lines as mainly rubbish, and that, in truth, is what it is. The only contributors to the volume who go to the trouble of stating plainly what Humanism is are Dr. Foerster and Prof. Babbitt. Dr. Babbitt, who has been in the movement for years, says that it represents an effort to set up a criterion of values which "the phenomenal world does not supply"—in other words, to add intuition to experience. The trouble with such a fellow, say, as Dreiser, is that he simply describes the world as he sees it, and lets it go at that. Ask him what meaning there is in the story of Jennie Gerhardt and he tells you that he doesn't know. Dr. Babbitt believes that, at least for many men, this is insufficient. They want some assurance, some certainty, some answer to the riddle. As for Dr. Babbitt himself, he believes that it is to be found in "religious insight." "For my own part," he says, "I range myself unhesitatingly on the side of the supernatural." And he believes that it would be a good thing to round up all persons who think the same way, that they may "move toward a communion" and become "an element of social order and stability." Dr. Foerster inclines the same way. He believes that man lives "on three planes, the natural, the human and the religious," and that Humanism "should be confined to a working philosophy seeking to make a resolute distinction between man and nature and between man and the divine."

In all this, of course, there is nothing new, though I fear Dr. Foerster is going beyond the facts when he says that Homer, Shakespeare and Goethe believed it. The same thing precisely has been preached in all the Little Bethels of the world since the invention of original sin, and is even today the theme of nine evangelical sermons out of ten—that is, when they deal with religion at all. More, it is at the bottom of all the secular schemes for getting rid of uncomfortable realities by conjuring up something grander and gaudier—for example, Rotarianism. George F. Babbitt, in fact, was quite as sound a Humanist as Dr. Foerster: he too yearned and panted for a sweet and simple arcanum and could see something divine in a bank cashier, or even a lawyer. Nor is it hard to understand why the Humanist theology should appeal powerfully to young college instructors, and to the colicky sophomores who admire them. It is the natural and inevitable refuge of all timorous and third-rate men—of all weaklings for whom the struggle with hard facts is unendurable—of all the nay-sayers of Nietzsche's immortal scorn. The hot sun is too much for them: they want an asylum that is reassuringly dark and damp, with incense burning and the organ playing soft and delicate hymns.

The demand for that asylum is couched in mellifluous terms, but it remains nonsense. The progress of the human race is not forwarded by any such vague and witless blather. It is forwarded by extending the range of man's positive knowledge, by grappling resolutely with facts, by facing life, not like a schoolma'm, but like a man. With that business the finishers of bond salesmen have no more to do today than their melancholy predecessors had to do in the past. It is the enterprise of far better men—most of them, though they may not always know it, creative artists. It is an enterprise demanding the highest capacities of mankind, and so it is naturally not comprehensible to campus Pollyannas.[18]

Within a few years the Humanists had been pretty much forgotten. Indeed, they affected the literature of the time only insofar as they increased reader interest in the books they bitterly opposed. It is also doubtful that many people in 1930 took Seward Collins, editor of the Humanist organ *The Bookman*, seriously when he wrote that Stuart Sherman had effectively annihilated Mencken back in 1917. It is interesting to read the remarks of Collins on Mencken; they express a hatred that, at times, borders on the pathological. There can be no doubt that Mencken was by far the best-hated writer in the little world of New Humanism.

III

It is generally believed that Mencken was prejudiced against the South. Nothing could be further from the truth. Actually, he preferred the southerner, as a man, to any other "regional" American. And for this reason, if for no other, he condemned the South unmercifully for its false pride, for its subservience to charlatans of all sorts (especially political and theological quacks), for its lethargy, for its artistic sterility. In his birching of the southern posterior, one detects something of the father chastising an errant and torpid son.

In "The Sahara of the Bozart," his most violent and telling excoriation of the South, first published in the New York *Evening Mail* in November, 1917, then revised and lengthened for the *Smart Set* of the same month, and finally expanded again for *Prejudices: Second Series* (1920), Mencken challenged the South to answer him if it could. First of all, he let it be known that he was a southerner. "I regard the surrender of General Robert E. Lee as the most calamitous human event since the discovery of America. I would rather be chained by the leg in the common jail of Yazoo City, Miss., fed only upon hoecake and coca-cola, than smothered in violets by all the gals of Boston."[19] This was quite obviously adding insult to injury to the average Confederate. Georgians, for example, were intensely proud of Asa G. Candler, the inventor of Coca-Cola; of Frank L. Stanton, a Georgia poet; of Mrs. Raynes, the first to promote a common United Daughters of the Confederacy; of Mrs. C. Helen Plane, the first to suggest a state historian of the United Daughters of the Confederacy; of Mrs. F. R. Goulding, the first to suggest putting to music Heber's "From Greenland's Icy Mountains"; and they were righteously proud of the fact that the first Sunday school was opened in Savannah. But for the Bolshevik Jew Mencken to claim membership in the southern fraternity was too much. After the appearance of the *Smart Set* article in 1917, a leading southern newspaper printed a long denunciation of Mencken's father, then dead nearly twenty years, assailing him as an ignorant foreigner of dubious origin, inhabiting "the Baltimore ghetto." Incidentally, the delusion that Mencken was Jewish persisted throughout the nineteen-twenties, and he did nothing to correct it. For several years he was listed in the Jewish *Who's Who* and was boisterously delighted every time the book came out. One of the most unwittingly comic aspersions of Mencken's "race" was made by G. K. Chesterton, who, after calling Mencken "a clever and better Jew," summed his philosophy up as "the sort of nihilistic pride which belongs to a man with a sensitive race and a dead religion."

In the finished version of "The Sahara of the Bozart," by now something of a classic, Mencken asserted that the South was incredibly sterile:

> Down there a poet is now almost as rare as an oboe-player, a dry-point etcher or a metaphysician. It is, indeed, amazing to contemplate so vast a vacuity. One thinks of the interstellar spaces, of the colossal reaches of the mythical ether. Nearly the whole of Europe could be lost in that stupendous region of fat farms, shoddy cities and paralyzed cerebrums: one could throw in France, Germany and Italy, and still have room for the British Isles. And yet, for all its size and all its wealth and all the "progress" it babbles of, it is almost as sterile, artistically, intellectually, culturally, as the Sahara Desert. There are single acres in Europe that house more first-rate men than all the states south of the Potomac; there are probably single square miles in America. If the whole of the late Confederacy were to be engulfed by a tidal wave tomorrow, the effect upon the civilized minority of men in the world would be but little greater than that of a flood on the Yang-tse-kiang. It would be impossible in all history to match so complete a drying-up of a civilization.[20]

Mencken admitted that there had been, in bygone days, a civilization down there, despite the Baptist and Methodist barbarism that reigns there now. Down to the Civil War, the main hatchery of ideas was in the South. It was there that the first signs of an American aristocracy were evident. Compared to the New England shopkeepers and theologians, the ante-bellum southerners stood out as truly superior men, "of delicate fancy, urbane instinct and aristocratic manner—in brief, superior men—in brief, gentry." The Ur-Confederate delighted in ideas; he was hospitable and tolerant; he possessed the vague thing we call culture.

> But consider the condition of his late empire today. The picture gives one the creeps. It is as if the Civil War stamped out every last bearer of the torch, and left only a mob of peasants on the field. One thinks of Asia Minor, resigned to Armenians, Greeks and wild swine, of Poland abandoned to the Poles. In all that gargantuan paradise of the fourth-rate there is not a single picture gallery worth going into, or a single orchestra capable of playing the nine symphonies of Beethoven, or a single opera-house, or a single theater devoted to decent plays,

or a single public monument (built since the war) that is worth
looking at, or a single workshop devoted to the making of
beautiful things.[21]

The best of the southern states, Mencken believed, was undoubtedly Virginia, and she had no art, no literature, no philosophy,
no mind or aspiration of her own. "Her education has sunk to the
Baptist seminary level; not a single contribution to human knowledge has come out of her colleges in twenty-five years; she spends
less than half upon her schools, *per capita*, than any northern state
spends. In brief, an intellectual Gobi or Lapland." There remained
from its golden days only a ghost of the old aristocracy, infinitely
charming but totally bereft of its former power. It would be as
difficult to imagine a Lee or Washington in present-day Virginia,
Mencken contended, as it would be to imagine a Huxley in Nicara-
gua. Whether or not Mencken included Virginia in the Bible Belt
(Mencken's coinage) was recently discussed in the *Norfolk-Virgin-
ian Pilot* (April 23, 1962). Literate southerners are still vividly
aware of Mencken's assault on the South.

Turning from the Old Dominion to such a commonwealth as
Georgia, one encounters even darker wastes. "Georgia is at once
the home of the cotton-mill sweater and of the most noisy and
vapid sort of chamber of commerce, of the Methodist parson
turned Savonarola and of the lynching bee. A self-respecting European, going there to live, would not only find intellectual stimulation
utterly lacking; he would actually feel a certain insecurity, as if
the scene were the Balkans or the China Coast." While the worst
characteristics of the South were to be found in Georgia and
Mississippi, the best were found in Virginia and, especially, North
Carolina. But in this essay Mencken was more interested in pointing out failings than in applauding successes.

Shortly after "The Sahara of the Bozart" appeared in book form,
Emily Clark brought out the first issue of *The Reviewer* in Richmond. She included a laudatory review of *Prejudices: Second Series*
and pleaded guilty to all the charges Mencken had made against
the South. Mencken wrote Miss Clark and offered her his assistance.
She accepted at once, and Mencken brought such contributors as
Hergesheimer, Rascoe, Boyd, Ellen Glasgow, Frances Newman,
and Gerald W. Johnson to her aid. He paid Miss Clark a visit in

Richmond and at the same time met James Branch Cabell, with whom he had corresponded for some time.

A few months later, he appraised the sudden awakening of the artistic impulse in the South in his *Smart Set* article "The South Begins to Mutter." He stated that the same thing was then going on in the South that went on in the Middle West of the eighteen-nineties; that is, a growing revolt of the more alert and competent youngsters against the constraints of an ancient, formalized, and no longer vital tradition. He further remarked that literary flower-ings, at least in modern history, are usually preceded by a number of little magazines. And three such periodicals were already at large: *The Reviewer* in Richmond, *The Double-Dealer* in New Orleans, and *All's Well* "out in trackless, unexplored Arkansas, a state still almost fabulous." He remarked parenthetically that though he had known New Yorkers who had traveled to Cochin China, Kafiristan, Paraguay, Somaliland, and West Virginia, he had yet to meet one who had penetrated the miasmatic jungles of Arkansas.

Although the mere existence of such magazines augured well, Mencken feared that *The Reviewer* had already gone soft. Its ninth number contained an essay by Cabell attacking three dunderheads —all of them English. There was also an essay that proved Poe was actually a temperance apostle. To such tame enterprises Menc-ken was violently opposed.

> What the South needs is not an onslaught by Cabell upon the tripe-sellers and cheese-mongers of England, but an onslaught by Cabell upon the tripe-sellers and cheese mongers of the South, of Virginia, of Richmond itself. And before an intelligent criticism may be set up down there—the one thing absolutely prerequisite to a civilized literature—the old mawkish criticism of talented literary ladies, mush-headed curates and idiotic pedagogues must be put down by *force majeure*, head-long, cruelly, riotously.[22]

No quarter should be given, heads must fall, the thing must be done with violence and without pity. To make war on the senti-mentalists and barbarians was naturally a dangerous enterprise, for they were firmly entrenched, especially in the South where they had gone unmolested for sixty years. Also, they were supported by both the mob and the forces of conventional respectability. So much the better. A good fight would justify anything. Besides, what could be more exhilarating than unmasking one mountebank after another? "What could be more charming than to tackle a gang of school-marms, male and female, all dressed up as artists—and haul off their disguises one by one?"

No sooner had the magazine hit the newsstands than a flurry of insults issued out of Arkansas. Mencken had described the "miasmatic jungles," the "dead brains," the "idiotic patriots," and the "brummagem mountebanks" of "a state almost fabulous," and he got just what he wanted and expected—an answer. The Little Rock *Daily News* demanded that action be taken against "Menne-ken." He was, according to that paper, the "one remaining relic of the Kultur Klub of the one-time Kaiser Bill." The editor printed a large section of Mencken's article (a very dangerous thing for a Mencken hater to do, since the Mencken *style* often convinces out of proportion to the content), and then asked if this sort of fellow should be allowed to run loose. The Little Rock *Trade Herald* seemed to think that Mencken's behavior was a result of syphilis. The *Herald* printed the most humorous, if not the most effective, answer to Mencken: "In the words of Scott's immortal hero, 'Lay on Macduff, and damned be he that cries "Hold, enough!" ' " There was talk about having Mencken, who was assumed to be an alien, deported; and Washington ambassadors from Arkansas were asked to look into the matter. Unhappily, it was found that Mencken was a native countryman and privileged to stick around as long as he liked.

There can be no doubt that Mencken's "destructive" criticism of the South was a leading cause of the rebirth of writing in that region. Van Wyck Brooks credits "The Sahara of the Bozart" with being the first cause of that reawakening.[23] Writing in the *Georgia Review* (Winter, 1952), Oscar Cargill commented on the powerful effect of Mencken on the South. Employing the most effective tool for breaking through the walls of Philistinism, Mencken proved once again that when pills won't work, a saw should be used, and when the saw won't cut, the critic must resort to the club. The fact that Mencken took to the club like a fish to water is beside the point. Furthermore, it should be obvious that the South was beyond normal medical aid.

Also, it appears evident that the South was as much a prey to Puritan influences as any other section of the country. A rabid, almost insane, Protestantism had completely strangled southern writers and would-be writers for two generations before Mencken tossed his bomb across the river Potomac. In "Puritanism as a Literary Force," he stated that Puritanism was as thoroughly national as the kindred belief in the devil. Moreover, it was in the South, rather than the North, that it took on "its most bellicose and extravagant forms." Mencken claimed that the tendency to locate Puritanism in New England was based, in large part, on a fallacy.

> Berkeley, the last of the Cavaliers, was kicked out of power in Virginia so long ago as 1650. Lord Baltimore, the Proprietor of Maryland, was brought to terms by the Puritans of the Severn in 1657. The Scotch Covenanter, the most uncompromising and unenlightened of all Puritans, flourished in the Carolinas from the start, and in 1698, or thereabout, he was reinforced from New England. In 1757 a band of Puritans invaded what is now Georgia—and Georgia has been a Puritan barbarism ever since.[24]

The early Cavaliers in control of the plantations clung to the seacoast; the inhabitants of the hinterland were the sons and heirs of the same moral philosophy that produced Cotton Mather. When the Civil War destroyed or put to flight the more civilized southerners, the already powerful Philistinism was able to thrive unchecked.

In an extraordinary article he wrote for the *Virginia Quarterly Review* (January, 1935), Mencken again showed his great interest in the problems of the South. "The South Astir" differs vastly from the writing done in the nineteen-twenties, primarily in that it is muted in tone, far less addicted to the frontal-assault method of the earlier essays. And it has, partially for that reason, been far less widely known. Though the essay is more concerned with disputing the theories of the Regionalists, or Fugitives as they were called, than with literature itself, I consider the essay worthy of more than a brief mention. In the opening paragraphs Mencken briefly traced the dogmas of the South, with which he agreed in part, remarking that the region reached its nadir at the beginning of the century with "the emergence of such mephitic shapes as Vardaman and Blease, the stampede to Bryan, the triumph of sentimentality in Southern letters, and the heyday of the evangelist." He then wondered at the end of such pestilences. A minority, certainly, was responsible for the great strides taken forward, but that minority was largely unknown. He attributed the victory of the radicals largely to university professors, particularly those at the University of North Carolina, for it was there that an outspoken antagonism to backward-looking southerners was most evident. It should be remembered, by the way, that Alfred Knopf credits Mencken with having encouraged W. J. Cash to write *The Mind of the South*, by far the best book yet done on the area. Though freedom of thought was anything but widespread in the South, still a minority of opinion was making itself heard throughout the land. "In brief, there is now in the South a minority of opinion that is quite as enlightened as that to be discovered in any other part of the country. To be sure, it seldom if ever prevails, at least on anything properly describable as a large scale, but that is only to say what is true everywhere else. The important thing is that it exists, and has managed to make itself heard, if not actually heeded."

After this disarming preface Mencken went on to say that, unfortunately, free thought was not always the same as wise thought, as was evidenced by the writings of the so-called Agrarians. Although they were earnest young rebels of good faith, possessing a certain kind of intelligence, what they had to offer was "only a little less absurd than the old balderdash that they seek to supplant." They erred in the same manner of social reformers at all times and everywhere: "They conjure up a beautiful Utopia, prove that life in it would be pleasant, and then propose that everyone begin to move in tomorrow. Carried away by their ardor, they overlook the massive detail that it really doesn't exist, and cannot be imagined as existing in the actual world." Mencken considered it absurd to attempt to revive the bucolic economy of the days before the Civil War, thus cutting loose from the industrialism that the Agrarians detested so vehemently. Such Agrarian dreams were comparable to those of some of the Russian experimentalists. Mencken's most severe criticism was reserved for those, particularly Donald Davidson, who insisted that the South cut itself off from the rest of the country and go its own way without regard to the nation at large.

It can, in point of fact, no more cut itself off from the rest of the country than it can cut itself off from the industrial organization of Christendom. Its best interests are bound to be colored and conditioned, not only by the best interests of the North and West, but also by their notions as to what would be good for it, and what it deserves to have. And its canons of taste can no more be formulated in a vacuum than its principles of politics can be so formulated. As Haeckel—a foreigner, and hence a scoundrel—long ago pointed out, the cell does not act, it *re*acts, and that is quite as true of the cells in the human cortex as it is of the amoebae in a test-tube. When the flow of ideas from without is cut off, or hampered by filters and barriers, then the bubbling of ideas within slows down. That, in brief, was what was the matter with the South during the long half-century after the war. Too many cultural Tibets were set up, and too many survive to this day. Certainly it would be folly to try to get rid of them by surrounding the whole region with new Himalayas.

For example, Davidson believed that the Dayton trial was made a farce by the New York atheists and that Tennessee should have been allowed to settle its own problems.

> He seems to believe in all seriousness that the Bryan obscenity at Dayton was a private matter, on which the rest of the country had no right to an opinion. What he overlooks is that it was made an indubitably and even vociferously public matter by the deliberate (if idiotic) act of the very "believers in God" he now defends, and that before it came to an end the whole world was looking on. Having been invited to the show, the world pronounced a verdict upon it, and what that verdict was he may discover by going to Capetown, or Samarkand, or Bogotá, and telling the first literate man he meets that he is from Tennessee.

Mencken went on to defend "New York" against the charge that it was attempting to dictate to the hinterlands and was attempting to undermine the "believers in God." Having been designated a "New Yorker"—that is, a member of the Godless North—by Davidson, Mencken accepted the designation for the sake of argument, but protested that it was not the North which was intolerant. "The opinion of New York, like that of any other cultural capital, is always immensely tolerant, and you will never detect in it any genuine missionary spirit. It may find the Hinterland, on occasion, uncouth and preposterous, but its disposition is to laugh, not to call the police." In fact, the currents of the Uplift all ran the other way; it was the hinterland that attempted to deprive the cities of their freedoms; for example, the freedom to drink legally. Mencken's comments on the problems surrounding states' rights are as applicable today as they were thirty years ago. For example:

> The fundamental trouble with the Regionalists seems to be that they do not differentiate between a civil right and logical rightness. Starting out from the sound position that any self-contained section of the country should be left as free as possible to frame its own institutions and develop its own folkways, they blunder into the imbecility of arguing that whatever it chooses should be beyond criticism. To be sure, they may not do this consciously, but nevertheless they do it, and the fact is sufficient proof of their general muddleheadedness.

Moreover, the Agrarians were begging the question when they sought to find enemies on the outside when the enemy was in camp. Davidson had attacked, as the sort of thing advocated by the North, "German Expressionism, French Dadaism, the erotic primitivism of D. H. Lawrence, the gigantic *fin de siècle* pedantries and experimentalisms of James Joyce, the infantilism of Gertrude Stein," and "all the choicest remains of the literary bordellos of the ancient and modern world" (the quotations are from Davidson). To begin with, Mencken had no objection to Davidson's bugbears since, as he admitted, he had attacked the same fads when they were popular in the nineteen-twenties; but the objections were actually beside the real issue.

> The real business before the Southern publicists is not to drive the damyankee back to his theological speakeasies and "literary bordellos," but to clean up their own dooryard. They are never going to get anywhere by deploring his atheism and immorality, for if he chose to defend himself he could answer very readily that even the naughtiest atheism is measurably more consonant with civilization than the demonology prevailing in rural Tennessee, and that nothing advocated by the customers of Lawrence, Joyce and La Stein is half so barbaric as the public frying of blackamoors. It shows a poor hand at the dialectic to expose one's self to such obvious ripostes, yet that is precisely what some of the more cocksure young men are doing all the time. In brief, their ideology is hard to distinguish, in its more lyrical moments, from that of the incense-swingers they have presumably displaced. They show the same old petulance with outside opinion, and the same incapacity for turning it to profit.

Mencken concluded his essay by remarking that he would begin to take seriously the prophets of Regionalism when he heard that they had "ceased to fever themselves over the sins of New York, and applied themselves courageously to clearing the ground in their own Region." Here, as everywhere else in Mencken, there is the admonition to face the harsh facts of the present rather than engage in theorizing or wrap oneself in a dreamy haze of escapism. Like Thoreau, Mencken never tired of insisting that the terms of existence were *present* terms, never of the past or the future.

It is worth noting further that the so-called Agrarians were essentially the same men who edited and wrote *The Fugitive: A Magazine of Verse* (1922–1925). In their advertisements the editors proudly quoted Mencken's remark, from the Baltimore *Sun*, that their magazine represented almost the entire literature of Tennessee. Knowing Mencken's opinion of Tennessee, however, they were cautious about accepting his comment as undiluted praise. Their next concerted effort was a symposium, *I'll Take My Stand* (1931), which Mencken criticized severely at the time. In his *Mercury* review (March, 1931) he objected to the wistful sentimentalizing of the past in the book, and he denied that industrialism was, in itself, degrading. After all, the South's "most highly industrialized State, North Carolina, is today, in many ways, its most civilized, whereas its least industrialized, Mississippi, is its most barbaric." He asked that the twelve contributors to the volume stop "blowing pretty soap-bubbles and devote themselves honestly and courageously to concrete evils and workable remedies." So far as can be determined, the Agrarian movement was stillborn. (Recently a paperback edition of *I'll Take My Stand* appeared, the first in thirty years. Reading the essays today, one is often moved by the beauty of the prose and at the same time a bit incredulous that anyone could ever have taken the movement seriously.)

An extremely resilient group, the Agrarians, alias Fugitives, next appeared as leaders in the New Criticism, *circa* 1940. Much of the Agrarian animosity for the bitter facts of modern life is written into the tenets of that criticism; for example, the divorce of literature from philosophy, history, biography, psychology, society, and so on. Running throughout is a suspicion, or even fear, of science, which is combated—or, rather, ignored—by removing literature from the market place entirely and placing it in the hands of "experts." In many ways, this has made for a better criticism, particularly in the quarter of analysis, but it has had the harmful effect of driving criticism back into the ivory tower from whence Mencken and Huneker and Brooks and Wilson and other kindred spirits had rescued it nearly half a century ago. What was that about a cyclic theory?

CHAPTER TEN

The Devil's Advocate

I

DURING his fifteen years on the *Smart Set*, ten of them as its coeditor, Mencken was generally out of step with his fellow American critics. He never "followed" other men, though he learned much from various critics both at home and abroad, nor did he cater to public demand or taste. He constantly expressed minority opinions on the writers of his day. Indeed, he seemed to relish his role as a majority of one. When the literature he whooped for became overwhelmingly popular in the decade following World War I, he began to lose interest in literary criticism. This is not to say that he lost interest *because* he had ceased to be a "loner," or *because* he could not stand prosperity, as it were. Quite simply, he became more interested in nonaesthetic affairs than in belles-lettres. For example, his contribution to the rather famous symposium on *Civilization in the United States* (1922), edited by Harold Stearns, was the essay on "Politics." Van Wyck Brooks wrote the essay on literature. In his autobiography, *The Street I Know* (1935), Stearns discussed the rather large part Mencken played in obtaining contributors to the symposium. As early as 1920 Mencken had written Louis Untermeyer that they lived, "not in a literary age, but in a fiercely political age," remarking further that he was trying to "escape" from literary criticism: "The wider field of ideas in general is too alluring." He wrote Ellery Sedgwick in 1923 that he had been trying to get rid of the *Smart Set* for five years; that is, since the end of the war. It should be evident that those years before the founding of the *Mercury* were by far his most important as far as literary criticism is concerned; and it is doubly ironic that in assessing Mencken's literary criticism today, people should go back, not to the *Smart Set* years, but to the twenties, when Mencken reached his height as a national force in other areas of inquiry. Mencken must bear part of the responsibility for this distorted view, since he has been instrumental in deciding what part of his writing should be handed down to posterity; but the scholars have shown themselves unwilling to disinter the earlier criticism.

In his final article for the *Smart Set* (December, 1923), Mencken composed what might be taken as his valedictory to literary criticism. Looking back over the preceding fifteen years, he was struck most forcibly by the great change and improvement in the situation of American writers. "In 1908, strange as it may seem to the literary radicals who roar so safely in Greenwich Village today, the old tradition was still powerful, and the young man or woman who came to New York with a manuscript which violated in any way the pruderies and prejudices of the professors had a very hard time getting it printed." The early years had been a time of complacency and conformity. "Hamilton Wright Mabie was still alive and still taken seriously, and all the young pedagogues who aspired to the critical gown imitated him in his watchful stupidity." The critics in power had silenced Dreiser for eleven years after the ill-starred publication of *Sister Carrie*. Harriet Monroe, Amy Lowell, and Willa Cather were just beginning their careers and as yet offered little evidence of what they were later to do or represent in the world of art. The popular writers were Richard Harding Davis, Robert W. Chambers, and James Lane Allen. Looking back from 1923, the first decade of the century appeared almost fabulous. After the *"pianissimo* revolt of the middle 90's—a feeble echo of the English revolt—had spent itself, the Presbyterians marched in and took possession of the works."

> The American Idealism now preached so pathetically by Prof. Dr. Sherman and his fellow fugitives from the Christian Endeavor belt was actually on tap. No novel that told the truth about life as Americans were living it, no poem that departed from the old patterns, no play that had the merest ghost of an idea in it had a chance. When, in 1908, Mrs. Mary Roberts Rinehart

printed a conventional mystery story which yet managed to have a trace of sense in it, it caused a sensation. (I reviewed it, by the way, in my first article.) And when, two years later, Dr. William Lyon Phelps printed a book of criticism in which he actually ranked Mark Twain alongside Emerson and Hawthorne, there was as great a stirring beneath the college elms as if a naked fancy woman had run across the campus.

A number of writers addressed themselves to the dispersal of the fog shrouding American letters, but their efforts lacked a concerted purpose. "The more contumacious of the younger critics, true enough, tended to rally 'round Huneker, who, as a matter of fact, was very little interested in American letters, and the young novelists had a leader in Dreiser, who, I suspect, was quite unaware of most of them." But it was Dreiser, Mencken felt, who gave the movement what little form it had, even though he was not writing novels during the period. Rather, it was his steadfastness before his critics that appealed to the younger rebels. Mencken felt that Frank Norris, had he lived longer, would eventually have compromised with the traditionalists who had wooed and ruined Garland before him. But Dreiser was made of sterner stuff. Moreover, he had never had to face the seductions which won Garland and threatened Norris. Instead, the critics had fallen on him with violence the moment he appeared, and he was to be the storm center of a battle which lasted twenty years.

> The pedagogues tried to scare him to death, they tried to stampede his partisans, and they tried to put him into Coventry and get him forgotten, but they failed every time. The more he was reviled, sneered at, neglected, the more resolutely he stuck to his formula. That formula is now every serious American novelist's formula. They all try to write better than Dreiser, and not a few of them succeed, but they all follow him in his fundamental purpose—to make the novel true. Dreiser added something, and here following is harder; he tried to make the novel poignant—to add sympathy, feeling, imagination to understanding.

Mencken's remarks may be backed by the testimonial of almost every important American novelist since Dreiser. It should be remembered that Lewis and Anderson and Fitzgerald and Wolfe were all followers. And Faulkner, certainly different from Dreiser in manner, stated a few years ago that Dreiser was the root from which sprang the main branch of modern American fiction. Oddly enough, though, F. R. Leavis, who appears to know slightly less than nothing about American literature, has written that Dreiser belongs to no tradition (Leavis' favorite word) and that nothing properly called literature could come from what he represented. He goes on in the same place (in his introductory note to Marius Bewley's *The Complex Fate*) to remark that Scott Fitzgerald was disqualified as "a novelist and a creative writer" by the accounts of his life! We are in all seriousness asked to believe that "in Fitzgerald's world, no vestige, and no suspicion, of any standard of maturity exists. [. . .] There is nothing in his writings to contradict what we know of the life." All of which attests to the fact that Anthony Comstock is not really dead after all; he has just ceased to roar about sex and has begun to concentrate on the behavior of artists as a means of appraising their art.

Mencken believed the enormous changes that had taken place in drama, the novel, and poetry during the last twenty years were largely beneficial changes, and they were in large part the result of the artist's newly acquired freedom to depict the life about him as he saw it and to interpret that life as he pleased. Mencken even went so far as to remark that American publishers, "once so fearful of novelty, are now so hospitable to it that they constantly fail to distinguish the novelty that has hard thought behind it from that which has only some Village mountebank's desire to stagger the *booboisie*." Our stage was perhaps the freest in the world, and "Our poets get into print regularly with stuff so bizarre and unearthly that only Christian Scientists can understand it." There were those who found it hard to believe that so much freedom could have been gained in such a short time, and they thus continued to cry out at the few taboos and inhibitions that remained. But Mencken doubted that the comstocks ever actually suppressed a book of consequence. Ironically, his *Mercury* was to be suppressed within two years. But then Mencken was, as I have remarked before, a man marked by the comstocks. Moreover, it was a "sex" violation that got the *Mercury* banned in Boston; and Mencken admitted that the comstocks were confining their operations to the single field of sex, which was of least importance to the freedom of the artist.

It was against the so-called "American tradition" that the important battles had been fought—and won. For example, Dos Passos' *Three Soldiers* "was far more subversive of that tradition than all the stories of sex ever written in America—and yet *Three Soldiers* came out with the imprint of one of the most respectable of American publishers, and was scarcely challenged." *Babbitt* had scored an even easier victory than *Three Soldiers,* and yet it was doubly subversive in that it attacked the two most sacred of the American sacred cows: American business and American Christianity. Even the "alfalfa *Gelehrten*" (Mencken's abusive term for the academic critics; he was probably thinking particularly of Sherman) praised *Babbitt,* "apparently on the theory that praising Lewis would make the young of the national species forget Dreiser. Victimized by their own craft, the *Gelehrten* thus made a foul attack upon their own principles, for if their principles did not stand against just such anarchistic books, then they were without any sense whatever, as was and is, indeed, the case." No one could doubt that immense changes had taken place between the suppression of *Sister Carrie* and the deification of *Babbitt.* What is more, there was a large audience eager to read the latter book, just as there were numerous critics capable of recognizing its worth and willing to support its author. The chief enemy of the creative artist was no longer the censor, but was now himself. He fell victim to the popular magazines, Hollywood, or politics. Twenty years later Mencken told James Farrell that the three greatest pitfalls of the creative artist were women, booze, and politics. On that he never varied.

Since he had been embroiled in the literary wars of the previous fifteen years (and quite obviously he did not intend to be much concerned with literary criticism thereafter), Mencken felt it was natural that his criticism should have seemed unduly tart to many a reader. But on re-examination of his early criticism, he doubted that his harshness had been unjust. And in his ensuing comments, we get a good view of his attitude toward the necessity of *judgment* in criticism:

> I have overpraised books, and I have applauded authors incautiously and too soon. But, as the Lord God Jahveh is my judge and I hope in all humility to be summoned to sit upon His right hand upon the dreadful and inevitable Day of Judgment, when all hearts are bared and virtue gets its long-delayed re-

ward, I most solemnly make my oath that, with the single exception noted on a previous page, I can't remember a time when I ever printed a slating that was excessive or unjust. The quacks and dolts who have been mauled in these pages all deserved it; more, they all deserved far worse than they got. If I lost them customers by my performance I am glad of it. If I annoyed and humiliated them I am glad of it again. If I shamed any of them into abandoning their quackery—but here I begin to pass beyond the borders of probability, and become a quack myself. Regarding false art, cheap cant, pious skullduggery, dishonest pretense—regarding all these things my position is this: that their practitioners have absolutely no rights that anyone is bound to respect. To be polite to them is not to be tolerant; it is simply to be silly. If a critic has any duty at all save the primary duty to be true to himself, it is the public duty of protecting the fine arts against the invasion of such frauds.

He went on to admit that he had been led by his private tastes quite as much as by any sense of professional duty. Furthermore, the writer who endeavored "to subjugate beautiful letters to the puerile uses of some bucolic moral scheme, or some nonsensical notion of the national destiny, or some petty variety of new-fangled politics is a man who is congenitally and incurably offensive to me." Such a man had a right to be heard, but not in the field of belles-lettres. Though they said it in a much quieter tone, later critics were to make names for saying the same thing; I am thinking, of course, of the New Critics.

Mencken concluded his "farewell address" (a part of which he included in his essay on "The American Novel" in *Prejudices: Fourth Series*) by commenting on the great need for more and better evaluations of American literature and the forces that shaped it. Mencken's interest in cultural and psychological "causes" is evident in his comments on Poe and Emerson and Whitman, all of whom were in need of more attention than they had received. Again, he attacked the belief that Poe was a great poet and inventor of the short story ("Nine-tenths of his poetry is so artificial that it is difficult to imagine even college tutors reading it voluntarily; as for his tales, they have long since passed over to the shelf of juveniles"), but he insisted the criticism was important and the mind which conceived it was worthy of close examination. Even more ironic than the fate of Poe was the apotheosis of Emerson as

a kind of philosophical milquetoast, when he was actually one of
the great American rebels.

> It was obviously Emerson's central aim in life to liberate the
> American mind—to set it free from the crippling ethical obsessions
> of Puritanism, to break down herd thinking, to make liberty
> more real on the intellectual plane than it could ever be on the
> political plane. It is his tragic fate to be mouthed and admired
> today chiefly by persons who have entirely misunderstood his
> position, in brief, by the heirs and assigns of the very prigs
> and dullards he spent his whole life opposing. Certainly it would
> be difficult to imagine a greater irony than this. Emerson paved
> the way for every intellectual revolt that has occurred since his
> time, and yet he has always been brought into court, not as a
> witness for the rebels, but as a witness for the militia and the
> police.

Mencken was probably thinking of the New Humanists, who liked
to invoke the prestige of Emerson for support of their extreme
conservatism.

Some of the credit for the great interest in Melville, Twain,
Bierce, Poe, Stephen Crane, and Whitman during the nineteen-
twenties must be given Mencken, since the *Mercury* published
articles on all of them. Fourteen appeared on Whitman alone.
Mencken himself wrote rather extensively on all these writers with
the exception of Melville, whose novels were rediscovered in the
twenties, following Frederick O'Brien's *White Shadows in the South
Seas* (1919). Mencken wrote in 1920 that Melville's career offered
"tempting invitations to the psychological explorer"—a statement
that is agonizingly true. He also remarked that Melville was "being
over-praised as greatly as he was once under-praised." *Moby Dick*
should have appealed mightily to him, for in that masterpiece may
be found precisely the struggle and quest that, according to
Mencken, concerned the great writers of all periods: that is, the
struggle of man against his destiny. It is difficult to believe that
Mencken could fail to be fascinated with Ahab, the noble rebel
against the indifference of the universe, the deep-down diver, the
undaunted titan who refused to compromise with life and settle
for less than truth. And yet so it was: assuming he ever really read
Melville, Mencken seems to have been little moved by his art. By
the time Melville was read again, Mencken had moved too far in
the direction of the American Voltaire to practice the sort of literary

criticism which he himself had been advocating for years. Satire was now his forte. Literature gave way to the gaudy spectacle: the Republic in upheaval. Why seriously concern oneself with the novel when there stood Boobus Americanus, blown full of pride and provincial ignorance, just waiting to be deflated? . . . The time had passed when man thinking could engage in narrow pursuits.

In December, 1922, a year before the founding of the *Mercury*, Mencken admitted in a rather too self-effacing article that his criticism had been devoted, in the main, to attacking and tearing down the "formal ideas" which oppressed American literature during the first two decades of the century—ideas of form and method, of aim and purpose, of mere fashion and propriety. His constant attacks on formalism of all sorts had got him, he admitted, the name of a professional ruffian. He was constantly accused of tearing down without building up, of murdering a theory without offering a new and better one to replace it. "My business, considering the state of the society in which I find myself, has been principally to clear the ground of mouldering rubbish, to chase away old ghosts, to help set the artist free. The work of erecting a new structure belongs primarily to the artist as creator, not to me as critic." Once free from restrictions, the artist sometimes had nothing to say; but, Mencken wrote, "it is certainly better to utter nonsense as a free man than to keep on repeating formulae like a boy in school."

Immediately, the tender-minded reader might file another objection. If Mencken was so interested in freedom, why did he belabor writers whose only crime was the expression of honest ideas in a banal manner? Did they not deserve the right to say what they wished unhindered by the police—or by Mencken? The answer was simple—perhaps a bit too simple. Banality was not their sole crime. They were, in effect, endeavoring to deny other men *their* honest opinions. Mencken belabored them, he argued, for trying, whether consciously or unconsciously, to set up standards and taboos that would hinder the free play of the creative impulse. The writer who became popular as the result of a bad book is certainly a standard-maker, and the standard he sets will definitely stand in the way of a better writer who comes after him. Mencken insisted, moreover, that the essence of sound art is freedom. (As I have pointed out, at the heart of all his writing in whatever area is this demand that man be allowed freedom to explore and create.

This demand explains Mencken's objections to religions and governments as well as critical theories which set out to control, if not actually coerce, the individual's mind and his expression. It should be noted, for example, that he never attacked the religious impulse; only the fanatic who propounded his religion as "absolute" and endeavored to force his beliefs on others drew his scorn. A nun working as a nurse in a hospital was one thing; an archbishop telling thousands what they can and cannot read or see in the theater is something entirely different.) Above all, the artist must be allowed the freedom to experiment, and he must be granted his own subject matter. He "must be allowed his impish impulse, his revolt, his perversity." Echoing Huneker, Mencken insisted that the artist is by nature opposed to Philistine correctness; when he is bound to tradition he is nothing. Though he by no means agreed with all artists and their revolts, he opposed all those who sought to censure the artist through the ballot, the policeman's club, the schoolmaster's rattan, the bishop's miter.

> I am even against proscriptions on purely aesthetic grounds. Thus when Miss Lowell and her friends essayed to set up the doctrine that the only decent way to write poetry was the way they personally wrote it, and that all exponents of other ways were ignoramuses—when this theory appeared in the learned groves and barber-shops I joined the professors in opposing it. But the great majority of such attacks upon freedom are not made by revolutionists, but by advocates of an established order: for one Futurist who launches bulls like a pope there are a hundred pedagogues who issue proscriptions like an American Attorney-General—for one Miss Lowell there are whole herds of Comstocks. Thus my critical labors, in the main, have been on the side of the younger generation. I have protested *sforzando* against the schoolmastering of letters—against setting the artist in bondage to his inferiors.[1]

II

Considering Mencken's critical credo, his skepticism, and his *Weltansicht*, one should be able to guess correctly which artists most appealed to him. It should be noted, however, that Mencken never praised a writer because his philosophy happened to agree with that of Mencken. Rather, the artistic presentation of the writer's world view determined his worth. Mencken admired Nietzsche, but he was contemptuous of most Nietzschean novelists. He abhorred socialism, but he praised many socialistic novels. In a sentence, the best art was that which represented accurately and interpreted convincingly and was imbued with a current of feeling that co-ordinated and informed the whole work. The contemporary artist who came closest to embodying Mencken's credo was, of course, Joseph Conrad.

Long before Conrad had an American audience, Mencken hymned him in the *Smart Set* articles. Though Conrad's philosophy, which is clearly revealed in everything he wrote, appealed to Mencken, it was his artistic excellence, not his thought, which evoked Mencken's highest praise. Conrad was forever fascinated by the "immense indifference of things" (a phrase from *Nostromo* which Mencken liked to quote), the tragic vanity of human aspiration, the profound meaninglessness of life. He had no answers to any of the puzzles which beset man; he was pre-eminently *not* a moralist. As Mencken put it, he swung as far from revolt and moralizing as is possible, for he did not even criticize God.

> He neither protests nor punishes; he merely smiles and pities. Like Mark Twain he might well say: "The more I see of men, the more they amuse me—and the more I pity them." He is *simpatico* precisely because of this ironical commiseration, this infinite disillusionment, this sharp understanding of the narrow limits of human volition and responsibility. . . . I have said that he does not criticize God. One may even imagine him pitying God.[2]

Mencken felt that Conrad was unwilling to "explain" his characters for the simple reason that he did not competely understand them himself. The little that the reader learns about Lord Jim or Kurtz or Nostromo is learned fortuitously and unexpectedly. We view the characters dimly from varying angles, but we are never given clear portraits of the essential nature of a character. And "in that very dimness, so tantalizing and yet so revealing, lies two-thirds of Conrad's art, or his craft, or his trick, or whatever you choose to call it. What he shows us is blurred at the edges, but so is life blurred at the edges." Conrad certainly could paint a scene; he could make the reader see and feel an event, an object, a personage, as probably no other artist in the realm of fiction could do, but the mere outward show of the phenomenal world was secondary to his art. He was concerned with "the inextricable movement of phenomena and noumena between event and event"; with "the obscure genesis, in some chance emotion or experience, of an extraordinary series of transactions"; with the "effect of some gigantic and fortuitous event upon the mind and soul of a given man"; with showing "how cause and effect are intricately commingled, so that it is difficult to separate motive from consequence, and consequence from motive." And in all his works it was the process of the mind rather than the actual fact that interested him. He was concerned foremost with subjective impulses and only secondarily with the objective acts resulting from the impulses. Again, Conrad fitted Mencken's early belief that the artist in fiction was more concerned with causes than with effects. It may well be, of course, that Mencken developed his theory *after* coming under the influence of Conrad. Which is to say, his aesthetic, like Aristotle's theory of tragedy, was derived empirically.

In reviewing *Under Western Eyes,* in January, 1912, Mencken first presented a detailed summary of the story. Then he admitted that, after all, this gave only the gross framework. "The real concern of the author is with the genesis and conflict of ideas in the mind of Razumov. What he is always trying to make clear is that Razumov is essentially a Russian, that his ideation follows routes unfamiliar, and often almost impassable, to the man of the West." The novel was really a study of racial psychology, aiming to clarify "the processes of thought which eventuate in the astounding Russian act—the elaborately planned, artistically perfect, wholly savage assassination; the piling up of spy upon spy, of spy upon the spy of spy; the childlike following of false and motley leaders; the sudden appearance of the Tartar chieftain, fresh from the steppes, in the frock coat of the bespectacled doctor of philosophy." Moreover, the bizarre characters never lost their plausibility. "Razumov's slow progress, through doubt and terror, to what must be accepted, perhaps, as actual insanity, has the convincing flow of an equation." In effect, Mencken insisted that Conrad had given his tale that sense of inevitability which makes for fascinating reading rather than just idle pleasure. Finally, he judged *Under Western Eyes* inferior to *Lord Jim* and some of the shorter things, but as representative of the average Conrad canon, which still put it on a level that few other novelists of the time could reach.

Mencken considered *Victory,* reviewed in the April, 1915, *Smart*

Set article entitled "The Grandstand Flirts with the Bleachers," an overt attempt on Conrad's part to appeal to a large reading public, or at least to a larger one than he had theretofore enjoyed. Was he, Mencken asked, actually lending a "covert hand to those shameless Barabbases of Garden City, L.I.," who advertised him "as if he were some new brand of breakfast food or touring car?" Evidently so. The debauchery was complete. The damning evidence was on hand. *Victory* was "a fiction that even a tired business man might conceivably enjoy and understand. Gone are all the Conradean indirections of yesteryear: the backings and fillings, the endless interludes and by-the-ways, the amazing snarls and subtleties. In place of them there is a narrative that gets under way on the very first page and proceeds uninterruptedly to a *sforzando* and melodramatic close." The "meticulous and merciless anatomizing of motive and emotion," found in such novels as *Lord Jim, Almayer's Folly,* and *Under Western Eyes,* had been replaced by "a skilful and deliberate piling up of dramatic suspense," similar to that of *Germinal* or *McTeague* or even *Treasure Island.* Mencken then summarized the story down to the landing of Mr. Jones and party on Heyst's island of Samburan, remarking the rapidity of the action —in comparison, that is, with other Conrad novels. "From the moment that Jones and Ricardo reach the crazy jetty, sun-blistered, purple-faced, half dead of thirst—from this moment to the last scene of all, with Heyst dead, Alma dead, Jones and Ricardo dead, the apeman dead and Wang vanished into the jungle, there is no halting or turning aside in this inexorable tragedy of blood. Put upon paper by a lesser man it would become a mere penny-dreadful, almost a burlesque." But in the hands of Conrad the story was almost as vivid and haunting as *Heart of Darkness.* Mencken compared Mr. Jones to Kurtz, finding in both characters a depravity "grown so vast that it takes on an aspect of the heroic. And in both of them, at bottom, there is humor—humor infinitely ironic, infinitely horrible."

Although he saw in *Victory* a concession to the mass reader, Mencken still thought it "an authentic contribution to the Conrad opera, despite its novelty of plan and treatment, and an example of unadorned storytelling that challenges the most galloping of the best-sellers on their own ground." Moreover, the novel may have been Conrad's way of answering those critics who charged him with falling victim to his own meticulousness. In conclusion, Mencken noted what he considered an "obvious blemish" in Conrad's omitting to clarify his use of the island volcano, "that glowering symbol of the whole sordid drama." At the beginning of the novel, one hears much of it, but then it is forgotten. "It dominates and menaces Heyst's lonely island; it is the beacon that brings Jones and Ricardo to the crazy jetty. And then, unaccountably, one hears of it no more."

In Conrad, Mencken saw an excellent yardstick for measuring the difference between melodrama and the true work of art. If an incident or a series of incidents is properly prepared and accounted for, if it comes at the end of a chain of connected and comprehensible, albeit amazing and unprecedented, causes, then it is deserving of study by thoughtful men. On the other hand, incidents that are unaccounted for are fit only for melodrama. (The strong believers in free will or choice will, of course, deny that this criticism is valid, since it smacks of behaviorism.) In Conrad's novels and stories there are all sorts of spectacular, even fabulous, happenings: shipwrecks, revolutions, anarchist plottings, suicides, killings, violence of all sorts. But his events always have "elaborate and plausible causes behind them"; he shows not only the thing done, but the why and wherefore of it.

His *Nostromo*, in its externals, is merely a tale of South American turmoil, and not unrelated to *Soldiers of Fortune*. But what great differences between the methods, the points of view, the psychological material of the two stories! [Richard Harding] Davis is content to show us the overt act; Conrad goes behind it for the motive, the process of mind. The one achieves an agreeable romance, and an agreeable romance only; the other achieves an extraordinarily incisive study of the Latin-American temperament—a study of the ideals and passions which lead presumably sane men to pursue each other like wolves, and of the reaction of that incessant pursuit upon the men themselves. I do not say that Conrad is always accurate. I do not know, in point of fact, whether he is or isn't. But I do say that he is wholly convincing, that the men he sets into his scene hang together; that the explanations he offers for their acts are at least plausible; that the effects of those acts upon actors and immediate spectators alike, are such as might be reasonably expected to follow; that the final impression is one of almost uncanny reality.[3]

The naturalistic demand for causal relationships, which in turn lend that sense of "reality" without which no art can survive the prejudices and penchants of its day, is nowhere better stated than in Mencken's criticism of Conrad. After all, it is this same relationship which makes the stream-of-consciousness novels of Faulkner, for example, seem real. The numerous time shifts (the backing and filling) in Conrad (and in Faulkner) heighten the plausibility of the transactions of the story to the point, at times anyhow, where the "seemingness" becomes actual "being." This is what Mencken was saying when he constantly wrote that to read Conrad was to undergo *experience*. The reader is, for a time, taken out of his chair and placed in the midst of the story; and while he is being thus "fooled," he is also being enriched. Experience makes the man, determines his size and shape. I refer, of course, to experience in the broadest sense, and not to mere physical titillation. To assume that a man may know that which he has never experienced is the same as assuming that something may come from nothing. Or, as Nietzsche put it: "A man has no ears for that to which experience has given him no access." It might be plausibly argued, furthermore, that in the world of art lies the broadest and deepest depository of experience.

In his reviews of Conrad's novels (and he reviewed all that appeared after 1908 when he joined the *Smart Set*), Mencken constantly endeavored to show how Conrad's method of telling a story, rather than the story itself, was responsible for his greatness. The story, or "raw material of fiction," as Mencken phrased it, often sufficed to make excellent reading, just as the melody, the raw material of music, was sometimes enough to make good hearing. But because of the paucity of good stories or melodies, the artist normally depended on his skill in telling an old story rather than on his invention of new stories, which were usually inferior to those already at hand. This triumph of skill over materials was best observed in music, the knowledge of which stood Mencken in good stead for analyzing fiction:

> The opening movement of the greatest orchestral work ever written, Beethoven's Fifth Symphony, has nothing at the bottom of it save a little melody of two tones, one of them three times repeated—a melody so childishly simple that one has to stretch the meaning of the term to call it a melody at all. And yet, out

of that austere material, Beethoven constructed a piece of music so noble and so beautiful, so rich in imagination and so lofty in style, that it remains today, after more than a century, a masterpiece that no other man has ever equalled, and that few have even so much as approached. But this same Beethoven, in the symphony immediately following, made a failure almost as noteworthy as his success in the incomparable Fifth. Here, in the so-called Pastorale, he started out with a melodic idea of decided grace and charm—in other words, with what seemed to be excellent material—but when he essayed to embellish and develop it, his usual resourcefulness failed him, and all he managed to do was to repeat it over and over again, with inconsiderable changes in tonality and instrumentation. The result was a composition which remains famous to this day, despite many beauties in its other movements, chiefly for its forbidding monotony. It is hard hearing, just as certain books by undoubtedly competent authors are hard reading.[4]

All this was by way of introduction to his three-thousand-word examination of *Chance*. Here, as in most other of his stories, what mattered was not the story so much as what the author thought about it, and particularly it was "the great laws of conduct and destiny that he sees within and behind it, that make it on the one hand a work of art and on the other hand a profound study of human motive, instinct and emotion." The fascination of *Typhoon*, Mencken added, lay not in the storm that battered the *Nan-Shan* or even in the melodramatic battle among the terrified Chinese in her hold, "but in the action and reaction of these external phenomena upon the muddled mind of Captain MacWhirr." Again, a story like *Youth*, told by an O. Henry or even a Kipling, whom Mencken admired, would be little more than an exciting story. "But told by Conrad it is at once a subtle philosophy of life and a stately poem, with something in it of the eternal wisdom of Ecclesiastes and something of the surge and thunder of the Odyssey."

The danger of employing this method of creation lay in the artist's temptation to forego the story (or the melody) and fall back on *just* his manner or method. Mencken believed Conrad had fallen into this trap in *Chance*; he went through the motions of saying something when he actually had nothing to say. The result was, of course, painful to the faithful reader, who "gets a specious effect of profundity, a sonorous and deceptive soothing. He is ready, and even eager, to believe that he is being led down tortuous and enchanting paths. But the truth is, of course, that he is standing stock still, or rather, revolving like a teetotum, and after a while his head begins to swim and his knees to give way, and he presently falls into a fitful and unrefreshing slumber."

It is not at all remarkable that Conrad appreciated the service Mencken performed for him. In a letter to George T. Keating dated December 14, 1922, Conrad spoke at great length of Mencken's criticism. It is interesting to note that he was sensitive to Mencken's views of his Slavic, aristocratic background. Mencken made the guess that Conrad had been influenced by the great Russian novelists; Conrad denied any such influence and even stated that he knew no Russian. Part of his feigned ignorance doubtless results from his hatred of the Russian revolutionaries and his strong nationalistic love of Poland. The letter warrants quoting:

> Mencken's vigour is astonishing. It is like an electric current. In all he writes there is a crackle of blue sparks like those one sees in a dynamo house amongst revolving masses of metal that give you a sense of enormous hidden power. For that is what he has. Dynamic power. When he takes up a man he snatches him away and fashions him into something that (in my case) he is pleased with—luckily for me, because had I not pleased him he would have torn me limb from limb. Whereas as it is he exalts me almost above the stars. It makes me giddy. But who could quarrel with such generosity, such vibrating sympathy and with a mind so intensely alive? What, however, surprises me is that a personality so genuine in its sensations, so independent in judgment, should now and then condescend to a mere parrot talk; for his harping on my Slavonism is only that.[5]

There follows a long denial that he was in any way Slavic, but rather had derived from a "Western Roman culture," was southern in temperament, etc. Then he casts an angry eye on the implication that he was influenced by the Russians: "I suppose [Mencken] means Russian; but as a matter of fact I never knew Russian. The few novels I have read I have read in translation." Russia, Russians, and Russian literature were totally repugnant to him (he did admit elsewhere that he had read Turgenev). Conrad concluded his remarks on this point by saying that Mencken might have given him credit for being an individual somewhat out of the common, instead of ramming him into a category which he did not fit anyhow. He then ended his discussion of Mencken:

This outburst is provoked, of course, by dear Mencken's amazing article about me, so many-sided, so brilliant and so warmhearted. For that man of a really ruthless mind, pitiless to all shams and common formulas, has a great generosity. My debt of gratitude to him has been growing for years, and I am glad I have lived long enough to read the latest contribution. It's enough to scare anyone into the most self-searching mood. It is difficult to believe that one has deserved all that. So that is how I appear to Mencken! Well, so be it.

Mencken's "amazing article" was probably the one which constituted a part of the December, 1922, *Smart Set* article, "The Monthly Feuilleton." Mencken chose this particular article, incidently, for inclusion in the *Chrestomathy*—a good choice since it is much more concise than the long essay in *A Book of Prefaces* and is more conclusive than any of the reviews of specific novels—reviews which invariably included discussions of the body of Conrad's work. In this essay, Mencken defended Conrad against the charge that his English was not always of the King's variety; and in the defense he remarked that Conrad remained a Slav to the end, adding that the people of his tales were also as much Slavs as he was. (Conrad's objection on this point was certainly just.) In the *Chrestomathy*, Mencken saw fit to admit in a footnote that Conrad had objected to this idea when it was first set forth in the *Smart Set* of December, 1919 (not in a criticism, but in *"Répétition Générale"*), and had "remonstrated politely." That was exactly three years before the article which elicited Conrad's complaint to Keating. Mencken refused to be swayed by Conrad's disclaimer, concluding his footnote: "But I stick to my guns." Actually, the point is a minor one, whether Mencken was right or wrong. Much more important were the remarks on Conrad's free-wheeling use of the language, his refusal to force his style to "roll along in the old ruts." It was, Mencken felt, his avoidance of those ruts that made him the unique genius he was.

No Oxford mincing is in him, despite his curious respect for Henry James. If he cannot find his phrase above the salt, he seeks it below. His English, in a word, is innocent. And if, at times, there gets into it a color that is strange and even bizarre, then the fact is something to rejoice over, for a living language is like a man suffering incessantly from small internal hemorrhages, and what it needs above all else is constant transfusions of new blood from other tongues. The day the gates go up, that day it begins to die.[6]

This delight in language, in the color and "clang-tint" of words, as Mencken expressed it, may be found in all the criticism. In an early book review of the last novel of George Meredith, Mencken remarked the novelist's great delight in the language, and in doing so said much about his own love affair with words: "Here, indeed, was a man who understood to the full the wonderful fluency and elasticity of that noblest of human inventions, the English language. What joy he must have got out of writing it!"[7]

In a brilliant little essay (in the *Nation,* August 20, 1924), written shortly after Conrad's death, Mencken pointed with great insight to the core of the novelist's works and the guiding impulse behind them. Later writers have written reams on Conrad, only to arrive at substantially the same conclusions. Mencken insisted, first of all, that Conrad was not a romancer—a popular belief of the time—but was the opposite of one in that he was a realist. And that realism was not of the naturalistic sort, not so much of Zola's dissecting table as of the questioning and serenely skeptical kind. Conrad went beneath meticulous representation to "the inner reality of things." Though the world of Conrad's time had gotten rid of many of its old certainties, it had taken on others almost as bad ("As the ethics of Tupper had gone out the politics of H. G. Wells had come in").

Men no longer believed in an anthropomorphic Deity, half amiable grandpa and half prohibition-enforcement officer, but they still believed that they knew the purpose of human life, the destiny of man—they were still full of a new and pseudo-scientific cocksureness, as idiotic at bottom as the worst dogmatism of a Calvin or a Swedenborg. It was against this dogmatism that Conrad launched himself, and against whatever was left of the older brand. Upon it he played the hose of his irony. Against it he patiently arrayed his devastating facts. His execution was excellent. Certainties dissolved into doubts, and then into absurdities. A whole theory of knowledge went to pieces, and with it a whole canon of ethics. There emerged at last his own aloof skepticism—not complacent and attitudinizing, like Anatole France's, nor bitter and despairing, like Thomas Hardy's or Mark Twain's, but rather the serene skepticism of the scientist, with no room in it for any emotion more violent than curiosity.

Where critics of the last twenty years have either depicted Conrad as a forlorn existentialist, weeping over the dilemma of man placed in a godless universe, or considered him an ultramoralist passionately concerned with showing man the nature of right and wrong, Mencken saw him as the author of great novels, "all of them studies of human motive, and all of them ending with question marks." Which is to say, Mencken saw him as psychologist and skeptic—and above all as artist. He quoted the last sentence of *Lord Jim* as illustrative of the central thesis of Conrad: "He passes away under a cloud, inscrutable at heart, forgotten, unforgiven, and excessively romantic." In an excellent little essay on Conrad, E. M. Forster pointed to the misty center of the novels, concluding that Conrad actually had *no* creed whatsoever, but only opinions which he could throw overboard the moment they were contradicted by facts. Unlike Forster, Mencken considered this absence of creed as an example of the "novelist wholly purged of his old omniscience. But none the less illuminating for all that. For if Conrad never answered the riddle, then he at least stated it superbly; he at least took off all its wrappings of false assumption, and revealed its inner essence." Moreover, Conrad's matter was intimately wedded to the manner:

> *Youth,* in the ordinary sense, gets nowhere. The protagonist is a youth who does not act logically, but only instinctively. What he does would surely shock a school-teacher. But he comes out of his fantastic adventures in the end as the most real boy, perhaps, in all fiction, save only Huckleberry Finn. It is, indeed, an almost faultless piece of representation, for in it the author performs the difficult feat of getting rid of himself entirely.

Mencken remarked that Conrad began writing at a time when "the methods of the laboratory began to invade the ivory tower of the novelists." Since he did not accept the new fashion of the Freudian novel, however, he was out of step and hence not widely read. Some of his books, because they tell such good stories, had a mild vogue, but his best work remained unpopular with the majority of readers. "He remains, for the most part, a sort of affectation, like James and Proust." And this alienation was not, as some critics had maintained, a result of his style, which, Mencken claimed, was extraordinarily vigorous and clear: "There is never the slightest doubt about his meaning, and more often than not he expresses that meaning in phrases that are full of melody and color." Rather than the style, it was the content that threw the reader off and made him wary. "The thing before [Conrad] is not a demonstration but a problem. He is trying to throw light upon it from all sides, to get at the mystery that is in it. It interests him enormously, but it also puzzles him. He does not dogmatize about it; he speculates. The whole proceeding is as disconcerting in a novelist, to the ordinary novel reader, as it would be in a surgeon or a politician." Moreover, the endings of Conrad's stories offer little comfort for the reader: "The reader, having gone to the book to learn something, is dashed at the end by being asked something. More, there is a dismaying tone in the question, as if no answer were really expected. Such violations of the code do not make for popularity in novelists." It was precisely this violation that disturbed Forster; more unhappily, it was this violation that opened the gates to lesser critics to read their own meanings into Conrad. Only the man who is skeptical to the extent that he says there are no answers to the major questions can take Conrad *on his own terms.*

More than any other American, Mencken was responsible for spreading the news that Conrad was a great writer—not only that he was a master storyteller but that he furnished other writers with an almost perfect model. To perform this service, Mencken called upon his powers of persuasion as well as his critical acumen—another instance of the great advantage the good writer has over the fervorless critic or scholar. William McFee, whose sea stories, especially *Casuals of the Sea* (1916), Mencken had reviewed favorably, concluded his introduction to *A Conrad Argosy* (1942) by quoting a statement Mencken made on Conrad's death: "There was something almost suggesting the vastness of a natural phenomenon. He transcended all the rules. There have been, perhaps, greater novelists, but I believe that he was incomparably the greatest artist who ever wrote a novel."

When Mencken wished to compare a work of art with another of its kind (and he constantly compared men to men, books to books; his articles are drenched with names and titles), he often called upon Conrad to set the standard by which others might be judged. In *Man and Superman,* Shaw, with typical grandiloquence, pointed out that the artist was a ruthless man who would readily let his aged mother scrub floors if his freedom to create depended on it. In an interview with a *Paris Review* reporter, published in *Writers at Work* (1958), Faulkner stated that a good writer was a completely ruthless man who could have no peace until his dream was down on paper. And until his book was written, everything went by the board: honor, pride, decency, security, happiness, all. "If a writer has to rob his mother," Faulkner said, "he will not hesitate; the 'Ode on a Grecian Urn' is worth any number of old ladies." In like manner, Mencken scoffed at "The Good Citizen as Artist":

> Again, there is the bad author who defends his manufacture of magazine serials and movie scenarios on the ground that he has a wife, and is in honor bound to support her. I have seen a few such wives. I dispute the obligation. . . . As for the biological by-products of this fidelity, I rate them even lower. Show me 100 head of ordinary children who are worth one *Heart of Darkness*, and I'll subside. As for *Lord Jim*, I would not swap it for all the children born in Trenton, N.J., since the Spanish War.[8]

III

In March, 1911, when Mencken was thirty, Theodore Dreiser gave him the manuscript of a new novel. From what followed, one may imagine the high state of excitement with which he sat down to his ancient Corona to write Dreiser. Not only was *Jennie Gerhardt* by a personal friend, but it was the first American novel of importance that Mencken would have an opportunity to review. His letter began with fulsome praise:

> When *Jennie Gerhardt* is printed it is probable that more than one reviewer will object to its length, its microscopic detail, its enormous painstaking—but rest assured that Heinrich Ludwig von Mencken will not be in that gang. I have just finished reading the ms.—every word of it, from first to last—and I put it down with a clear notion that it should remain as it stands. The story comes upon me with great force; it touches my own experience of life in a hundred places; it preaches (or perhaps I had better say exhibits) a philosophy of life that seems to me to be sound; altogether I get a powerful effect of reality, stark and unashamed. It is drab and gloomy, but so is the struggle for existence. It is without humor, but so are the jests of that great comedian who shoots at our heels and makes us do our grotesque dancing.[9]

He compared the new work with *Sister Carrie*, commenting that it was, structurally at least, a superior piece of fiction. In the earlier work, Dreiser had allowed his central protagonist to be replaced in the latter half of the novel by Hurstwood; but in *Jennie* the two main characters—Jennie and Kane—were drawn in relation to each other: "The reaction of will upon will, of character upon character, is splendidly worked out and indicated." In his review of the novel for the *Smart Set*, Mencken repeated this criticism. What most impressed him, just rising from his first reading of the book, was the impression "of a living whole, not of a fabric that may be unravelled and examined in detail. In brief, you have painted so smoothly and yet so vigorously that I have no memory of brush strokes." He found the dialogue particularly successful, especially that of Jennie's father. Mencken was later to state that Dreiser's greatest skill lay in his handling of aged persons and his capturing their poignant frustration in the face of changing times. In the long letter to Dreiser, he remarked that he was most interested in the subjective nature of the characters rather than in the objective events of their lives: "Here you have got very close to the very wellsprings of action. The march of episodes is nothing: the slow unfolding of character is everything." Furthermore, the work fitted Mencken's definition of the good novel in that it was at once "an accurate picture of life and a searching criticism of life."

Mencken's few objections showed the care he took with details that are necessary to heighten the appearance of reality in the work of art. He doubted, for example, that a man of the world like Kane would remain ignorant of the fact that Jennie had had a child: "Child-bearing leaves physical marks, and those marks commonly persist for five or six years." But then he did not think many readers would raise the point (so far as I know, no one else has). Finally, he felt that Jennie was the least satisfactory personage in the novel. "Not that you do not account for her, from head to heels —but I would have preferred, had I the choice, a more typical kept woman. She is, in brief, uncompromisingly exceptional, almost unique, in several important details." Would Mencken, one wonders, have been more pleased had she resembled Becky Sharp, who was hardly so praiseworthy, or Anna Karenina, who was not so exceptional, or Nana, who was more nearly a typical kept woman? Perhaps. Reading the novel today (and it stands as a major accomplishment), one is aware that Jennie's essential goodness is difficult to accept completely. Mencken believed nonetheless that Dreiser had written a novel that no other American, and no more than half a dozen Englishmen, of the time could have matched.

In his *Smart Set* review, which appeared in November, 1911, under the title "A Novel of the First Rank," Mencken called it "the best American novel I have ever read, with the lonesome but Himalayan exception of *Huckleberry Finn*"—praise which Harper and Brothers used in their advertising of the book. Pretty obviously, Mencken had never read *Moby Dick*, or if he had, he had failed to appreciate its greatness. The review itself is a minor masterpiece; no other American critic of his day could have brought more persuasiveness, feeling, and insight to a book review. Mencken had another laudatory review ready for simultaneous appearance in Willard Wright's Christmas Book Section of the Los Angeles *Times* and the Baltimore *Evening Sun* and still others for any periodical or newspaper that would print them. Dreiser was at first bewildered by Mencken's overwhelming praise, not at all sure it was warranted. Soon afterward, a few other critics, notably Huneker and Floyd Dell, joined Mencken in hailing the book, and for the first time Dreiser had a respectable following (though not a best seller, the book did sell five thousand copies the first month). For services rendered, Dreiser allowed Mencken to choose one of his original manuscripts (he chose *Sister Carrie*) and, with unwonted foresight, designated him officially his literary executor and unofficially his agent and manager.

In his *Smart Set* review Mencken admitted that *Jennie* was not as graceful or humorous (there was no need to admit that!) or well constructed as various other American novels,

> but taking it as it stands, grim, gaunt, mirthless, shapeless, it remains, and by long odds, the most impressive work of art that we have yet to show in prose fiction—a tale not unrelated, in its stark simplicity, its profound sincerity, to *Germinal* and *Anna Karenina* and *Lord Jim*—a tale assertively American in its scene and its human material, and yet so European in its method, its point of view, its almost reverential seriousness, that one can scarcely imagine an American writing it.

What most appealed to him was the philosophy of life which the novel illustrated—by implication, though not by forthright statement. That "philosophy" is by now perhaps too well known and too generally accepted—that is, among people who read and write—to cause much furor, but at the time of Mencken's writing it was still not widely known and was viewed with something like abhorrence. There was in the novel "the same profound pessimism which gives a dark color to the best that we have from Hardy, Moore, Zola and the great Russians—the pessimism of disillusion—not the jejune, Byronic thing, not the green sickness of youth, but that pessimism which comes with the discovery that the riddle of life, despite all the fine solutions offered by the learned doctors, is essentially insoluble." The book was thus more than the ordinary novel in that it offered both a criticism and an interpretation of life. While comparing the *story* of Jennie to that of Carrie, Mencken showed that the tragedy of both heroines was not that they had been seduced and left forlorn. It was, after all, through their lovers that they were able to escape the physical miseries of the struggle for existence "only to taste the worse miseries of the struggle for happiness."

> With the rise from want to security, from fear to ease, comes an awakening of the finer perceptions, a widening of the sympathies, a gradual unfolding of the delicate flower called personality, an increased capacity for loving and living. But with all this, and as a part of it, there comes, too, an increased capacity for suffering—and so in the end, when love slips away and the empty years stretch before, it is the awakened and supersentient woman that pays for the folly of the groping, bewildered girl. The tragedy of Carrie and Jennie, in brief, is not that they are degraded but that they are lifted up, not that they go to the gutter but that they escape the gutter.

As always in his reviews of Dreiser's novels, Mencken concluded by commenting on the style, particularly the hackneyed diction. But even the naïveté of the trite expressions was, in the long run, an asset: "The narrative, in places, has the effect of a series of unisons in music—an effect which, given a solemn theme, vastly exceeds that of the most ornate polyphony." It was impossible, Mencken said, to imagine *Jennie* "done in the gipsy phrases of Meredith, the fugual manner of James. One cannot imagine that stark, stenographic dialogue adorned with the brilliants of speech." As it stood, it depicted better than any other novel of its day the life that was being lived in America.

Given Mencken's premise that the great novel was a criticism and an interpretation of life, it is difficult to argue against his notion that Dreiser outstripped his contemporaries of the early years of the century. As a craftsman, of course, he was the inferior of several of his fellow countrymen.

It would be hard to find two men who were at once more alike and more different than Mencken and Dreiser. As a youth Dreiser had been greatly influenced by two of Mencken's masters, Herbert Spencer and T. H. Huxley. He early adopted a somewhat deterministic view of man's place in nature; he agreed completely with Thomas Hardy that "we are to the gods as flies to wanton boys." But with what a different effect did the two men come to their identical conclusions! Mencken, who was a freethinker by inheritance, was intoxicated with a joyous skepticism; Dreiser was left morose and subdued, an apostate to the Catholic Church. Mencken delighted in existence and gleefully damned it as idiotic; even in the witless and obscene gambolings of the gods he found wry humor, profound irony. So far as I know, he was the only pessimist who could at the same time denounce life and make you want to live. The daily miracle of a fresh egg was enough to rouse his unbounded joy and wonder at the gift of life. Dreiser possessed little if any humor, nor could he see any in the unraveling of man's fate.

In their long friendship Mencken appears to have been the stronger and more influential of the two. After all, Mencken *knew* what he believed, at the same time admitting that he might be wrong. Dreiser searched constantly for belief, for a Rock. For example, Mencken constantly chided Dreiser for worrying over every unanswerable problem that the imagination could conceive. By the time he met Dreiser the general outline of his own skeptical view of things was drawn. Dreiser's mental journey appeared to be without direction, a kind of groping in the dark. During their early friendship, Mencken asked him to read his book on Nietzsche if he wished to be free from his petty questionings. Dreiser read the book and was greatly impressed; there is more than one evidence of Nietzsche to be found in the novelist's most artistically satisfying work, *The Titan*. What influence Mencken may have had in helping Dreiser escape the furies of doubt was short-lived, however. In a particularly revealing review (revealing of Mencken's view of things as much as of the book) of Dreiser's *Hey Rub-a-Dub-Dub*, a collection of essays that appeared in 1920, after Dreiser had become *the* major American novelist, the man other novelists looked to as leader of the cause for artistic freedom, Mencken concentrated

on Dreiser's wayward journeying through the metaphysical mists.
The book was, Mencken stated, the natural offspring of the sentient man's urge to unload his ideas. "If he is at that end of the
scale which touches the rising ladder of the *Simiidae* he becomes
a Socialist on a soap-box or joins the Salvation Army; if he is literate
and has a soul he writes a book." Mencken used the word "soul,"
incidentally, much as Joyce used it in *A Portrait of the Artist as a
Young Man.* He then "imagined" Dreiser "sitting up all night in his
sinister studio down in Tenth street, wrestling horribly with the
insoluble, trying his darndest to penetrate the unknowable." And in
the "imagining," Mencken caustically depicted a man wasting his
time.

> One o'clock strikes, and the fire sputters. Ghosts stalk in the
> room, fanning the yellow candle-light with their abominable
> breath—the spooks of all the men who have died for ideas since
> the world began—Socrates, Savonarola, Bruno (not Guido, but
> Giordano), Ravaillac, Sir Roger Casement, John Alexander
> Dowie, Dr. Crippen. Two o'clock. What, then, is the truth about
> marriage? Is it, as Grover Cleveland said, a grand sweet song,
> or is it, as the gals in the Village say, a hideous mockery and
> masquerade, invented by Capitalism to enslave the soul of
> woman—a legalized *Schweinerei*, worse than politics, almost as
> bad as the moving-pictures? Three o'clock. Was Marx right or
> wrong, a seer or a mere nose-puller? Was his name, in fact, ac-
> tually Marx, or was it Marcus? From what ghetto did he es-
> cape, and cherishing what grudge against mankind? Aha, the
> Huneker complex: *cherchez le Juif!* (I confess at once: my
> great-grandpa, Moritz, was rector of the Oheb Shalon *Schul* in
> Grodno). Three o'clock. . . .
> Back to Pontius Pilate! *Quod est veritas?* Try to define it.
> Break it into its component parts. What remains is a pale gray
> vapor, an impalpable emanation, the shadow of a shadow. Think
> of the brains that have gone to wreck struggling with the prob-
> lem—cerebrums as large as cauliflowers, cerebellums as perfect
> as pomegranates. Think of the men jailed, clubbed, hanged,
> burned at the stake—not for embracing error, but for embracing
> the *wrong* error. Think of the innumerable caravan of Burlesons,
> Mitchell Palmers, Torquemadas, Cotton Mathers. . . . Four
> o'clock. The fire burns low in the grate. A gray fog without.
> Across the street two detectives rob a drunken man. Up at Tar-
> rytown John D. Rockefeller snores in his damp Baptist bed,
> dreaming gaudily that he is young again and mashed on a girl
> named Marie. At Sing Sing forty head of Italians are waiting to

be electrocuted. There is a memorial service for Charles Garvice in Westminster Abbey. The Comstocks raid the Elsie books. Ludendorff is elected Archbishop of Canterbury. A poor working-girl, betrayed by Moe, the boss's son, drowns herself in the Aquarium. It is late, ah me: nearly four thirty. . . . Who the deuce, then, is God? What is in all this talk of a future life, infant damnation, the Ouija board, Mortal Mind? Dr. Jacques Loeb is the father of a dozen bullfrogs. Is the news biological or theological? What became of the Albigenses? Are they in heaven, in purgatory or in hell? . . . . Five o'clock. Boys cry the *Evening Journal*. Is it today's or tomorrow's? The question of transubstantiation remains. There is, too, neo-transcendentalism. . . . In Munich they talk of *Expressionismus*. . . . Poof! . . .[10]

It was easy enough to ponder such questions and phenomena, but working them out on paper was not so simple a business. Dreiser probably had at some time thought of composing novels that were "full of ideas, saying something, teaching something, exposing something, destroying something." But the artist in him prevented that pollution. So he gathered the ideas which the artist had rejected and put them in *Hey Rub-a-Dub-Dub*. Well, were the ideas worthy of survival in book form? Mencken seriously doubted it. To begin with, Dreiser lacked "the mental agility, the insinuating suavity, the necessary capacity for romanticising a syllogism." Having gone this far in the direction of pure skepticism, Mencken went the final step when he wrote:

Ideas themselves are such sober things that a sober man had better let them alone. What they need, to become bearable to a human race that hates them and is afraid of them, is the artful juggling of a William James, the insurance-agent persuasiveness of an Henri Bergson, the boob-bumping talents of a Martin Luther—best of all, the brilliant, almost Rabelaisian humor of a Nietzsche. Nietzsche went out into the swamp much further than any other explorer; he left such pallbearers of the spirit as Spencer, Comte, Descartes and even Kant all shivering on the shore.

Nietzsche had made skepticism charming, a delight to the eye and ear; Dreiser's skepticism was merely despairing. Dreiser simply took the sorrows of the world on his own shoulders and then passed them on to his reader. In effect, he was a novelist, not a philosopher; and, Mencken strongly implied, he should stick to his last. I do not give this review as a good example of Mencken's criticism of a book; it is no such thing. But it is excellent criticism of Dreiser.

While the review satisfies the first premise of Mencken's critical credo—to wit, that it be a work of art, that it interest the reader in and for itself, and that it make some sort of judgment against a relevant standard—it also is addressed to Dreiser, who, doubtless, was outraged. For the two men's many differences of opinion, often expressed with hostility, one should consult Mencken's *Letters* (1961) and *Letters of Theodore Dreiser* (3 volumes, Philadelphia, 1959).

After the rather successful *Jennie*, Dreiser's next novel, *The Financier* (1912), was a definite failure. His faults, which were so glaring that Mencken called them "methods," stood out clearly in this first volume of a proposed trilogy on the life of Frank Cowperwood, who had a real-life counterpart in Charles T. Yerkes (1837–1905), an American financier who in the manner of the robber baron gained control of the street-railway system in Chicago and later formed a syndicate to build the London underground railway. While pointing out its faults, Mencken praised the novel and again called attention to Dreiser's extraordinary ability to depict old men. In *Jennie*, there was old man Gerhardt; in *The Financier* was Edward Malia Butler, the father of Cowperwood's mistress.

Mencken considered *The Titan* (1914), as far as its structure was concerned, the best of Dreiser's novels, nor did he see any reason for revising his estimate with the publication of *An American Tragedy*, which he reviewed so severely that he and Dreiser were estranged for years. There were, Mencken said, fewer of the typical faults—clumsiness, bad diction, verbosity—in *The Titan* than in any other of his books. Cowperwood was admirably presented as "a blend of revolutionist and voluptuary, a highly civilized Lorenzo the Magnificent, an immoralist who would not hesitate two minutes about seducing a saint, but would turn sick at the thought of harming a child."[11] In *The Financier*, his sordid character was simply repellent, but in the second installment of his life he became Dreiser's greatest creation. Like the protagonists in Conrad's best novels, he was a completely "round" (a term later employed with great effect by E. M. Forster in his *Aspects of the Novel*) character—accounted for in every detail, and yet, in the final analysis, not accounted for at all. The conundrum of life hung about him to the end, veiling his inner self from human understanding. Indeed, Cowperwood never knew himself. He was capable of change, in other words, since his character was in a state of growth. Mencken considered him the complete and indubitable male—the complement, in a sense, of the eternal female depicted in Jennie. "His struggle with the inexorable forces that urge him on as with whips, and lure him with false lights, and bring him to disillusion and dismay, is as typical as hers is, and as tragic." Mencken wrote Dreiser (March 23, 1914) that he considered *The Titan* the best thing he had done, with the possible exception of *Jennie Gerhardt,* which was more poignant but less satisfactory in its form. Four days later he wrote Dreiser again, remarking that though Cowperwood did not appeal to the sympathies or "grip the more responsive emotions," as Carrie and Jennie did, he still thought the book "better planned and better written than either of the others."

Mencken felt that Dreiser's next novel, *The "Genius,"* marked the nadir of his achievement, as *The Titan* had reached the apex. Interrupting his Cowperwood trilogy (the third volume, *The Stoic,* did not appear until 1947), Dreiser endeavored in an overly long and turgid novel to tell the story of an amatory artist, Eugene Witla. In his *Smart Set* review of the novel, Mencken paid special attention to its formlessness and to Dreiser's bad writing and his laborious and relentless meticulousness ("the Dreiser manner devours and defeats itself"). In *A Book of Prefaces* he called the novel "flaccid, elephantine, doltish, coarse, dismal, flatulent, sophomoric, ignorant, unconvincing, wearisome." In his biography of Dreiser, F. O. Matthiessen stated that Mencken's adjectives still fit. Throughout the biography Matthiessen quoted Mencken's assessments of Dreiser's works—assessments which he found virtually impregnable.

There is no doubt that the novel was, as Mencken put it, "as gross and shapeless as Brünnehilde." Still, the work obviously came from the pen of a major writer and, with all its faults, deserved mention among the best fiction of that year. Besides, Dreiser, like all other artists, should be allowed to misfire now and then:

> But let it go! A novelist capable of *Jennie Gerhardt* has rights, privileges, prerogatives. He may, if he will, go on a spiritual drunk now and then, and empty the stale bilges of his soul. Thackeray, having finished *Vanity Fair* and *Pendennis,* bathed himself in the sheep's milk of *The Newcomes,* and after *The Virginians* he did *The Adventures of Philip.* Zola, with *Germinal, La Débâcle* and *La Terre* behind him, recreated himself horribly with *Fécondité.* Tolstoi, after *Anna Karenina,* wrote

What Is Art? Ibsen, after *Et Dukkehjem* and *Gengangere,* wrote *Vildanden.* The good God himself, after all the magnificence of Kings and Chronicles, turned Dr. Frank Crane and so botched his Writ with Proverbs. . . . A weakness that we must allow for.[12]

If *The "Genius"* represented no great achievement for Dreiser, it did assume a symbolic value that was of immense concern to American literature. For the ban placed on this novel by the New York Society for the Suppression of Vice in 1916 had the effect of clearly drawing the battle lines, of setting two opposing forces face to face. Before the suppression of the book, however, Mencken and Dreiser had all but come to a parting of ways. There is reason to believe that Mencken's criticism of *The Titan* while it was in manuscript form did much to make that Dreiser's most dramatic and best-constructed work. The book was praised by several critics and sold relatively well. But when Mencken criticized the manuscript of *The "Genius,"* Dreiser refused to listen, and the book was published, in October, 1915, as he first wrote it. When the smuthounds pounced on it in the summer of 1916, Dreiser realized that his Baltimore friend was still necessary.

At first, Mencken proposed to Dreiser that he allow the objectionable phrases to be taken out of the novel and then recirculate it. The war in Europe was in its third year, and anti-German sentiment was rampant in America. Mencken did not at all relish the role of martyr—indeed, he had little if any respect for martyrs, believing that they were often pathologically inclined to masochism; and he knew that Dreiser's very name would be a strike against him if the publisher, the John Lane Company, took the matter to court. Dreiser, however, was in no mood to compromise. He promptly enlisted the aid of a group of his radical friends, who organized a Committee of One Hundred in his support. Seeing that Dreiser would not back down in any way, Mencken came to his aid. First, he wrote the Authors' League of America and asked if it would join in the defense. It agreed, and Mencken and John Cowper Powys then drafted protests for writers and artists to sign. J. Jefferson Jones, the American agent of Lane's, a British firm, wrote London for support from English authors. Willard Wright debated the issue publicly with John S. Sumner, executive secretary of the New York Society for the Suppression of Vice; and Ezra Pound threw the weight of his *Egoist* against the censors. Harold Hersey, a Dreiser admirer, did much of the spadework, while Mencken wrote the more conservative and famous authors and convinced Dreiser that the names of his "tenth-rate Greenwich Village geniuses" be kept off the list, lest they alienate the writers he was most anxious to enlist. He sent the following note to the conservatives:

> Perhaps you believe, as I do, that The *"Genius"* is anything but a great novel. But here we have a battle that involves an issue far greater than the merits or fate of The *"Genius"*, and that is, the issue of freedom in letters. I know Dreiser to be an honest man, and I think he deserves to be let alone. His case is the case of all of us. We should at least support him as firmly as the authors of France supported Zola.[13]

The list of signers, about four hundred in all, was impressive. It included such names as Alfred A. Knopf, Nathan (of course), William Rose Benét, Robert Frost, Edward Arlington Robinson, Willa Cather, William Allen White, James Montgomery Flagg, Winston Churchill (the novelist), Booth Tarkington, Ellery Sedgwick, and Lawrence Gilman. Equally impressive, from England came the names of Arnold Bennett, Hugh Walpole, W. L. George, and H. G. Wells. There were some, of course, who refused to sign the protest for various reasons: William Lyon Phelps, Howells, Brander Matthews, Hamlin Garland, and Edith Wharton (who gave her ignorance of Dreiser's works as excuse).

Mencken felt that victory was in sight; with such overwhelming support the ban would have to be lifted. He had not taken into account, however, the bullheadedness of Dreiser. Assuming that his battle was won, Dreiser composed, in the fall of 1916, *The Hand of the Potter*, a four-act play about a sex pervert who violates and then murders an eleven-year-old child and then commits suicide. Mencken naturally protested the publication of such a play at that time (it was eventually published in 1918); indeed, he objected to such an outburst on artistic grounds as well. He wrote Dreiser a long letter,[14] listing his multifarious reasons for not thinking it advisable to have the play printed or staged. He began by saying that not only was the subject "impossible on the stage" but the handling of it lacked dramatic effectiveness, being little more than a series of speeches after the first act. "The whole thing is loose, elephantine and devoid of sting. It has no more dramatic structure than a jelly-fish." As for the subject matter, Mencken insisted that there were limits to artistic freedom in the theater, as in books. Actually, he seemed to contradict his frequently iterated defense of artistic freedom. It might be said in his defense, however, that he was more concerned with winning the fight over the banning of *The "Genius"* than he was with being placed in the position of fruitlessly aiding a martyr. Indeed, he later admitted to Dreiser[15] that his objection was not so much to the play intrinsically as to the folly of giving ammunition to the comstocks. A few months later he wrote Burton Rascoe[16] that he was much less against the play than he had been when it was first shown him. "But I think I did Dreiser a valuable service when I induced him to withhold it while the Comstock case against him was still before the courts. The idiot wanted to print it at once, to show how brave he was. He wrote it with the same aim." Considering the plays of greatest popularity during the last twenty years, one must chuckle over Mencken's initial letter to Dreiser on the subject:

> You and I, if we are lucky, visit the bowel-pot daily; as for me, I often have to leave a high-class social gathering to go out and piss; you, at least, have been known to roll a working girl on the couch. But such things, however natural, however interesting, are not for the stage. The very mention of them is banned by that convention on which the whole of civilized order depends. In no country of the world is such a thing as sexual perversion dealt with in the theatre. Even in Germany and Russia, where Wedekind's *Fruehlingserwachen* is played regularly, a touch of Krafft-Ebing would bring up the polizei.

Finally, Mencken felt that nothing was more abhorrent to the average man than sexual perversion: "He would roar against it in the theatre." At the time that may have been true.

Mencken argued further that the cause of the attack on *The "Genius"* was "not that Witla works his wicked will upon the girls, but that you make him insert his thumb into Angela's (as yet) virgin person. Copulation may go down, but the decencies must be observed. You and I, I hope, are good friends. I would not hesitate to tell you that I had fallen from virtue. But I would surely not recite for you the precise details of the act. This is a distinction to be remembered." Arguing further, he anticipated Dreiser's answer that he was hedging. Freedom, yes—but not without license.

If the thing were possible, I'd advocate absolutely unlimited freedom in speech, written and spoken. I think the world would be better off if I could tell a strange woman, met at a church social, that I have diarrhoea—if the stage could be used to set up a more humane attitude toward sexual perverts, who are helpless and unhappy folk—if novels and other books could describe the precise process of reproduction, beginning with the hand-shake and ending with lactation, and so show the young what a bore it is. But these things are forbidden. The overwhelming weight of opinion is against them. The man who fights for them is as absurd as the man who fights for the right to walk down Broadway naked, and with his gospel pipe in his hand. Both waste themselves upon futile things while sound and valuable things remain to be done.

Dreiser answered this outburst with a lengthy defense of the play on the grounds that it was a tragedy, and the subject matter was beside the point. He admitted Mencken was within his rights as a critic to denounce the play as "a hopeless botch," but that he was certainly not within those rights when he tried to tell Dreiser what the "artistic or moral limitations of the stage" were or what the American people would stand for. In other words, Mencken had gone beyond the realm of criticism and entered the domain of the artist, who, after all, must have more respect for his own judgment than for that of any critic. In this, Dreiser was right, of course, as Mencken later admitted; but then, Mencken was writing as friend and not as critic alone. He answered that Dreiser's stand would injure his case, then pending, before the comstocks: "Fully half of the signers of the Protest, painfully seduced into signing by all sorts of artifices, will demand that their names be taken off. You fill me with ire. I damn you in every European language. You have a positive genius for doing foolish things. Put the ms. behind the clock, and thank me and God for saving you from a mess." If they were nothing else, they were candid in their mutual respect.

Dreiser was at times stupid, and his memory was often weak, but he was not altogether unappreciative. Moreover, Mencken's outspoken remarks in the letters and in the published reviews were not designed to pacify him. Forgetting his grievances, he wrote Mencken on November 14, 1920: "And looking back on myself I know now that except for your valiant and unwearied and even murderous assaults and onslaughts in my behalf I should now be little farther than in 1910." Mencken answered: "You greatly over-estimate my services to you. You were squarely on your legs before I came into contact with you or wrote a line about you, and you would have made the same progress if I had been hanged in 1902, perhaps more." His determinism, a wise and perhaps irrefutable philosophy, had degenerated into something not far from fatalism, which refuses to acknowledge the importance of the *cause* in cause-effect sequences. After their cordial exchange in November, 1920, the disagreements appeared again within weeks. For example, Dreiser wrote a sarcastic note (December 6, 1920) to Mencken that *Hey Rub-a-Dub-Dub*, which Mencken disparaged, was out-selling *Twelve Men*, which Mencken praised, particularly the sec-tion on Dreiser's brother, Paul Dresser. He also defended *The "Genius,"* for which he always had a peculiar fondness, against Mencken's belief that it was weaker than the early novels. Mencken answered immediately (it is well known that he never left a letter unanswered for more than twenty-four hours), repeating former re-marks that he did not object to *The "Genius"* because of its realism, which seemed to him "harmless," but rather on the ground that "parts of it seem to me to be excessively dull" (obviously, Mencken's memory is here a bit vague, since he had objected to some of the "realistic" detail). Nor did he object, he wrote, to *Hey Rub-a-Dub-Dub* because it was unintelligible, but because much of it seemed to him unintelligent, "that is, far out of accord with my private notion of what is important and interesting and true." Finally he answered the boast that *Hey Rub-a-Dub-Dub* was outselling *Twelve Men:*

> The fact that [*Hey Rub-a-Dub-Dub*] outsells *Twelve Men* supports my view. *Twelve Men* is a vastly better piece of work. *Hey Rub-a-Dub-Dub* largely appeals, I believe, to the defec-tively educated. It certainly can't seem as wonderful to a man who has read, say, Nietzsche, Schopenhauer, Spencer, Huxley, Ostwald, Haeckel and Sumner as to one who has not read them. I don't think you argue well. I could have done the book much better myself, whereas I couldn't have done a single chapter of *Twelve Men* or *Sister Carrie.*
>
> But all this is unimportant. You are writing your books, and I am writing mine. Do your damnedest, and may the Good Lord Jesus watch over you. When you offend my pruderies I shall bawl, but I'd consider you an ass if you let it influence you.[17]

Three years later Dreiser declared in a widely publicized open letter to Gelett Burgess, vice-president of the Authors' League, that he had fought and was still fighting the battle of The "Genius" singlehanded without aid from any quarter. Mencken wrote him a furious letter (May 31, 1923), saying in part: "With all due respects, you lie like an archbishop. Young [Harold] Hersey sweated for you like a bull, and there was a critic in Baltimore who, as I recall it, laid out $300 in cash to round up the authors of the United States on your side. Most of them, true enough, ratted, but that was surely not his fault." He then concluded his letter: "How are you, anyhow? I am thinking of giving up literature and returning to the cigar business."

Dreiser responded, admitting he was "a victim of the archepiscopal failing." Ostensibly, the Protest was a failure, for the comstocks did not lift the ban until 1923, when Dreiser made his silly brag. Before then Mencken had acted as an arbitrator, meeting with Sumner in an effort to work out a policy agreeable to both sides. Although he was successful in getting the number and length of the "objectionable" passages greatly reduced, he was unable to convince Dreiser that he should allow the book to be reprinted. Dreiser had asked Mencken in 1922 to meet with Sumner again in hopes that the novel might be reissued. Mencken obtained a greatly abbreviated list of objections this time, and Dreiser seemed ready to go ahead with the slightly expurgated version. When Mencken heard that Dreiser planned to allow an unexpurgated edition to be printed the next year, he wrote Dreiser that he would like to know in advance if what he heard was true, since he did not want Sumner, who had "acted very decently," to think that Mencken "was fooling him about the cuts."

Though no aesthetic judgment can be definitive, Mencken came as close as a mortal can get to stating the last word in his essay on Dreiser in A Book of Prefaces. After glancing briefly at the influences on his thought and style (H. B. Fuller was, according to Mencken, the only American who seemed to be a forerunner; Thomas Hardy had the most profound effect on him), Mencken examined the Dreiser method of prose composition: "an endless piling up of minutiae, an almost ferocious tracking down of ions, electrons and molecules, an unshakeable determination to tell it all. One is amazed by the mole-like diligence of the man, and no less by his exasperating disregard for the ease of his reader." All of his faults were pinpointed and held up to public view; Mencken was especially short with Dreiser's poor diction, the tendency to indulge in banalities, the working to death of trite phrases. He never imitated Flaubert by writing for *"la respiration et l'oreille"*: "There is no painful groping for the inevitable word, or for what Walter Pater called 'the gipsy phrase'; the common, even the commonplace, coin of speech is good enough."

Turning then to his general philosophy, Mencken showed the similarity between Dreiser and, among others, Conrad. Like Conrad, Dreiser was a skeptic, but with a major difference. Dreiser, who was born a peasant and, in many ways, remained one all his life, was constantly groping for hidden meanings and was perfectly willing to employ the Ouija board to aid in the search. Mencken once remarked that if Dreiser became ill and walked along a street where there were two signs, one reading Dr. Osler and the other Dr. Quack, you could bet all your money that he would go in to see Dr. Quack every time. On the other hand, Conrad, an aristocrat by birth and training, possessed the gift of emotional detachment. "The lures of facile doctrine do not move him. In his irony there is a disdain which plays about even the ironist himself." But Dreiser was the product of different forces and traditions and could "no more shake off the chains of his intellectual and cultural heritage than he can change the shape of his nose." There was, Mencken felt, vastly more intuition than intellect in Dreiser. His ideas seemed to be always deduced from his feelings. For this reason, Mencken believed that his talent was essentially feminine, as Conrad's was masculine.

To illustrate his belief, Mencken compared Dreiser to Schubert, "an ignoramus, even in music; he knew less about polyphony, which is the mother of harmony, which is the mother of music, than the average conservatory professor." Still, Schubert "had such a vast instinctive sensitiveness to musical values, such a profound and accurate feeling for beauty in tone, that he not only arrived at the truth of tonal relations, but even went beyond what, in his day, was known to be the truth, and so led an advance." Dreiser had done the same thing with the novel of his own day. To be sure, Dreiser was disorderly, sometimes chaotic, but his effects were often overwhelming. "One swiftly forgets his intolerable writing, his

mirthless, sedulous, repellent manner, in the face of the Athenian
tragedy he instils into his seduced and soul-sick servant girls, his
barbaric pirates of finances, his conquered and hamstrung supermen, his wives who sit and wait." All this is evident today, but at
the time Mencken was almost alone in his belief.

Mencken then examined the individual works, pointing out that
no development, after the first two novels, was evident in Dreiser's
manner (*Jennie* was followed by *The Financier,* which was followed by *The Titan,* which was followed by *The "Genius"*—from
very good to average to the best to the worst). In these novels were
the magnificent characters of Cowperwood, Jennie and, especially,
the old men. "Dreiser is at his best, indeed, when he deals with old
men. In their tragic helplessness they stand as symbols of that un-
fathomable cosmic cruelty which he sees as the motive power of
life itself."

Much of this long (eighty-page) essay was taken up with
defending Dreiser against his attackers: the comstocks and the academic critics who considered Dreiser a mere recorder of unsavory
events in the lives of unsavory people. That Dreiser's realism was
abhorrent to many Americans raised on the sugared nothings manufactured by the popular novelists was in no way a competent criticism of Dreiser. One thinks of the story concerning the American
tourist who, on leaving the Louvre, remarked to a guard that he
saw nothing inside that was worthy of admiration. The guard simply informed the tourist that the pictures inside were no longer on
trial; it was now the viewer who stood before the judge.

Mencken always insisted that it was impossible to pigeonhole
Dreiser; that, in fact, he did not fit any contemporary theories of
realism or naturalism. "His aim is not merely to record, but to
translate and understand; the thing he exposes is not the empty
event and act, but the endless mystery out of which it springs."
He found the most apposite analogy in these lines from *Oedipus
Rex:* "O ye deathward-going tribes of man, what do your lives mean
except that they go to nothingness?" In Dreiser's novels, as Mencken
pointed out, there is a quality that is often absent from pure representation. In reviewing a novel (for the *Mercury* in April, 1924)
that the "Young Intellectuals" admired and begged him to read,
Mencken remarked that the work, an imitation of Dreiser, fell short
because it merely reported the acts and words of its characters.

It failed to do what all good novels must do; that is, it did not move the reader or make him feel for and with the people of the story. Going on to explain what made Dreiser an extraordinary artist, Mencken used *Jennie* to illustrate his belief that the evocation of emotion was the central business of the novelist, as of all other artists. In a way that was hard to analyze, Dreiser made us see the world through Jennie's eyes, thereby giving us an understanding of her tragedy.

> Superficially, [Jennie] is simply a girl of loose morals, living in contempt of the Mann Act. But actually, in Dreiser's highly skillful hands, she becomes a representative of the agony of all womankind. The last scene of the book, with Jennie looking through the train-gate as Lester's carcass is loaded into the baggage-coach, is surely not mere photography; it is poignant and unforgettable tragedy. To argue that it cannot be tragedy because Jennie is a poor simpleton—in other words, that simple folk cannot know disaster and despair—is to argue plain nonsense.

To read Dreiser unmoved, Mencken said, is to confess that there is nothing moving in the eternal tragedy of man.

IV

With the possible exception of the eighteen-fifties, no ten-year period in American history has been so productive of literary art as the decade following World War I and terminating with the stock market crash in October, 1929. America not only came of age, after an almost fantastically long adolescence, but began to set the pace, in literary matters anyhow, for other nations. American writers possessed more freedom to experiment and more freedom of subject matter than ever before. There were, indeed, almost as many first-rate novels written in that decade as had been written in the preceding three hundred years since the landing at Jamestown. American poetry, as written by Jeffers, Frost, Robinson, Millay, Stevens, Aiken, Eliot, Sandburg, Pound, and Cummings, so far exceeded the poetry of any other period that one might almost assume that American poets had, like Rip Van Winkle, snoozed for an age, to wake suddenly all together.

If the writers of the nineteen-twenties had any one thing in common, it was the feeling of discontent with their homeland.

America, settling "in the mold of its vulgarity, heavily thickening to empire," was viewed as a Wasteland, a Perishing Republic, the home of the Beautiful and Damned. Soldiers returning from Europe found that A. Mitchell Palmer was rounding up enemy aliens to cultivate our prison farms, read in the papers that George F. Babbitt had just been elected head of Rotary (by unanimous vote, his only detractors being absent from the meeting), found that the rotgut sold in the corner speak-easy was infinitely inferior to and outlandishly more expensive than the cooling vintage of European bistros and sidewalk cafés, felt outraged at the puritanical repressions of everything physiological,[18] were nauseated by the grotesque hypocrisy of American politics, manners, morals, business—and decided not to unpack after all. Not everyone, of course, greeted his homeland with the salutation of hail and farewell; a man's freedom is dependent, in large part, on his bank statement. Still, there were enough solvent citizens of artistic, and pseudoartistic, bent to fill the boats to overloading, and the boats left every day.

But where was Mencken, the man who found so much to decry in the throat-parched Republic? He was standing quietly on the dock, wrapped in the flag, bidding fond farewell to his younger countrymen who had no taste for the obscene pranks of one-hundred-per-cent Americans. I take a sentence from his apologia:

> Yet here I stand, unshaken and undespairing, a loyal and de-voted Americano, even a chauvinist, paying taxes without com-plaint, obeying all laws that are physiologically obeyable, accepting all the searching duties and responsibilities of citizen-ship unprotestingly, investing the sparse usufructs of my miser-able toil in the obligations of the nation, avoiding all commerce with men sworn to overthrow the government, contributing my mite toward the glory of the national arts and sciences, enrich-ing and embellishing the native language, spurning all lures (and even all invitations) to get out and stay out—here am I, a bachelor of easy means, forty-two years old, unhampered by debts or issue, able to go wherever I please and to stay as long as I please—here am I, contentedly and even smugly basking beneath the Stars and Stripes, a better citizen, I daresay, and certainly a less murmurous and exigent one, than thousands who put the Hon. Warren Gamaliel Harding beside Friedrich Bar-barossa and Charlemagne, and hold the Supreme Court to be directly inspired by the Holy Spirit, and belong ardently to every Rotary Club, Ku Klux Klan, and Anti-Saloon League, and

choke with emotion when the band plays "The Star-Spangled Banner," and believe with the faith of little children that one of Our Boys, taken at random, could dispose in a fair fight of ten Englishmen, twenty Germans, thirty Frogs, forty Wops, fifty Japs, or a hundred Bolsheviki.[19]

Why did he remain at home? Because nowhere else on earth could a man of his general weaknesses, vanities, appetites, prejudices, and aversions be half so happy as he could be right here where "the general average of intelligence, of knowledge, of competence, of integrity, of self-respect, of honor is so low that any man who knows his trade, does not fear ghosts, has read fifty good books, and practices the common decencies stands out as brilliantly as a wart on a bald head, and is thrown willy-nilly into a meager and exclusive aristocracy." Moreover, the daily panorama of human existence here was "so inordinately gross and preposterous, so perfectly brought up to the highest conceivable amperage, so steadily enriched with an almost fabulous daring and originality, that only the man who was born with a petrified diaphragm can fail to laugh himself to sleep every night, and to awake every morning with all the eager, unflagging expectation of a Sunday-school superintendent touring the Paris peep-shows."

After admitting that a "certain sough of rhetoric may be here," Mencken went on to comment on a variety of topics, all of them concerned with the nation's accomplishments, its present status, and its destiny. He discussed the fallacious belief that art and poverty go hand in hand (the Greenwich Village Complex again), the difficulty of being civilized in America, the bogus hardships (comparatively speaking) of the pioneers, the traits of the American peasant, the national morality and its savage taboos, the rise of mobocracy, the lack of an intellectual aristocracy, the continued dependence on England, the absurd bragging over America's military history ("The combats with Mexico and Spain were not wars; they were simply lynchings"), the American Legion, and America as the Greatest Show on Earth. One of the most joyously, even uproariously, cynical essays in our literature, "On Being an American" is also one of the most perceptive appraisals of the national weaknesses that I know of. Proof is readily seen in the fact that the essay may be read today and its contemporaneousness be immediately felt. Exaggerated it was. But it was not without its central truth. Furthermore, it did what is no longer done, perhaps cannot any longer be done: it insulted precisely those myths and myth-makers that were thought to be most secure. Mencken was "de-lighted" (and dismayed, of course) by all things American—espe-cially, and above all, by America's colossal showmanship. Where else on earth, he asked, could a man be afforded the joy of having Harding as President for only eighty cents a year—his private share of the expense of maintaining the Chief Executive? He estimated that the United States Senate would cost him about eleven dollars for the year, and, as a journalist, he would receive the *Congres-sional Record*, regularly priced at fifteen dollars, for nothing. Thus, for four dollars less than nothing he would be entertained as Solo-mon never was by his hooch dancers. What really endeared America to Mencken, though, was the political campaign.

> Consider, for example, a campaign for the Presidency. Would it be possible to imagine anything more uproariously idiotic—a deafening, nerve-wracking battle to the death between Tweedle-dum and Tweedledee, Harlequin and Sganarelle, Gobbo and Dr. Cook—the unspeakable, with fearful snorts, gradually swal-lowing the inconceivable? I defy any one to match it elsewhere on this earth. In other lands, at worst, there are at least intel-ligible issues, coherent ideas, salient personalities. Somebody says something, and somebody replies. But what did Harding say in 1920, and what did Cox reply? Who was Harding, any-how, and who was Cox? Here, having perfected democracy, we lift the whole combat to symbolism, to transcendentalism, to metaphysics.[20]

Have presidential campaigns changed remarkably in the last forty years?

For all his mock sympathy for the Young Intellectuals who fled the shambles for foreign scenes, Mencken actually regarded the expatriate with a somewhat jaundiced eye. He believed that the professional writer functioned best in his own back yard. It is true that he delighted in the circus spectacle of American life, but that delight was always darkly tinged with satiric scorn. For one thing, he was seriously concerned with the development of a native American literature. He felt, for example, that Henry James, whom he admired as a craftsman, had made the mistake of going the wrong way when he set out to escape the desiccated culture of New England. "In London he was in exactly the same situation as a young Westerner in Boston—that is, he was confronted by a culture more solid and assured than his own. It kept him shaky all his life long; it also kept him fawning, as his letters inconveniently reveal. He died a sort of super-Howells, with a long row of laborious but essentially hollow books behind him." This estimate will doubtless appear outrageously harsh to James votaries; but it should be remembered that while he refused to place James on the same level with Conrad, Mencken placed him far above Howells and the vast majority of his contemporaries. I am convinced Mencken was correct when he stated that James's "painful psychologizings, when translated into plain English," turned out to be chiefly kittenishness, "an arch tickling of the ribs of elderly virgins—the daring of a grandma smoking marijuana."

Mencken's concern for a nationalistic literature was one reason why he admired Willa Cather's novels, and why he admired Willa Cather. In her work, as in the work of Dreiser, Lewis, Lardner, Anderson, and Ruth Suckow, he perceived something distinctly American. In *Alexander's Bridge* (1912), her first novel, Mencken saw great promise. *O Pioneers!* (1913) showed a definite advance, and *The Song of the Lark* (1915) offered proof that she was a true professional. Mencken considered *My Ántonia* (1918) her best novel and the best ever written by an American of her sex. Her later work was never as moving as that story of a young Bohemian girl's life on the Nebraska plains and the hardy strength she displayed in meeting the adversities of pioneer life. Moreover, Miss Cather made no effort to "teach" or reform; she had no pet theory for the cures of the world's aches and pains; she was a pure artist. In his review of that novel, Mencken remarked her extraordinary ability to create something beautiful out of the apparently sordid:

> The whole enchantment is achieved by the simplest of all possible devices. One follows a poor Bohemian farm girl from her earliest teens to middle age, looking closely at her narrow world, mingling with her friends, observing the gradual widening of her experience, her point of view—and that is all. Intrinsically, the thing is sordid—the life is almost horrible, the horizon is leaden, the soul within is pitifully shrunken and dismayed. But what Miss Cather tries to reveal is the true romance that lies even there—the grim tragedy at the heart of all that dull, cowlike existence—the fineness that lies deeply buried beneath the peasant shell.[21]

There is no way of accurately estimating Mencken's influence on the nineteen-twenties. It is a demonstrable fact, however, that the writers, almost without exception, who gained a large and lasting audience in the early years of that decade—and of the preceding decade—owed at least part of their popularity to Mencken. In turn, they were unanimous in their praise of the critic—a rarity, indeed, when the defendant kisses the hand of his judge! The three most influential writers of that day, Dreiser, Lewis, and Sherwood Anderson, were all indebted to Mencken. The influence of Dreiser and Anderson on other writers was incalculably great, and Lewis' books colored the thought of American readers for a generation. Nathan and Mencken accepted stories from both Anderson and Lewis for the *Smart Set* as early as 1916. Reviewing *Winesburg, Ohio* in 1919, Mencken felt "all the joy that goes with the discovery of something quite new under the sun—a new order of short story, half tale and half psychological anatomizing, and vastly better than all the kinds that have gone before." Although he was not as enthusiastic over Anderson's novels as he was over the short stories, Mencken saw at once that Anderson was a first-rate artist. He also saw that there were *two* Andersons, sharply differentiated and warring with each other.

> One is the artist who sees the America of his day as the most cruel and sordid, and yet at the same time as the most melodramatic and engrossing of spectacles—the artist enchanted by the sheer barbaric color of it all, and eager to get that color into living pages—the artist standing, as it were, above the turmoil, and intent only upon observing it accurately and representing it honestly, feelingly and unhindered. The other is a sort of uncertain social reformer—one appalled by the muddle of ideas and aspirations in the Republic, and impelled to do something or say something, however fantastic, however obvious, to help along the slow and agonizing process of reorganization—in brief, a typical American of the more reflective sort, full of inchoate visions and confused indignations.[22]

If the second of the two Andersons generally triumphed in the novels, the former won hands down in such short-story collections as *Winesburg, Ohio* and *Horses and Men*. That criticism is universally accepted today.

In Sinclair Lewis' respect for Mencken there was a strong flavor of hero worship. He not only considered Mencken the greatest critic

America had produced but went so far as to write novels, and the best ones he was ever to write (*Babbitt* and *Elmer Gantry*), on subjects recommended by Mencken. Nathan has humorously described the first meeting between Lewis and the two *Smart Set* editors—a meeting which promised anything but the close friendship which was to follow. A mutual friend, T. R. Smith, then managing editor of the *Century Magazine,* had invited Mencken and Nathan to drop by his apartment for a drink one evening in 1920. On arrival they were greeted by a tall, skinny, redheaded loudmouth, whom they knew only as the author of a short story they had published four years earlier and of a serial that had first appeared in the *Saturday Evening Post* and then later been gathered between book covers. Lewis, too drunk to stand without aid, at once entwined a long arm around the neck of Mencken and another around the neatly cravated neck of Nathan and began yelling at the top of his voice:

> So you guys are critics, are you? Well, let me tell you something. I'm the best writer in this here gottdam country and if you Georgie, and you, Hank, don't know it now, you'll know it gottdamn soon. Say, I've just finished a book that'll be published in a week or two and it's the gottdamn best book of its kind that this here gottdamn country has had and don't you guys forget it! I worked a year on this gottdamn thing and it's the goods. I'm a-telling you! Listen, when it comes to writing a novel, I'm so far ahead of most of the men you two think are good that I'll be gottdamned if it doesn't make me sick to think of it! Just wait till you read the gottdamn thing. You've got a treat coming, Georgie and Hank, and don't you boys make no mistake about that![23]

After a half-hour of such roaring, Lewis tired, and Mencken and Nathan ran for the door. Proclaiming "that red-headed numskull" the greatest idiot he had ever laid eyes on, Mencken set about trying to forget the unpleasant fellow as rapidly as possible. Dropping by the office the next morning, previous to catching a train back to Baltimore, Mencken was amazed to find proofs of a novel by the redhead waiting for him, along with a note from the publisher thanking him for the praise he had allegedly bestowed on the author at Smith's the day before. Having nothing else to read on the train, Mencken reluctantly set forth with *Main Street* under his arm. By the time the train reached Baltimore, he had undergone a shock which threatened to undermine his religious faith. He wrote Nathan at once:

> Dear George: Grab hold of the bar rail, steady yourself for a terrible shock! I've just read the advance sheets of the book of that *Lump* we met at Schmidt's and, by God, he has done the job! It's a genuinely excellent piece of work. Get it as soon as you can and take a look. I begin to believe that perhaps there isn't a God after all. There is no justice in the world.
>
> Yours in Xt.,
M.[24]

In his review of the novel, Mencken praised its exactness of detail, its almost perfect dialogue, its accurate presentation of a typical American family in a typical American town. Although Carol's revolt against the stuffiness of her surroundings was not typical of the average American housewife, she and Will Kennicott were in other respects "triumphs of the national normalcy—she with her vague stirrings, her unintelligible yearnings, her clumsy gropings, and he with his magnificent obtuseness, his childish belief in meaningless phrases, his intellectual deafness and near-sightedness, his pathetic inability to comprehend the turmoil that goes on within her." In this "disparate cultural development of male and female," Mencken saw the essential tragedy of American life, or, at any rate, the sardonic farce. Lewis' rendering of the struggle between Will and Carol was especially pleasing to Mencken.

> [Lewis] is far too intelligent to take sides—to turn the thing into a mere harangue against one or the other. Above all, he is too intelligent to take the side of Carol, as nine novelists out of ten would have done. He sees clearly what is too often not seen—that her superior culture is, after all, chiefly bogus—that the oafish Kennicott, in more ways than one, is actually better than she is. Her war upon his Philistinism is carried on with essentially Philistine weapons. Her dream of converting a Minnesota prairie town into a sort of Long Island suburb, with overtones of Greenwich Village and the Harvard campus, is quite as absurd as his dream of converting it into a second Minneapolis, with overtones of Gary, Ind., and Patterson, N. J.[25]

Ironically, Lewis probably intended Carol to appeal more to the reader's sympathy than Mencken would have us believe. Here is an excellent example of an author's intention not being fulfilled, since nearly all readers of the novel today will agree with Mencken that Carol's "superior culture" was, indeed, mainly bogus. On the debit side of the ledger, Mencken noted that Lewis' characters were sometimes "flat," that is, two-dimensional, and that the author was unable to give his creations the poignancy that Dreiser managed so well: "One seldom sees into them very deeply or feels with them very keenly." Still, Lewis' satire was quite effective and, though done with malice, never went beyond the bounds of probability. He concluded his criticism: "I have read no more genuinely amusing novel for a long time. The man who did it deserves a hearty welcome. His apprenticeship in the cellars of the tabernacle was not wasted."

When *Babbitt* (1922) appeared, Mencken quite rightly hailed it as a great advance for Lewis. Babbitt was more than a character in a novel; he was a type of Everyman. There was far more, Mencken felt, than just humor in the novel; there was searching truth. Nor had Lewis written a coldly analytical novel; he had done more than just "represent." In *Main Street* he had very nearly gone too far in the direction of emotion-dry representation; here there was more imagination and less "bald journalism." Above all, Lewis had a better grip on the characters in the later novel. Babbitt lived and breathed: "The fellow simply drips with human juices. Every one of his joints is movable in all directions. Real freckles are upon his neck and real sweat stands upon his forehead." His saga was hardly even "fiction." Lewis had abandoned all the tricks of the trade, including plot and character development. He gave the reader people who underwent no more change in the two years covered by the story than you or I have changed in the last two years.

> Every customary device of the novelist is absent. When Babbitt, revolting against the irksome happiness of his home, takes to a series of low affairs with manicure girls, grass-widows and ladies even more complaisant, nothing overt and melodramatic happens to him. He never meets his young son Teddy in a dubious cabaret; his wife never discovers incriminating correspondence in his pockets; no one tries to blackmail him; he is never present when a joint is raided. The worst punishment that falls upon him is that his old friends at the Athletic Club—cheats exactly like himself—gossip about him a bit. Even so, that gossip goes no further; Mrs. Babbitt does not hear it. When

she accuses him of adultery, it is simply the formal accusation of a loving wife: she herself has absolutely no belief in it. Moreover, it does not cause Babbitt to break down, confess and promise to sin no more. Instead, he lies like a major-general, denounces his wife for her evil imagination, and returns forthwith to his carnalities. If, in the end, he abandons them, it is not because they torture his conscience, but because they seem likely to hurt his business. This prospect gives him pause, and the pause saves him. He is, beside, growing old. He is 48, and more than a little bald. A night out leaves his tongue coated in the morning. As the curtain falls upon him he is back upon the track of rectitude—a sound business man, a faithful Booster, an assiduous Elk, a trustworthy Presbyterian, a good husband, a loving father, a successful and unchallenged fraud.[26]

Though Mencken was to state two years later, in defense of *Babbitt*, that the *pity* in the novel was worth all its humor (and certainly Babbitt is a pitiable creature, since he is essentially helpless), his enthusiasm doubtless derived from the criticism which the book made of American society—of its herd morality, mob politics, standardized habits of all kinds—in brief, of the abject surrender of the individual to the mass. And these are precisely the criticisms that Mencken had been making of Americans for years. Moreover, he felt the novel had the utilitarian value of accomplishing a thousand times better what writers like Walter Lippmann had endeavored to do in such volumes as *Public Opinion*. Needless to say, *Babbitt* is often taught in sociology courses, evidently as a sort of "case history" of other-directedness. Though Mencken was later to write of the pity in the novel, of Babbitt's impotent attempt to gain freedom, his initial criticism is sound: Babbitt was, and is, a hollow fraud. That Lewis may have had a kind of sympathy for him is beside the point.

Mencken realized that Lewis, like Dreiser, was often very uneven; he could be very good and very bad in the same book. And then he could be almost incredibly bad, as in *Mantrap* (1926), which left Mencken amazed: "I have presented *Mantrap* to my pastor, and return joyfully to a rereading of *Babbitt*." In *Elmer Gantry* (1927) Lewis created a character that was dear to Mencken, that was drawn for and dedicated to him. As Carl Van Doren remarked in his little book on Lewis (1933): "In a sense, Gantry is Mr. Mencken's criticism rendered in flesh and blood, put into drama, and set moving." Aside from the fact that the novel is an extraordinarily vivid and incisive portrait of a highly successful rogue—probably the best pure satire ever written by an American —it was still inevitable that Mencken, considering his contempt for vice crusaders, would be delighted by the book. In his *Mercury* review, Mencken placed it on the same shelf with *Babbitt*, even remarking that it was superior in some respects. He considered Babbitt's momentary dalliance with "the Liberal heresies" hardly credible; Babbitt was not, in effect, a perfect example of Babbittry. (Lewis, of course, had used the "dalliance" as a means of providing Babbitt with a saving grace; but again, Mencken was right: Babbitt is not the sort who would contemplate revolt from his natural order.) But Gantry was a flawless creation.

> The story is beautifully designed, and it moves with the inevitability of a fugue. It is packed with observation, all fresh, all shrewd, all sound. There is gargantuan humor in it, and there is also something not far from moving drama. It is American from the first low cackle of the prologue to the last gigantic obscenity—as American as goose-stepping or the mean admiration of mean things. And out of it leaps the most vivid and loving, the most gaudy and glorious, the most dreadful and perfect portrait of a man of God that has got between covers since Rabelais painted Friar John.[27]

The enraged outcries that greeted the publication of *Elmer Gantry* exceeded those surrounding the advent of any other book in our history. Mark Schorer, who considers *Gantry* a major achievement, thinks the "hot feelings" it aroused have caused it to be Lewis' one novel which has been consistently underrated. Naturally enough, Lewis was criticized for overstating his case against Babbitt and Gantry, among others. After all, Gantry is hardly representative of most clergymen; *ergo* (so the argument goes), Gantry is not a valid creation. The same logic would deny the worth of Chaucer's lecherous summoner and obscene pardoner, not to mention Molière's Tartuffe. In defending Lewis, Mencken pointed out the obvious when he stated that Lewis never intended Gantry to be taken as the archetype of *all* clergymen. But he did possess all the characteristics, dramatically revealed for artistic purposes, of the vice-crusading clergyman of the Billy Sunday vintage. Mencken did not think, either, that Gantry was overdrawn;

indeed, he had known just such a Tartuffe in Baltimore in 1916
(about whom he had written at the time, incidentally). He was a
powerful regulator of public morals, and it was generally believed
that he would rise fast in his chosen field of saving souls. However, the police, who were, according to Mencken, terrorized by
the man, took the liberty of checking into his private life and uncovered evidence of vices unspeakable.

> Shortly afterward he left town between days, and has never
> been heard from since. Curiously enough, the recreations which
> the cops unearthed were not unlawful under the liberal laws
> of the Maryland Free State, a commonwealth much given to
> carnal exercises. But he cleared out nevertheless, and so the
> Methodist connection lost a powerful and consecrated bishop,
> and the Anti-Saloon League an enthusiastic supporter.

While reviewing *Dodsworth*, and finding it inferior to Lewis'
three best novels, Mencken summed up the novelist's rare ability
as our most acute observer, while at the same time denying the
charge that Lewis was nothing more than a reporter (it will be
recalled that he had also felt obligated to defend Dreiser against
the same absurd criticism):

> No novelist in practice among us observes so accurately, or has
> so vast a talent for putting what he sees into pungent phrases.
> He is, by long odds, the best reporter ever heard of—not, as
> incompetent critics so often allege, because he is only a re-
> porter, but because he is so much more than a reporter. Bab-
> bitt shaving, Dr. Kennicott operating, Gantry drunk—these are
> little masterpieces that no rival has ever matched.[28]

Of the *Letters of H. L. Mencken* so far published, several are
to Lewis. Of special interest is one (dated October 15, 1945)
written in an effort to bolster the spirits of the extremely melancholy
novelist. Mencken also offers, in as unobstrusive a manner as possible, some good advice to the artist that was almost dead in Lewis.
The letter, which Mark Schorer quotes at great length in his
biography, begins:

> In am not going to tell you that *Cass Timberlane* is comparable
> to *Babbitt* or *Elmer Gantry* (all except the last 30,000 words,
> which you wrote in a state of liquor), but it seems to me to be
> the best thing you have done, and by long odds, since *Dods-
> worth*. It has the same defects that *Dodsworth* had: the woman

is such a bitch that it is hard to imagine a sensible man falling
for her. But you have a right to set your own story, and in
Cass Timberlane you have managed it admirably. There is not
a trace of the banality that I howled against in *Ann Vickers*.
There is none of the patriotic fustian that made me sick in
It Can't Happen Here. There is no going to pieces toward the
end, as in *Gideon Planish*. In brief, a well-planned and well-
executed book, with a fine surface. I liked the Assemblages of
Husbands and Wives especially. The authentic Red, foul and
full of sin, shows up in them. They are searching and swell
stuff, though I protest that frigging is much less important in
marriage than you seem to make it out. The main thing is
simply talk. It is boredom that makes the lawyers fat.

After this opening praise, Mencken asked Lewis to consider for
his next novel the numerous types in America that begged to be
embalmed in his amber: "the rich radical, the bogus expert, the
numskull newspaper proprietor (or editor), the career jobholder,
the lady publicist, the crooked (or, more usually, idiotic) labor
leader, the press-agent, and so on." While there were many writers
of "love stories and Freudian documents," there was no other
writer to compare with Lewis as an "anatomist of the American
Kultur." The fact that Lewis was sixty—a fact that he brooded
over—meant nothing. After all, he was writing better books at
sixty than he was at fifty. Turning then to the sad news that Lewis
had given up his bibulous ways, Mencken remarked: "Seeing you
on the water-wagon affects me like seeing you on your knees.
It is intolerably obscene. But if it is necessary, then let us forget
it. At any moment the quacks may order me to join you. If so, I
shall thank them for their advice—and retire to a brewery." After
commenting again on what Lewis might write next and paying a
Menckenian compliment to the sort of women who are worthy of
a man's devotion (like so many writers, Lewis was constantly in
trouble with the ladies), Mencken concluded: "I hope that *Cass*
is selling well, and that you are not laying out all your lucre on
ice-cream sodas. If you had any fixed place of abode, like a decent
Christian, and it were near to Baltimore we might meet now and
then and think up nasty names for our enemies. But God seems
determined to keep us apart. Maybe we will meet in Heaven. I
surely hope not."

V

Dreiser, Miss Cather, Anderson, and Lewis were but four masters whom Mencken aided. A list of the others—James Branch Cabell, Floyd Dell, Ruth Suckow, Ring Lardner, F. Scott Fitzgerald, John Dos Passos, Edgar Lee Masters, Joseph Hergesheimer, Carl Van Vechten—is very nearly a list of the best American writers at work in 1920. Among those appearing in the *Smart Set* between 1916 and 1923 were Dreiser, Willa Cather (three times), Anderson, Lewis, Cabell, Ruth Suckow (several times), Fitzgerald (ten times, including "May Day" and "Diamond as Big as the Ritz"), Masters (poetry), O'Neill (three plays), J. W. Krutch, Howard Mumford Jones, Lewis Mumford, Maxwell Anderson, Anita Loos, John Hall Wheelock, Ben Hecht, Dorothy Parker. Waldo Frank, Thomas Beer, Julia Peterkin, John Peale Bishop—all these writers more than once and several of them, especially Hecht and Jones, numerous times. Fitzgerald, incidentally, raged that he had to sell his best stories, the ones he really sweated over, to Mencken for a paltry three hundred dollars or so, while the ones he knocked out in a day and a night brought two thousand dollars and up from other magazines.

In 1920 Mencken stated that he could not imagine any competent novel going unpublished in America for longer than six months. Only four years earlier he had been fighting Dreiser's war; now the comstocks were on the defensive, and, Mencken believed, the American novelist had as much freedom as he needed. What is more, the style of novels was undergoing a great change in the years following the war in Europe. In a review of Evelyn Scott's *The Narrow House* in November, 1921, Mencken predicted that an entirely new novel form was forthcoming.

> The old-time novel, with its neat plot, its slow tempo and its discursive and undistinguished style, has begun to enter its dotage; there is probably nothing more to be pumped out of the form; it sickens as the epic sickened. The new novel will be at closer grips with life, and it will attempt a more succinct and vivid representation.

For example, the war novels being written by young men were almost entirely different, in style and temper, from those that went before. Dos Passos' *Three Soldiers* (1921), an honest attempt to depict the sordidness of army life and the cheap idealism behind the war, was well received by the critics and the readers. Mencken remarked the vast difference in tone between *Three Soldiers* and Willa Cather's patriotic war novel, *One of Ours* (1922), winner of the Pulitzer prize for 1923. He stated that Dos Passos probably knew what he was writing about and wished that Miss Cather would confine her talents to other topics.

The high hopes of 1921 had turned a bit sour, however, by 1927, when he wrote in a *Mercury* editorial that though writers were making more money than ever before in any country of the world, the art of letters had not kept pace with the prosperity of the literary trade. There was, indeed, evidence that the easy money had done as much harm as good, since it had become so easy to sell second-rate work. Furthermore, why should an author strive to write another *Lord Jim* when he could expect a sale of no more than 25,000 copies, with no serial, stage, or movie rights to add to his bank account? The best fiction was being written by the older men "who were already beginning to oxidize ten years ago; the youngsters, debauched by the experiments of such men as James Joyce, wander into glittering futilities." Their novels, though often competent, never reached below the diaphragm: "Reading them is a diversion, not an experience. There is no moving passion in them; they leave the withers unwrung." It is pretty evident that he had reached that stage in life when the *memory* of experience was more deeply felt than the new experience. Yet he could remark with some justice: "No first book as solid and memorable as *McTeague* or *Sister Carrie* has come out since the annunciation of Coolidge." Well, what *first* book was published between 1923 and 1927 to compare with the two Mencken mentioned? I can think of none. Still, one critic has found the foregoing opinion incredible: "Today it seems somewhat unbelievable that Mencken wrote this at a time when Hemingway, Wolfe, Faulkner, Fitzgerald, and Dos Passos were publishing fairly regularly."[29] The author of this amusing comment should be taken gently aside and told to be more careful in the future with dates of publication. Wolfe's first book came out two years *after* Mencken made his statement! *One Man's Initiation—1917* and *This Side of Paradise* both appeared in 1920, *The Marble Faun* in 1924, and *In Our Time* in 1925.

In 1922 Mencken was able to say that American criticism and

fiction were at last divorced from English models and that the
American products were palpably superior. Such books as *Jurgen*
and *Winesburg, Ohio* and *Chicago Poems* and even *My Ántonia*
were, he felt, almost incomprehensible to the average Englishman.
In "An Open Letter to H. L. Mencken" in the *Bookman* (May,
1922), Hugh Walpole very kindly asked Mencken to visit England
and renew his acquaintance with the English novel, which he had
been neglecting. At the same time, the English could learn about
the Americans, who were writing novels that the average Englishman had difficulty in understanding. As examples, Walpole listed
My Ántonia, Main Street, Moon-Calf, and *Three Soldiers*—novels
which presented problems both in diction and in cultural setting.
"When you get to the works of Don Marquis or Ring Lardner they
might, for most English readers, be just as readily written in
Russian or Chinese." Mencken answered Walpole in the next issue
of the *Bookman*, stating that of the novels he had reviewed, not
just briefly noticed, during the past year nearly a third were
English. He then asked for the name of any English critic who
could claim so high a percentage of American novels. On the same
topic he wrote again, in 1925:

> Certainly no reviewer in practise in the Republic has spent
> more time and energy, during the past twenty years, whooping
> up English books of sound merit. But I confess that I grow
> weary of the doctrine that English books are good, even when
> they are bad. And of the twin doctrine that it is impossible for
> an American to write better ones. Americans are actually doing
> it every day; they will do it more copiously, I believe, as year
> chases year.

There can be no doubt of the correctness of those views, now that
we have the fiction of the last forty years before us.

As for American criticism, Mencken wrote that it had become
so amenable to innovation that a Walt Whitman, come to earth in
1922, "would get a reception almost fit for a bootlegger. A new
Poe would be deluged with adulation, and even with money."
Only ten years before, the reviewing of books had been done by
college professors who looked for sweetness and light in all new
books, and, "failing to find them, they either blasted the contumacious violator of the canon with a Presbyterian anathema, or
cloaked him in silence and laid him away to die." To break through

their guard and find an audience, as Stephen Crane and Frank Norris had done, was a feat of no small proportions. Cabell, for example, had been soundly hoofed by the comstocks for years, but he emerged as a great favorite with critics and readers alike in the nineteen-twenties. It is noteworthy that Mencken has been "accused" by his detractors of overpraising Cabell, who is now almost forgotten. Actually, he never considered Cabell the equal of Dreiser or Lewis, for example, but he did insist that he was much more than just an average novelist. As early as June, 1909, Mencken called attention to Cabell's style, his "feeling for form and color." In 1917 he stated that *The Cream of the Jest* had "a French smack" from beginning to end with overtones of Anatole France and J. K. Huysmans. *Jurgen* (1919), Cabell's most popular or notorious novel, was an extended version of "Some Ladies and Jurgen," a short story which appeared in the *Smart Set* in July, 1918. While remarking in his review that the novel was obviously padded, Mencken again praised the Cabellian style: "How charmingly the fellow writes! What a hand for the slick and slippery phrase he has! How cunningly he winds up a sentence, and then flicks it out with a twist of the wrist—a shimmering, dazzling shower of nouns, verbs, adjectives, adverbs, pronouns and prepositions!" In his little book on Cabell (1927), Mencken stated that future historians of the Great Debunking should certainly remember the part played by the Virginia aristocrat.

When gained overnight, freedom leads inevitably to all sorts of excess. It is a truism that the nineteen-twenties were the epitome of extravagance. American literature was in many ways similar to the little boy who had been cooped up in Sunday school and church for two hours, sweating under the constraint imposed by a tight necktie, immaculate breeches, and an aged lady instructor in the virtuous ways of restraint and angelic nicety. With church over, he bounds forth into the heady air of freedom, intent on making up for lost time. There are times when his intention is realized in a row of dirty words chalked on the back fence. Thus the young writers after the war. They had lived through a period of idiotic repressions, especially in matters of sex, so it was all but inevitable that they should decide to recompense themselves by "telling all." Sex was "discovered," so to speak; then it was discussed; finally it was exploited. The younger generation went on an emotional binge which had all the qualities, or characteristics, of a Dionysian holiday. Did the human body serve certain physiological functions necessary to propagation? Then let's hear about them, by all means. Furthermore, in the name of Truth and Freedom, let's hear about them in detail. And in the beginning was Sex. The coin minted by the Puritan fathers had two sides: on the one side, long displayed for the edification of all, was the face of hypocrisy and deceit; on the other side, at long last turned up for public view, was the face of a laughing and empty-headed satyr. The two faces of an American heritage. After all, it would be impossible to have a one-sided coin. On the changing status of sex in novels, Mencken wrote:

> As a book-worm I have got so used to lewd and lascivious books that I no longer notice them. They pour in from all directions. The most virtuous lady novelists write things that would have made a bartender blush to death two decades ago. If I open a new novel and find nothing about copulation in it, I suspect at once that it is simply a reprint of some forgotten novel of 1885, with a new name. When I began reviewing I used to send my review copies, after I had sweated through them, to the Y.M.C.A. By 1920 I was sending all discarded novels to a medical college.[30]

Above all things else in the world, Mencken believed in freedom of expression—freedom to the utmost limits of human endurance. He remarked in one place: "The only thing I respect is intellectual honesty, of which, of course, intellectual courage is a necessary part. A Socialist who goes to jail for his opinions seems to me a much finer man than the judge who sends him there, though I disagree with all the ideas of the Socialist and agree with some of those of the judge." More than any other American, Mencken joined hands with the eighteenth-century Frenchman who said: "I am opposed to every one of your beliefs but will uphold to the end your right to express them." Still, Mencken was often reticent where others were outspoken. For example, one searches in vain for any discussion of sex in the *Days* books. (He still praised the "confessions" of Frank Harris and the *Tropics* of Henry Miller.) When Alfred Knopf asked him to follow up *Happy Days*, which covered the first twelve years of his life, with a series of reminiscences, each covering a decade, he shied from the idea. He wrote Dreiser that since his teens "were full of loud alarms" it would be idiotic to treat them as he had dealt with his first ten years. He went on to say that in his twenties he "was gay again, and also in my thirties, but since the age of forty I have been full of a sense of human sorrow. This sense has frequently taken the virulence of an actual bellyache."

Unlike the older traditionalists, Mencken never shouted about the obscenity of the writer who gave detailed descriptions of seduction; he merely stated that an overemphasis on sex in no way made a novel more lifelike, and it often injured the writer's reputation insofar as it helped create a false impression of his actual merits. After all, a writer could be injured by acclaim as well as abuse; for example, the man who was taken up by the Greenwich Village crowd usually had more reason to lament than to rejoice. Among the novelists whom Mencken mentioned in this context were Joyce, Dreiser, Cabell, and Sherwood Anderson. The gaudy handling of sex hurt Dreiser, "if only by convincing him that depicting the obvious pawings and snufflings of human courtship is a novel and difficult art, and that those persons who esteem it are mellow aesthetes and advanced thinkers—worse, that those who laugh at it are all Methodists at heart, and probably secret contributors to the Comstock Society." He believed that Dreiser was actually very inept in his handling of sex.

> He will be remembered, not for the trivial carnalities described in *The "Genius,"* but for the astounding story of Hurstwood's decay, the dazzling analysis of Cowperwood's soul, the unforgettable pictures of Muldoon, old Gerhardt, Jennie, and the author's brother, Paul Dresser. In this department he is absolutely without a rival in our letters; as a sexual anatomist and physiologist he is exceeded by scores.[31]

Anderson also had a following to live down. Until he "depicted an old maid perambulating her front lawn in the dead of night, stark naked and defying God, he attracted little notice from the Freudian sisters; since then he has been one of their heroes. But that 'Nude Descending the Ladder to Hell' is certainly not one of his best pieces." (The reference is to the story "Adventure," from *Winesburg, Ohio*.) The publication of *Jurgen* had given Cabell a celebrity which became annoying. Mencken thought *Jurgen* a fine novel, but certainly not because of the passages that happened to "arrest the Comstocks and enchant the women's clubs and finishing schools. Cabell was an artist of sound abilities and high achievements long before *Jurgen* was put on paper. The folks who admired him then still admire him. He is not aided, nor is he flattered, by the additional admiration of the imbeciles who have since set up a gabbling about him." Of all the contemporary American novelists of the first rank, only Willa Cather avoided such notoriety.

> Those who are intelligent enough to admire *My Ántonia* admire it simply because it is a very beautiful piece of work, and not because there is anything in it that can be distorted into support for the imbecilities of Greenwich Village. If Dreiser were shrewd he would write a novel devoid of fornication, and so get rid of a whole army corps of his customers. Cabell has done it, and plainly feels the better for it.[32]

Mencken was convinced that much of D. H. Lawrence's popularity was due to his sole concern with sex, which was of infinitely less importance than the individual's grappling with the forces outside him and the weaknesses inside. He read the Lawrence canon assiduously (and published some of his early short stories in the *Smart Set*), but could find nothing to warrant exalted praise. He considered Lawrence's characters either incredible or boring or both. Certainly it is true, as Mencken believed, that Lawrence's people, when they are more than just stage props, are forever fluctuating between the pathological poles of sadism and masochism, as if they were not quite sure whether the greatest joy in life is to be derived from delivering someone a psychic smack or from receiving one. His characters are oftentimes little more than perambulating phallic symbols. Mencken found Lawrence's extreme irrationalism simply revolting, just as did Bertrand Russell. He concluded his review of *Aaron's Rod* by refusing to take the work seriously in any respect:

> A great nose-blowing, grunting and eye-rolling about nothing. At the primary business of a novelist it seems to me that he fails: he cannot make me believe in his characters. Now and then, of course, they interest me vaguely, but I never find myself assuming that they are real. They look to me to be simply a set of marionettes for discharging the ideas of their creator—and the ideas of their creator, in so far as I can comprehend them at all, strike me as extremely dubious. A few months ago, so the papers say, *A Lost Girl* was awarded a prize in England as the best

novel of the year. Well, we can match that in America. On the Tuesday following the first Monday in November, 1920, Warren Gamaliel Harding, of Marion, Ohio, was elected President of the United States.[33]

Like many another before him, Lawrence began as an artist and ended as a victim of his own messianic delusion, or, at least, so Mencken thought. But there can be no doubt, no matter what one thinks of Lawrence, that Mencken places his finger on a highly vulnerable spot when he speaks of Lawrence's using his characters to mouth his own ideas. Further, Mencken's censure is entirely consistent with his critical credo.

At the height of his renown, the New York *Times* called Mencken "the most powerful private citizen in America." Walter Lippmann called him "the most powerful personal influence on this whole generation of educated people." Borrowing from "Wynken, Blynken, and Nod," Berton Braley made sardonic comment (in the New York *Sun*, December 3, 1920) on "Mencken, Nathan and God."

> There were three who sailed away one night
> Far from the maddening throng
> And two of the three were always right
> And everyone else was wrong.
> But they took another along, these two,
> For He was the only One ever knew
> Why the other two should be.
> And so they sailed away, these three—
>
> Mencken,
> Nathan
> And God.
>
> And the two they talked of the aims of art,
> Which they alone understood,
> And they quite agreed from the very start
> That nothing was any good,
> Except some novels that Dreiser wrote
> And some plays from Germany.
> When God objected, they rocked the boat
> And dropped Him into the sea,
> "For You have no critical facultee,"
>
> Said Mencken
> And Nathan
> To God.

The two came cheerfully sailing home
Over the surging tide,
And trod once more on their native loam,
Wholly self-satisfied.
And the little group that calls them great
Welcomed them fawningly.
Though why the rest of us tolerate
This precious pair must be
Something nobody else can see

But Mencken,
Nathan,
And God!

Though Mencken was looked upon as a demigod by the vast majority of young writers and by the older realists, there were naturally a number of dissenters who bemoaned his position as a taste-maker. Academic critics, moralists, uplifters, professional patriots were all horrified at the spectacle of young Americans quoting Mencken and reading the books he praised. There was truth in the belief that he was our first literary dictator, or, as one academician put it, "the Mussolini of American Letters." Professor F. L. Pattee was more outspoken: "One Mencken in a generation is positively all that we can endure." Which is probably true, but I think it regrettable that America has so far produced no one to assume the vacant throne. For really vicious condemnation, one should go to *Menckeniana, a Schimpflexikon.*

In one of the many credos he furnished at the request of leading magazines of the period, he remarked that he believed (1) in telling the truth, (2) in being free, and (3) in acquiring knowledge— notions which had often got him attacked:

> I have been denounced on the floor of Congress by statesmen from the Bible Belt, and in blistering terms. The wowsers dislike me and have tried to jail me. I have been barred from the mails. During the late War for Human Freedom I was on the suspect list of the celebrated Department of Justice, along with Sacco and Vanzetti, and one of my own partners was put to watching me. The evangelical Protestant papers charge me with favoring the Pope's scheme to put a Catholic in the White House, and the Catholic papers damn me for atheism and anti-nomianism. The Red-hunters put me among the Radicals, and the Radicals belabor me as an intransigent Tory. In Greenwich Village I am thwacked as a medieval, and among college pro-

fessors I am regarded as an anarchist. During the twelve months of 1926 more than five hundred separate editorials upon my heresies were printed in the United States, and at least four hundred of them were hostile.[34]

All of this is by way of pointing out that Mencken's celebrity was more precisely a notoriety. One more example should suffice. Early in 1927 a number of suicides were reported from college campuses, and the newspapers, in typical fashion, played them up in a melodramatic manner and tried to show that there was an epidemic. On being interviewed by the Trenton, N.J., *Times*, the president of Rutgers, a man named Thomas, who later resigned his post and went into the insurance business, gave the cause of the suicides as "too much Mencken." Asked by the *Times* to comment on this, Mencken wrote that he could see nothing mysterious about the suicides, that the impulse to self-destruction was strong in everyone, especially in intelligent young people. In all probability, he wrote, the only thing that kept the reflective and skeptical man alive was his sense of humor. Besides, the college presidents, like the newspaper editors, would soon tire of the bogus epidemic and go yelling after some other phantasm. He ended the essay with a masterful stroke: "A college student, leaping uninvited into the arms of God, pleases only himself. But a college president, doing the same thing, would give keen and permanent joy to great multitudes of persons. I drop the idea, and pass on."

In his final years as a literary critic, Mencken became more and more convinced that the best novels were primarily character studies, were secondarily stories, and were least of all concerned with ideas. It is no wonder that Mencken, who became more and more interested in ideas as time passed, should have lost the enthusiasm for fiction that was evident during the first dozen or so years of his career. *Vanity Fair* is memorable for Becky Sharp; the novels of Dickens, Fielding, Tolstoi, Dostoevsky, and Jane Austen are remembered for their people rather than for the stories surrounding them or the ideas they emit. *Huckleberry Finn* and *My Ántonia* and *Babbitt* and *Jennie Gerhardt*—to say nothing of Conrad's novels—were favorites of Mencken for that reason. He also believed that the most memorable characters were those who were essentially average or normal. He called for fictional studies of certain types of men: policemen, lawyers (later to be portrayed so well by James

Gould Cozzens), insurance men, revivalists (Lewis, of course, answered this need), journalists, men of various trades and professions. In *Arrowsmith,* Lewis depicted the man of science (C. P. Snow has called it the best fictional treatment of a scientist in the English language). But nobody had ever painted the American politician adequately. Mencken felt that Harvey Fergusson's *Capitol Hill* (1923) was the only novel that had yet captured any of the true grandeur of the Washington scene. (He forgot to mention Henry Adams' *Democracy,* an excellent portrait of Washington politics.) He wondered that no effort had been made to draw the college president:

> I mean, of course, the university president of the new six-cylinder, air-cooled, four-wheel-brake model—half the quack, half the visionary, and wholly the go-getter—the brisk, business-like, confidential, button-holing, regular fellow who harangues Rotary and Kiwanis, extracts millions from usurers by alarming them about Bolshevism, and so builds his colossal pedagogical slaughter-house, with its tens of thousands of students, its professors of cheese-making, investment securities and cheer-leading, its galaxy of football stars, and its general air of Barnum's circus. Why has this astounding mountebank not got into a book? He fairly yells for loving embalming *à la* Babbitt.[35]

During those heady years of power in the nineteen-twenties, Mencken often told Nathan, "Whom the gods would destroy they first make popular." Certainly, the gods fattened Mencken to enormous size before the ax fell. By the middle twenties, indeed, the field of literary criticism had been occupied by other forces. Though Mencken's name continued to the end of the decade and on into the thirties to be invoked, particularly by his enemies, he was actually no longer on the field; only his ghost continued to haunt the scene. An empty fort, where Mencken held literary councils during the fifteen years on the *Smart Set,* was fired upon from both the Left and the Right. The fact that the fort was unguarded only intensified the ferocity of the attackers.

On occasion Mencken did recognize the New Humanists on the right and the proletarians on the left, but it was obvious that he was little concerned with what either of the parties thought or said. Reviewing T. S. Eliot's *For Lancelot Andrewes* in 1929, he was most concerned with the author's remarks on Humanism, which was, Mencken stated, little more than "a somewhat sickly and shame-faced Christian mysticism. The Humanist of the current model, at his best, is what Mr. Eliot seems to be himself: a natural Catholic who finds it impossible to swallow a church ruled by an Italian paleographer and so compromises on one ruled (at least transiently) by a Scotch labor agitator." At his worst, the New Humanist took the shape of a man who looked with horror upon the urbanization of modern life. The comments on Eliot are worth quoting:

> Mr. Eliot began life as one of Professor Babbitt's disciples, but hard study at the British Museum convinced him that the current Humanism was full of buncombe. His present point of view, he says, "may be described as classicist in literature, royalist in politics, and Anglo-Catholic in religion." Parts of this, as he himself confesses, are vague and savor of clap-trap; it is hard, for example, to think of the author of *The Waste Land* as a genuine classicist. But on the religious side there is no reason to doubt the author's seriousness. He proves it by exhuming various sacerdotal obscurities from oblivion, and arguing gravely that they were profound thinkers—nay, even gifted stylists. The enterprise is not new; I have heard Christian Scientists maintain that even Mrs. Eddy was a sound writer. But Mr. Eliot carries it off with more than the usual grace, for he writes very effectively himself, and is full of that odd and useless learning which gives an air of persuasiveness to otherwise bald and unconvincing disputation. For one, I remain unconvinced that either Bishop Andrewes or his brother Bramhall could write, but I confess that reading about them was pleasant, and did me no harm.[36]

It was Eliot's discussion of religion per se and of the Humanists' inability to avoid it that most impressed Mencken. He agreed completely with Eliot's description of Irving Babbitt's Humanism as "alarmingly like the very Liberal Protestant theology of the Nineteenth Century; it is, in fact, a product—a by-product—of Protestant theology in its last agonies." Mencken could imagine no definition which defined the movement more precisely. To call Babbitt and his cohorts Humanists was to warp the word beyond meaning.

In the nineteen-thirties Mencken's popularity declined abruptly, for he offered no panacea as a way out of the economic depression. Skepticism was not the wear. Saviors appeared in the streets again,

and the multitudes became disciples. In 1932 E. W. Howe called
Mencken the greatest writer in the country and added that he was
retiring from his role as American gadfly because the public no
longer listened to him. It was that simple. Thereafter, Mencken
devoted most of his time to his language studies and newspaper
work. He expressed his objections to the proletarian novelists in
1934 (in the *Saturday Review of Literature*), but there were few
listeners. He refused to believe that the social-reform novels were
good art. Marxian theology was no better than any other of the
ologies or isms that garnered and garner mass converts. Robinson
Jeffers perfectly described the temper of the age and the children
crying for a rock; for example, in these lines from "Thebaid,"
written in 1937:

> How many turn back toward dreams and magic, how many
>   children
> Run home to Mother Church, Father State,
> To find in their arms the delicious warmth and folding of souls.
> The age weakens and settles home toward old ways.
> An age of renascent faith: Christ said, Marx wrote, Hitler says,
> And though it seems absurd we believe.
> Sad children, yes. It is lonely to be adult, you need a father.
> With a little practice you'll believe anything.
>
> Faith returns, beautiful, terrible, ridiculous,
> And men are willing to die and kill for their faith.
> Soon come the wars of religion; centuries have passed
> Since the air so trembled with intense faith and hatred.
> Soon, perhaps, whoever wants to live harmlessly
> Must find a cave in the mountain or build a cell
> Of the red desert rock under dry junipers,
> And avoid men, live with more kindly wolves
> And luckier ravens, waiting for the end of the age.

His brow unclouded by "the fevers of faith," Mencken remarked
that the people who most ardently and dexterously performed the
mental acrobatics necessary to good standing in the Marxian school
were precisely those who had advocated the wilder theories of
sexology in the nineteen-twenties and the ones most likely to return
to Christian theology at a later date—those, in brief, who were
happily blessed with believing minds.

In an interview with Robert van Gelder of the New York *Times
Book Review* (it appeared later in *Writers and Writing*, 1946),

Mencken voiced some of his likes and dislikes concerning the novel. The main trouble with the writers of the nineteen-thirties was that they went into politics and thus lost their gift of disbelief. The shock of the Depression caused people to look about for "a rock of ages, a cave of brotherhood, a staff and diaper of belief." When college graduates could not find work, they turned naturally to messiahs like Russia and Roosevelt. The interview concluded with Mencken praising James Farrell, William Saroyan ("the only one of the 'advanced' writers with pungency, with something fresh to say and a new way of saying it"), and John Steinbeck, who had told a wonderful story in the *Grapes of Wrath* in spite of the "political essays" which "might have been written by one of the kept idealists on the liberal magazines that run on a deficit." He stated, with some accuracy, that Steinbeck would probably "outgrow the stupid politics."

Bernard Smith, a Marxist critic of the thirties and the author of *Forces in American Criticism* (1939), pretty well summed up that decade's objections to Mencken. After approving of Waldo Frank's remark that Mencken merely brought energy to despair—a glowing half-truth if ever there was one—Smith stated the Menckenian credo thus:

> Class distinctions are not economic and conventional, but con-genital and genuine. The few at the top of society are naturally aristocrats. Without them there can be no art, no disinterested thought, no fine manners, and none of the blessings of civilized society (good food, good wine, good conversation, and so on). The masses are essentially brutish, evil, and incompetent; they are instinctively hostile to culture, to rational conduct, and to esthetic discrimination. The first problem of politics is to keep them docile; the second is to prevent them from interfering with their betters. There are no such things as truth and progress. The superior man expects nothing but an opportunity to enjoy himself. One of his major pleasures is to laugh at the antics and idiocies of the herd.[37]

There is, oddly enough, a little truth in most of this credo, and then there are some dreadful botches. For example, Mencken certainly did *not* believe that the few at the head of American society were "naturally aristocrats"; indeed, he never tired of bemoaning the fact that there was *no* American aristocracy, but only a moneyed class or plutocracy. On the other hand, Mencken *did* believe in the existence, infinitesimal and sporadic though it was, of progress; and he shared the pragmatic view of truth with Charles Sanders Peirce and Nietzsche, which is to say that he believed in relative rather than absolute truths. Smith went on to say that

> to evaluate his criticism we must appraise his entire philosophy, for we subscribe to his literary opinions only if we agree with his interpretation of life. That is to say, we see in his favorites what he saw in them, we fail to see in them what he failed to see, and we refuse recognition to the writers he disliked, only if our beliefs about the nature of the universe and the history of the race coincide with his.

Not even the pedantic Marxist is often capable of such nonsense as this. Does one have to be an extreme liberal to agree with Vernon Parrington's praise of Roger Williams, and does he, *at the same time,* have to be a conservative to disagree with Parrington's estimate of Henry James? If we see in Dreiser or Conrad essentially what Mencken saw in them, must we then necessarily share Mencken's philosophy of life? And can we not agree with Mencken's philosophy and disagree with his estimate of, say, Robert Browning? But then even to answer such claptrap is to pay it an undue compliment. Again, like most of his humorless, millennium-hungry colleagues, Smith applauded Mencken for his promotion of realism in fiction, his attacks on the bourgeoisie (it should be remembered that Mencken often referred to himself as a bourgeois journalist), his war against the churches and their attendant mysticism and spiritualism, and his leading role in battering down the walls, erected by academicians and genteel critics, which separated literature from life. But, alas, Mencken could never be allowed entrance into Valhalla, for he was completely without sympathy for the noble common man. More, he was an "urban tory."

After it became clear to the worshipers at the Soviet shrine that no utopia lay in the direction of totalitarian governments, they let up in their attacks. One example: Michael Gold screamed at Mencken through the twenties and from his *New Masses* platform preached his funeral oration in September, 1931: "Rare Sam Johnson of our time: Farewell! Good-bye! Everything is finished between us. Your thunders do not awe us any longer. [. . .] You are a Tory who hates the Soviet Union. Worse than that, you are a white Nordic chauvinist who fears and hates the yellow races, and preaches war against the Soviet Union, because it is forging the brotherhood of all races." Twenty-two years later, in a more sober mood, Gold was one of the writers in a symposium who recalled Mencken as an editor and an encourager of new talent.[38] Gold could not understand why Mencken serialized and then praised *Jews Without Money,* since Gold considered Mencken a political reactionary. He was actually angry because Mencken acted decently.

For all that those of the Right and Left said to the contrary, Mencken was a *ja-sager,* a man who delighted in existence though he believed it was essentially meaningless (much in the manner of the modern-day existentialist like Paul Tillich). Though a skeptic, he never succumbed to the pessimistic view of the world. In reviewing Joseph Wood Krutch's *The Modern Temper* (1929), a profoundly pessimistic book on the plight of man in the scientific age, Mencken attributed the author's despair to his inability "to shake off the Christian delusion that human life is animated by some transcendental and grandiose purpose, that a mysterious divine plan runs through it, that there are lessons in it for philosophers, which is to say, for theologians." (In his autobiography, *More Lives than One,* Krutch wrote that he cherished above all other remarks that of his friend Mencken, who once commented on Krutch's natural failure to "come all the way from Tennessee to civilization in one generation." To be thus maligned by the great was no small compliment.) Human life, according to Mencken, was quite as charming and spacious today as it ever was in the past. The Greeks, for example, invented nothing to compare with the printing press; they discovered nothing as important as the cell; they produced no political document to equal the Bill of Rights. Mencken did not argue that the present century was the greatest of all; he actually preferred the eighteenth century to all others. But he had little patience with those who, finding no meaning or purpose in life, gave themselves up to despair. He believed "the one demonstrable aim of man is to hang on gallantly to his ball of mud, whirling through space. That hanging on, viewed realistically, is a superb adventure, and it has bred and developed, within the brief span of human history, a series of qualities that are sturdy, useful and noble." In the preface to the first volume of his autobiography, *Happy Days*

(1940), Mencken confessed that he had found existence on "this meanest of planets extremely amusing, and, taking one day with another, perfectly satisfactory":

> If I had my life to live over again I don't think I'd change it in any particular of the slightest consequence. I'd choose the same parents, the same birthplace, the same education (with maybe a few improvements here, chiefly in the direction of foreign languages), the same trade, the same jobs, the same income, the same politics, the same metaphysic, the same wife, the same friends, and (even though it may sound like a mere effort to shock humanity), the same relatives to the last known degree of consanguinity, including those in-law. The Gaseous Vertebrata who own, operate and afflict the universe have treated me with excessive politeness, and when I mount the gallows at last I may well say with the Psalmist (putting it, of course, into the prudent past tense): The lines have fallen unto me in pleasant places.

It is easy enough to show that Mencken's book criticism for the *Mercury* was less perceptive than his earlier criticism for the *Smart Set;* it has been shown numerous times before. He simply did not seem to comprehend the worth of much really first-rate fiction after 1925. But then he was no longer interested in "new" writers, as he had once been. He had, as he wrote Marquis Childs, simply "lost interest in fiction"—which is not, after all, a criminal offense. But even in his later criticism it has too often been the habit of writers to quote him out of context and thereby give a false impression of the final judgment he makes. For example, in the introduction to a recently published collection of essays on Scott Fitzgerald, Arthur Mizener, attempting to show that Fitzgerald's work was not well received in the nineteen-twenties, states that Mencken pronounced *The Great Gatsby* "no more than a glorified anecdote." To begin with, Mencken wrote that "in form" *Gatsby* was no more than a glorified anecdote. And he then went on to praise the novel highly as a great advance for Fitzgerald in the art of fiction! More than the story, it was the style that pleased in the novel. And as a social document on contemporary Philistia, it was sound and important. To be sure, Mencken did not praise without qualification, but he praised it nonetheless, and intelligently so. (Alfred Kazin includes the review in his collection, *F. Scott Fitzgerald: The Man and His*

Work). Mizner's completely misleading quotation is just one—the last I have seen—in a large catalogue of examples.

The first issue of the *Mercury*, in January, 1924, was in violent contrast to the *Smart Set*. There were only two short stories (by Ruth Suckow and John McClure) and four short poems (by Dreiser); the rest of the magazine was given to essays of various sorts: for example, a lengthy piece on Stephen Crane by Carl Van Doren; a "conversation" by Samuel Chew, entitled "Mr. Moore and Mr. Chew"; a mordant critique of the youthful dilettanti (which resulted in near rioting in Greenwich Village) by Ernest Boyd, entitled "Aesthete: Model 1924"; a sketch of George Santayana's years at Cambridge, by Margaret Munsterberg, daughter of philosopher Dr. Hugo Munsterberg; a philological essay by George Philip Krapp, entitled "The Test of English"; a piece on "The New Thought" by philosopher Woodbridge Riley. There were also some letters of Huneker, along with several other essays: "The Lincoln Legend" by Isaac R. Pennypacker, "The Drool Method in History" by Harry Elmer Barnes, "The Tragic Hiram" (on Hiram Johnson) by John W. Owens, "Two Years of Disarmament" by Miles Martindale, "The Communist Hoax" by James Oneal, and half a dozen others on equally diverse topics. Cabell, Boyd, and Isaac Goldberg helped Mencken review the books. Mencken's editorial, which must have set a record of some sort for its forthrightness, deserves more than brief mention. First of all, he made it clear that the editors (Nathan was coeditor for the first year of publication) were entirely devoid of messianic passion.

> The Editors have heard no Voice from the burning bush. They will not cry up and offer for sale any sovereign balm, whether political, economic or aesthetic, for all the sorrows of the world. The fact is, indeed, that they doubt that any such sovereign balm exists, or that it will ever exist hereafter. The world, as they see it, is down with at least a score of painful diseases, all of them chronic and incurable; nevertheless, they cling to the notion that human existence remains predominantly charming. Especially is it charming in this unparalleled Republic of the West, where men are earnest and women are intelligent, and all the historic virtues of Christendom are now concentrated. The Editors propose, before jurisprudence develops to the point of prohibiting skepticism altogether, to give a realistic consideration to certain of these virtues, and to try to save what is exhilarating in them,

even when all that is divine must be abandoned. They engage
to undertake the business in a polished and aseptic manner,
without indignation on the one hand and without too much
regard for tender feelings on the other. They have no set
program, either destructive or constructive. Sufficient unto each
day will be the performance thereof.

Mencken then stated that in the field of politics the magazine would
be antiutopian and iconoclastic, constantly assuming "that the more
ignorant a man is the more he knows, positively and indignantly."
He then addressed himself to the notion that he and Nathan were
Radicals proposing to undermine Americanism. In this section he
stated once more (and he had been saying the same thing for a
quarter of a century already) that the Editors viewed the capitalis-
tic system, "if not amorously, then at all events politely." It is remarkable that many people did not "discover" this until the
nineteen-thirties. Though he felt that capitalism may be replaced
elsewhere in the coming years, he believed it would survive longer
in America, "if only because the illusion that any bright boy can
make himself a part of it remains a cardinal article of the American
national religion—and no sentient man will ever confess himself
doomed to life imprisonment in the proletariat so long as the slightest hope remains, in fact or in fancy, of getting out of it."

After commenting at length on the nature of the Forgotten
Man—that is, the leading men of science and learning, the best
artists, the men of imagination—and remarking that neither the
Tories nor the Liberals had anything to say to this figure, Mencken
finally discussed the course which the *Mercury* would follow in the
field of the fine arts. The Editors belonged to no coterie and hoped
to propagate no aesthetic theory. "It is only when theories begin
to enter into the matter that counsels are corrupted—and between
the transcendental, gibberishy theory of a Greenwich Village aesthete and the harsh, moral, patriotic theory of a university pedagogue there is not much to choose." The middle road would be
followed in aesthetic matters. And precisely here do we have Mencken's abdication as literary critic, or more correctly as a major
literary critic. It is unthinkable that a great critic would set out with
the intention of occupying the middle of the road; the great critic
invariably occupies one side or the other of the road, until finally
he has built a road, or at least a path, of his own which others may

travel on. Mencken did just that during his *Smart Set* years. But now he was a man resting on his laurels. The battles were being fought in their fields, and there he would henceforth be found.

The worth of a critic is determined by two things: the soundness of his judgments and his influence on readers and writers. Mencken's influence both as critic and editor was tremendous. His successful battle for realism constitutes one of the major chapters in American literature. His popularity among writers was larger than that enjoyed by any other American critic before or since. In reading the vast amount of criticism he wrote between 1905 and 1925, I was astonished at how sound it appears from my vantage point in time. With rare exceptions (D. H. Lawrence is the major one), the writers he praised have lived and the writers he condemned have died; those who fell somewhere in between are the ones whom we "have heard of, but never read." In a lecture on "The Frontiers of Criticism," delivered in 1956, T. S. Eliot stated that "if in literary criticism, we place all the emphasis upon *understanding*, we are in danger of slipping from understanding to mere explanation" and "of pursuing criticism as if it was a science, which it can never be"; but that if, "on the other hand, we overemphasize *enjoyment,* we will tend to fall into the subjective and impressionistic, and our enjoyment will profit us no more than mere amusement and pastime." As I have shown through ample quotation, Mencken was saying essentially the same thing nearly half a century ago. More, he put the belief into practice. He dwelt between the two poles of understanding and enjoyment, touching now one and then the other, but never becoming shackled to either. He was, moreover, a man of the world, with a wide range of knowledge in other fields: another prerequisite for the major critic. Finally, he possessed the one enduring quality that all critics who live must have: he was a writer of the first rank. Indeed, he was an extraordinary artist, as is once more becoming clear to that happy minority of men who read books.

In *The Summing Up,* one of the best books in English on the craft of writing, Somerset Maugham made the remark: "If you could write lucidly, simply, euphoniously and yet with liveliness you would write perfectly: you would write like Voltaire." Mencken possessed those four traits as probably no other American critic has done. He was never obscure in the hopes that a murky passage would be interpreted as being too profound for clear statement. As Maugham remarked, fools can always be found to find some hidden meaning in a bad writer's outpourings. When *Heathen Days,* the third and last volume of Mencken's autobiography, was published, Joseph Wood Krutch compared him to Swift—a comparison that had been made numerous times before. Krutch added: "Time has served only to perfect a style which was always robust and exuberant, but which has grown with the years better balanced and better integrated until it has achieved now an almost classical perfection without losing its individuality."

Mencken was a rebel, but never a reformer. His vision was clear. He was, if such is possible, almost too commonsensical. He was a liberator par excellence, a pilgrim to the joy of living, a delighter in things beautiful. He was no Voltaire, and he was no Swift, but he was the nearest thing to those giants that America has produced.

Notes

CHAPTER ONE: *In the Beginning*

1 HLM, "Fifteen Years," *Smart Set*, 72:139 (December, 1923).

2 George Jean Nathan, "The Happiest Days of H. L. Mencken," *Esquire*, 48:146 (October, 1957).

3 Burton Rascoe, "Introduction," *The Smart Set Anthology*, edited by Burton Rascoe and Groff Conklin (New York, 1934), p. xxxiii.

4 In recalling, years later, that they met in May of 1908, Mencken and Nathan probably erred. In *The Man Mencken*, Isaac Goldberg dates the meeting as May, 1909. Carl R. Dolmetsch also gives 1909 as the correct date in his history of the *Smart Set*, published in 1966. The fact is that Channing Pollock did not resign as drama critic of the magazine until June, 1909. Nathan first appeared in the magazine in October, 1909, and his first critical article appeared a month later.

5 Quoted from a letter of Dreiser to Isaac Goldberg, August 4, 1925. See Goldberg's *The Man Mencken* (New York, 1925), pp. 379-380.

CHAPTER TWO: *The Sultry Atmosphere*

1 George Santayana, *Character and Opinion in the United States* (New York, 1955), p. 14.

2 *The Letters of Henry James*, edited by Percy Lubbock (New York, 1920), I, 136.

3 HLM, *Prejudices: First Series* (New York, 1919), pp. 52–53.

4 When the ellipsis marks are simple periods, as they are here, they belong to the author I am quoting; when I have made the deletion, the periods are enclosed in brackets. [. . .]

5 *Prejudices: First Series*, pp. 57–58.

6 Stedman quoted by Bernard Smith, *Forces in American Criticism* (New York, 1939), p. 250.

7 Wendell quoted by Smith, *op. cit.*, p. 264.

8 Maurice Thompson, "The Turning of the Tide," *Independent*, 48:238 (January, 1896).

9 Thompson quoted by Smith, *op. cit.*, p. 244.

10 *Ibid.*

CHAPTER THREE: *Moldings*

1 HLM, *Happy Days* (New York, 1940), p. 167.

2 *Letters of H. L. Mencken*, selected and annotated by Guy J. Forgue (New York, 1961), pp. 224–225.

3 HLM, *George Bernard Shaw: His Plays* (Boston, 1905), pp. xvi–xvii.

4 HLM, *Minority Report* (New York, 1956), pp. 292–293.

5 HLM, *Prejudices: First Series* (New York, 1919), pp. 182–183.

6 Stanley Weintraub, "Apostate Apostle: H. L. Mencken as Shavophile and Shavophobe," *Educational Theatre Journal*, 12:189 (October, 1960).

7 Archibald Henderson, "Literature and Science. A Dialogue Between Bernard Shaw and Archibald Henderson," *Fortnightly Review*, 122:512 (October 1, 1924).

8 *Living Philosophies*, edited by Will Durant (New York, 1931), pp. 179–180.

9 Edgar Kemler, *The Irreverent Mr. Mencken* (Boston, 1950), pp. 10–12.

10 Quoted by Isaac Goldberg, *The Man Mencken* (New York, 1925), p. 91.

11 *Minority Report*, p. 292.

12 *Letters of H. L. Mencken*, p. 189.

13 F. W. Nietzsche, *The Antichrist*, translated from the German with an Introduction by H. L. Mencken (New York, 1920), pp. 12–13.

14 Ludwig Lewisohn, *Expression in America* (New York, 1932), p. 350. For a minute treatment of Huneker's life and work, see Arnold T. Schwab's *James Gibbons Huneker: Critic of the Seven Arts* (Stanford, 1963).

15 HLM, *A Book of Prefaces* (New York, 1917), p. 193.

16 *Ibid.*, pp. 162–163.

17 HLM, *Prejudices: Third Series* (New York, 1922), pp. 66–67.

18 *Ibid.*, pp. 67–68.

19 *Ibid.*, pp. 72–73.

20 Benjamin De Casseres, *Mencken and Shaw* (New York, 1930), p. 64.

CHAPTER FOUR: *First Premise*

1 *Letters of H. L. Mencken*, selected and annotated by Guy J. Forgue (New York, 1961), p. 186.

2 *Ibid.*, p. 188.

3 Newton Arvin, "The Role of Mr. Mencken," *Freeman*, 6:382 (December 27, 1922).

4 HLM, "A Hot Weather Novelist," *Smart Set*, 31:153 (August, 1910).

5 HLM, " 'With Your Kind Permission—,' " *Smart Set*, 41:154 (October, 1913).

6 HLM, "The Novels That Bloom in the Spring, Tra-La!" *Smart Set*, 27:156 (April, 1909).

7 HLM, "From the Diary of a Reviewer," *Smart Set*, 61:141 (February, 1920).

8 HLM, *A Mencken Chrestomathy* (New York, 1949), pp. 541–542.

9 HLM, "*Répétition Générale*," *Smart Set*, 64:38 (March, 1921).

10 Benjamin De Casseres, *Mencken and Shaw* (New York, 1930), pp. 76–77.

11 HLM, " 'A Doll's House'—With a Fourth Act," *Smart Set*, 29:157 (December, 1909).

12 HLM, "The Books of the Dog Days," *Smart Set*, 29:154–155 (September, 1909).

13 HLM, "Sunrise on the Prairie," *Smart Set*, 58:143–144 (February, 1919).

14 HLM, "A Soul's Adventures," *Smart Set*, 49:153 (June, 1916).

15 " 'A Doll's House'—With a Fourth Act," p. 158.

16 HLM, "The Good, the Bad and the Best Sellers," *Smart Set*, 26:159 (November, 1908).

17 *Ibid.*

18 HLM, "Novels for Indian Summer," *Smart Set*, 60:144 (November, 1919).

19 HLM, "The Library," *American Mercury*, 19:122–123 (January, 1930).

20 "A Hot Weather Novelist," p. 158.

21 HLM, "A 1911 Model Dream Book," *Smart Set*, 35:153 (September, 1911).

22 *Letters of H. L. Mencken*, pp. 189–190.

CHAPTER FIVE: *Critical Credo*

1 HLM, "The Anatomy of the Novel," *Smart Set*, 43:153 (June, 1914).

2 HLM, "Novels for Indian Summer," *Smart Set*, 60:138–139 (November, 1919).

3 "The Anatomy of the Novel," p. 153.

4 HLM, "A Glance at the Spring Fiction," *Smart Set*, 30:153 (April, 1910).

5 *Ibid.*, p. 154.

6 HLM, *Prejudices: First Series* (New York, 1919), p. 28.

7 HLM, *The Bathtub Hoax and Other Blasts and Bravos*, edited by Robert McHugh (New York, 1958), p. 106.

8 *Ibid.*, p. 109.

9 HLM, "Zola," *Smart Set*, 37:154 (August, 1912).

CHAPTER SIX: *Criticism of Criticism*

1 See Spingarn's essay on "The Younger Generation" in the *Freeman* (June 7, 1922). After remarking that in his lecture in 1910 he had sought to destroy "moralism" and "the academic dry rot that was undermining the creative and intellectual spirit of the nation," Spingarn cautioned that this was not an effort to destroy discipline, character, morals, imagination, beauty, and freedom, but only "the sterile forms which were made to serve instead of these realities."

2 HLM, *Prejudices: Third Series* (New York, 1922), pp. 84–104.

CHAPTER SEVEN: *Götterdämmerung*

1 Vincent O'Sullivan, "The American Critic," *H. L. Mencken* (New York, 1920), pp. 16–17.

2 Benjamin De Casseres, *Mencken and Shaw* (New York, 1930), pp. 80–81.

3 Eric Bentley, *A Century of Hero-Worship*, Second edition (Boston, 1957), p. 3.

4 HLM, *Prejudices: Second Series* (New York, 1920), pp. 21–22.

5 When the *Nation* became very liberal in the nineteen-twenties, Mencken contributed numerous articles to it, including such things as "A Short View of Gamalielese" (reprinted in Edmund Wilson's *The Shock of Recognition* [Garden City, N.Y., 1943]), "In Tennessee" (on the Scopes trial), and reports on the political conventions of 1924 and 1928, entitled "Clown Show." Mencken was listed as a contributing editor of the *Nation* from May 11, 1921, to December 28, 1932. He accepted the unsolicited honor humbly, even gratefully, for though he had little faith in the panaceas of the liberals, he much preferred the liberal press to the red-baiting conservative organs. The liberals at least made an honest attempt to print the truth.

6 A. Mitchell Palmer, Attorney-General under Woodrow Wilson, was responsible immediately after World War I for the wholesale incarceration of thousands of people suspected of being socialists or Com-

munists, many of whom were kept behind bars for weeks without ever being charged with any crime. The Palmer raids of 1919 and 1920 were a menace to innocent citizens as well as to those who were "guilty" of belonging to labor unions or of being foreign-born. Needless to say, admirers of President Wilson look the other way when this is shown them. See Chapter 3 of F. L. Allen's *Only Yesterday* (New York, 1931).

7 *Prejudices: Second Series*, pp. 26–28.

8 *Ibid.*, pp. 31–32.

9 HLM, *Prejudices: Third Series* (New York, 1922), p. 17.

10 HLM, *Prejudices: Fifth Series* (New York, 1926), pp. 216–217.

11 *Prejudices: Second Series*, pp. 68–69.

12 *Ibid.*, pp. 72–73.

13 *Ibid.*, p. 78.

14 *Ibid.*, pp. 81–82.

15 *Ibid.*, pp. 85–86.

16 *Ibid.*, p. 61.

17 *Prejudices: Third Series*, p. 184.

CHAPTER EIGHT: *The American Hydra*

1 See the excellent preface to *The Puritans* (New York, 1938), edited by Perry Miller and Thomas H. Johnson.

2 HLM, "Variations upon a Familiar Theme," *Smart Set*, 66:139 (December, 1921).

3 HLM, *A Book of Prefaces* (New York, 1917), pp. 197–198.

4 *Ibid.*, p. 201.

5 *Ibid.*, pp. 212–213. It should be unnecessary to remind the reader that today many high government officials are waging, by their own frequent admissions, a "moral" war against the infidelity of Communism. Of course, the Communists are themselves fully aware of the effectiveness of moral judgments against the enemy. In his long introduction to *Patriotic Gore* (New York, 1962), Edmund Wilson composed a devastating indictment of all those who employ morality as a justification of or cloak for acts which are clearly motivated by self-interest. Although he did not exempt other nations from this disease, Wilson concentrated on the American's extraordinary ability in moral casuistry.

6 *Ibid.*, pp. 214–215.

7 *Ibid.*, pp. 217–218.

8 HLM, "From the Diary of a Reviewer," *Smart Set*, 66:142 (September, 1921). It is interesting to note that the friendship between Mencken and Van Doren was built almost entirely on correspondence. In his autobiography, *Three Worlds* (1936), Van Doren remarked that he had actually met Mencken only about a dozen times. When parts of Van Doren's *Contemporary American Novelists* (1922) appeared in the *Nation*, Mencken wrote him that he hoped Van Doren would not leave out two of Mencken's favorite novelists, Willa Cather and James Branch Cabell.

9 *A Book of Prefaces*, pp. 224–225.

10 Second edition (Boston: Little, Brown, 1859), p. xxvi. [Mencken's note.]

11 *A Book of Prefaces*, pp. 227–229.

12 *Ibid.*, pp. 231–232.

13 U.S. *vs.* Bennett, 16 Blatchford, 368–9 (1877). [Mencken's note.]

14 *Idem.*, 362; People *vs.* Muller, 96 N.Y., 411; U.S. *vs.* Clark, 38 Fed. Rep. 734. [Mencken's note.]

15 U.S. *vs.* Moore, 129 Fed., 160–1 (1904). [Mencken's note.]

16 U.S. *vs.* Heywood, judge's charge, Boston, 1877. Quoted in U.S. *vs.* Bennett, 16 Blatchford. [Mencken's note.]

17 *A Book of Prefaces*, pp. 263–265.

18 One of the most famous of censorship cases was fought in Boston in 1926 over the banning of Mencken's *Mercury*. J. Frank Chase, secretary of the Watch and Ward Society, had been stung sharply by various *Mercury* articles on his methods of censorship and had vowed revenge on Mencken. The chance came when a harmless essay on a pathetic small-town prostitute, entitled "Hatrack," by Herbert Asbury, appeared in the April, 1926, issue. The best description of the events surrounding the banning is to be found in William Manchester's *Disturber of the Peace* (New York, 1951) in the chapter entitled "Banned in Boston." Also see Asbury's acount: "The Day Mencken Broke the Law," *American Mercury*, 73:62–69 (October, 1951).

CHAPTER NINE: *A Trinity: The Prof. Drs., the Humanists, and Dixie*

1 Stuart P. Sherman, "Beautifying American Literature," *Nation*, 105:593 (November 29, 1917).

2 Carl Van Doren called Sherman the last of the academic critics, meaning, evidently, the last of the professorial critics of the genteel tradition.

3 The essay, in part a review of *Prejudices: Third Series* (New York, 1922), first appeared in the New York *Times* Book Review.

4 *Letters of H. L. Mencken*, selected and annotated by Guy J. Forgue (New York, 1961), p. 408.

5 In a long five-column review of *Life and Letters of Stuart P. Sherman* (two volumes, 1929), Mencken was overly kind to Sherman's ghost (Sherman died in 1926), saying that Sherman had a great future when he was cut off at forty-five.

6 HLM, "Critics Wild and Tame," *Smart Set*, 53:138 (December, 1917).

7 HLM, "The Mystery of Poe," *Nation*, 122:290 (March 17, 1926).

8 Edmund Wilson, *Classics and Commercials* (New York, 1950), p. 114.

9 HLM, *Prejudices: Sixth Series* (New York, 1927), pp. 94–95.

10 HLM, "On Controversy," *The Bathtub Hoax and Other Blasts and Bravos*, edited, with an Introduction and Notes, by Robert McHugh (New York, 1958), p. 277.

11 Among the professors and former professors who appeared in the *Mercury* during its first three years of existence: in literature and philology—Joseph Warren Beach, Bernard De Voto, Joseph W. Krutch, Emory Holloway (articles on Whitman, who interested Mencken more than any other American poet), Granville Hicks, J. Frank Dobie, Louise Pound, George P. Krapp, F. L. Pattee, and Samuel Chew; in history—Harry Elmer Barnes, Charles A. Beard, and Hendrik Willem van Loon; in anthropology—Robert H. Lowie and Franz Boas; in law—Zechariah Chafee, Jr.; in music—Virgil Thompson. For a conclusive listing of contributors to the *Mercury*, see Chapter 6 of M. K. Singleton's *H. L. Mencken and the American Mercury Adventure* (Durham, N.C., 1962).

12 H. M. Jones, "Professor Babbitt Cross-Examined," *New Republic*, 54:159 (March 21, 1928).

13 Edmund Wilson debunked this absurdity, once and for all, let us hope, in "Sophocles, Babbitt and Freud," which may be easily found in *The Shores of Light* (New York, 1952), pp. 468–475.

14 HLM, "From the Diary of a Reviewer," *Smart Set*, 61:139–140 (February, 1920).

15 HLM, "Books About Books," *Smart Set*, 65:142 (June, 1921).

16 *Ibid.*

17 HLM, *Prejudices: Third Series* (New York, 1922), pp. 178–179.

18 HLM, "The Library," *American Mercury*, 20:125–127 (May, 1930). Copyright 1930 by H. L. Mencken.

19 HLM, "Si Mutare Potest Aethiops Pellum Suam," *Smart Set*, 53:138 (September, 1917).

20 HLM, *Prejudices: Second Series* (New York, 1920), pp. 136–137.

21 *Ibid.*, p. 138.

22 HLM, "The South Begins to Mutter," *Smart Set*, 65:139 (August, 1921).

23 Van Wyck Brooks, *Days of the Phoenix* (New York, 1957), p. 107.

24 HLM, *A Book of Prefaces* (New York, 1917), p. 206.

CHAPTER TEN: *The Devil's Advocate*

1 HLM, "The Monthly Feuilleton," *Smart Set*, 69:141 (December, 1922).

2 HLM, *A Book of Prefaces* (New York, 1917), p. 17.

3 HLM, "Conrad, Bennett, James, Et Al," *Smart Set*, 36:153 (January, 1912).

4 HLM, "The Raw Material of Fiction," *Smart Set*, 42:154 (March, 1914).

5 G. Jean-Aubry, *Joseph Conrad, Life and Letters* (two volumes; Garden City, New York, 1927), II, 288–299.

6 HLM, *A Mencken Chrestomathy* (New York, 1949), p. 521.

7 HLM, "Meredith's Swan Song," *Smart Set*, 32:167 (October, 1910).

8 HLM, *Prejudices: Fourth Series* (New York, 1924), pp. 140–141.

9 *Letters of H. L. Mencken*, selected and annotated by Guy J. Forgue (New York, 1961) p. 12.

10 HLM, "More Notes From a Diary," *Smart Set*, 62:138–139 (May, 1920).

11 *A Book of Prefaces*, p. 114.

12 *Ibid.*, pp. 124–125.

13 Quoted by William Manchester in *Disturber of the Peace* (New York, 1951), p. 93.

14 Robert H. Elias gives a lengthy section of the letter in *Letters of Theodore Dreiser* (Philadelphia, 1959), pp. 238–240.

15 *Letters of H. L. Mencken*, pp. 141–142.

16 *Ibid.*, p. 156.

17 *Letters of Theodore Dreiser*, p. 319.

18 Waldo Frank summarized the attitude of the rebels about the Puritanism of provincial America when he spoke (in *Our America*

[1919]) of "the hypocrisy of the American who goes to church on Sunday and bleeds his brother on Monday, who leads a sexually vicious life and insists on 'pure' books, draped statues, and streets cleared of prostitutes, who preaches liberty and democracy and free speech and supports the subtlest oligarchy of modern times."

19 HLM, *Prejudices: Third Series* (New York, 1922), pp. 11–12.

20 *Ibid.*, p. 60.

21 HLM, "Mainly Fiction," *Smart Set*, 58:140–141 (March, 1919).

22 HLM, "Chiefly Americans," *Smart Set*, 63:138 (December, 1920).

23 George Jean Nathan, "The Happiest Days of H. L. Mencken," *Esquire*, 48:150 (October, 1957). Nathan also described this meeting, along with numerous other escapades of the three men, in *The Intimate Notebooks of George Jean Nathan* (New York, 1932).

24 *Ibid.*

25 HLM, "Consolation," *Smart Set*, 64:139 (January, 1921). Mencken's title was probably provoked by his unhappy introduction to Lewis.

26 HLM, "Portrait of an American Citizen," *Smart Set*, 69:138–139 (October, 1922).

27 HLM, "The Library," *American Mercury*, 10:506 (April, 1927).

28 HLM, "The Library," *American Mercury*, 16:506 (April, 1929).

29 Johnny L. Kloefkorn, *A Critical Study of the Work of H. L. Mencken As Literary Editor and Critic of The American Mercury* (Emporia, Kansas, 1959), p. 42.

30 *A Mencken Chrestomathy*, p. 352.

31 HLM, "Saving the World," *Smart Set*, 68:143 (July, 1922).

32 *Ibid.*, pp. 143–144.

33 *Ibid.*, p. 144.

34 HLM, "Testament," *American Review of Reviews*, 76:413 (October, 1927).

35 HLM, *Prejudices: Fifth Series* (New York, 1926), pp. 227–228.

36 HLM, "The Library," *American Mercury*, 18:123–124 (September, 1929).

37 Bernard Smith, *Forces in American Criticism* (New York, 1939), pp. 304–305.

38 "Bouquets for Mencken," *Nation*, 177:210–214 (September 12, 1953).

Index